Why Economies Grow

P21 - Central question
26 - " argument

Also by Jeff Madrick

Unconventional Wisdom:
Alternative Perspectives on the New Economy (editor)

The End of Affluence

Taking America

Why Economies Grow

*The Forces That Shape Prosperity and
How We Can Get Them Working Again*

Jeff Madrick

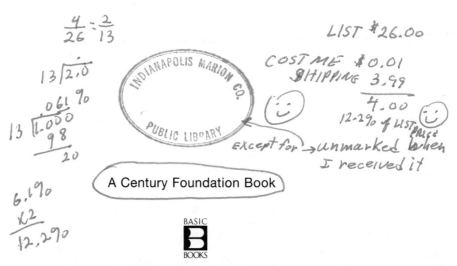

A Century Foundation Book

BASIC
B
BOOKS

A Member of the Perseus Books Group

Published by Basic Books,
A Member of the Perseus Books Group

Designed by Brent Wilcox

Library of Congress Cataloging-in-Publication Data

Madrick, Jeff
Why economies grow : the forces that shape prosperity and how we can
get them working again / Jeffrey Madrick.
p. cm.
"A Century Foundation book."
Includes index.
ISBN 0-465-04311-9
1. Economic development. 2. Commerce. 3. Information—Economic
aspects. 4. Economic history. 5. United States—Economic conditions.
6. United States—Economic policy. I. Title.
HD82 .M264 2002
338.9—dc21
2002008042

02 03 04 / 10 9 8 7 6 5 4 3 2 1

The Century Foundation

The Century Foundation, formerly the Twentieth Century Fund, sponsors and supervises timely analyses of economic policy, foreign affairs, and domestic political issues. Not-for-profit and nonpartisan, it was founded in 1919 and endowed by Edward A. Filene.

To my parents,
Cora and Milton Madrick

Contents

Foreword by Richard C. Leone   *ix*

Acknowledgments   *xiii*

1   Why Economies Grow   1

2   The Invention of the New Economy   13

3   The Importance of Economic Growth   31

4   The Causes of Industrial Revolution   47

5   The Drama of the American Industrial Revolution   69

6   The Productivity Slowdown of the Late Twentieth Century   87

7   Why We Grew Rapidly Again   115

8   The Challenges to Prosperity   133

9   Making America Grow: Challenges and Principles   143

10   Making America Grow: An Agenda   163

11   Why We Won't Do It   179

Notes   *199*

Index   *233*

Foreword

THE 1990s WERE FOR MANY THE BEST OF TIMES. AMERICAN popular culture, at least, suggested that success was rampant and helped to generate a remarkable degree of optimism. The sensational boom in technology stocks and in the broader market produced an unprecedented increase in equity values, especially in areas that seemed related to the revolution under way in computers and communications. Great fortunes were made and widely celebrated in the media. More important, a surge in productivity late in the decade seemed to fulfill some of the promise that had been long anticipated as a result of the widespread adoption of computers by businesses and individuals.

In the midst of what seemed like total enthusiasm, there were some analysts and scholars arguing for a more cautious assessment of the impact of these new technologies on the overall economy. They stressed that, although the computer revolution was undoubtedly important, it was still too early to forecast its long-term effects on growth and incomes. Still, as the valuation of the "computer stocks" skyrocketed, it was difficult not to be carried along by the pervasive exuberance. Finally, the inevitable market "corrections" at the end of the decade and during the early years of the new century forced a more sober calculation of the effects of the new communications technologies and the information revolution.

During the years before our current, more realistic view of the so-called new economy was arrived at, perhaps the greatest failure in our understanding of what was actually happening could be attributed to a routine deficiency in our knowledge of economic history. There were various reasons for this. Economics, as an academic discipline, moved during the past several decades to more intense concentration on theory and model building. Although this work often proved quite valuable, in many ways it has lessened our understanding of real world cases from both the present and the past. Economic historians generally have not picked up the slack, especially those with a primary focus on political and social developments. There are few in the field who combine a working knowledge of fundamental economic principles and a deep understanding of economic history; there are even fewer who can transform those insights into accessible and penetrating prose. The author of this volume, Jeff Madrick, is one.

This book is not the first project Madrick, who is editor of _Challenge_ magazine, author of *The End of Affluence: The Causes and Consequences of America's Economic Dilemma*, and a contributing columnist for *The New York Times*, has done with The Century Foundation. He served as the editor of our collection of essays on the economic developments of the past decade: *Unconventional Wisdom: Alternative Perspectives on the New Economy*.

The strength of this book comes from Madrick's ability to see the interaction of social, legal, technological, and other cultural change with the economic growth that he is explaining. Far from the mechanical modeling of some economists (who would divide economic growth into the percentage due to capital deepening and the remainder due to technology), Madrick's analysis incorporates the complex changes that occurred during the evolution of capitalism.

As he notes, raw materials have nothing or almost nothing to do with the acceleration of growth. Raw materials, which have been around throughout human existence, have become more useful economically only because our knowledge and imaginations have developed new ways to extract and use them. Indeed, even wider exchange, migration, and growing markets—which Madrick assigns the central place as prime mover of economic growth—ultimately depend on new means of transportation, communication, and warfare, themselves the fruit of accumulated knowledge. Madrick never lets us forget that we are unimaginably rich and long-lived by historical standards only because of the gradual and organic evolution of institutions of governance and commerce, cultural developments that have enabled us to trade, urbanize, and invent.

Madrick's analysis also points up the sluggishness of income for most workers. The most recent generation of Americans experienced a sharp increase in wealth and income inequality, something that was basically unexpected and is increasingly troubling. Although some analysts have attributed this to a statistical fluke caused by not taking account of the young people who move up the income ladder in the course of their lifetimes, more careful research has indicated that this has been taken into consideration. The current consensus is that starting in the early 1970s income inequality increased. Although many had hoped that productivity gains and the widespread dissemination of computers would help alleviate inequality, evidence to that effect is lacking.

How then should we view today's economy? Madrick argues persuasively that the new economy hype of the late 1990s was just that. The fundamental driving forces and institutions of capitalist economic growth have not changed. The new inventions, cheaper communication, and better organization of knowledge that developed so rapidly in the 1990s no more repeal the laws of motion of capitalism than the invention of the internal combustion engine or the electrical motor did. To focus on major technological innovations and ignore the myriad adaptations, extensions, and financial accommodations that markets breed is to trivialize the process of economic growth and remove its fundamental continuity. Madrick's contribution, then, is to place our recent economic growth in a historical and institutional perspective. If we are not in a breathless new economy, we still have reason for confidence in the long-run robustness of capitalist economic growth.

Economic developments have been a major area of study for this organization from its founding. This book is a part of a wide range of examinations of various aspects of the American economy we have supported over the past decade, including the essay collection edited by Madrick, *Unconventional Wisdom,* mentioned previously; Robert Kuttner's *Everything for Sale*; Jamie Galbraith's *Created Unequal*; Barry Bluestone and Bennett Harrison's *Growing Prosperity*; Paul Osterman's *Securing Prosperity*; Alan Blinder and Janet Yellen's *The Fabulous Decade;* and the volume of essays we cosponsored with the Russell Sage Foundation, *The Roaring Nineties.* We also are looking at economic policy in a number of forthcoming studies: Simon Head's examination of the impact of technology on economic inequality; Jonas Pontusson's study of what the United States can learn from other nations about the workforce, economic inequality, and public policy; and Edward Wolff's analysis of skill, work, and inequality.

The final verdict on the new economy is far from clear. Both real world experience and rigorous analysis are at a preliminary stage. Still, it seems quite certain that for many years to come Madrick's work will provide a critical guide to our understanding of what we have been and where we are headed. We look forward to his continuing work in this fundamental area of public policy and American life.

Richard C. Leone, President
The Century Foundation
May 2002

Acknowledgments

WHEN A BOOK RUNS AGAINST THE CONVENTIONAL WISDOM, IT requires the support of brave people. This book was conceived when almost everyone believed that a new economy had swept the nation towards a prosperity of unprecedented proportion and unending duration. To the question, why do economies grow, the chorus answered that it was technology, of course, aided by a return to unregulated markets.

This book offers a decidedly different answer. I must first thank Richard Leone, president of the Century Foundation, for his continuing support of this at times unpopular venture. Second, I must thank his lieutenant, Greg Anrig, for similarly undiluted support. Beverly Goldberg, director of publications at the Century Foundation, was critical to its publication. The Century Foundation economist Bernard Wasow, not always in agreement, provided important suggestions for the book. Further sincere thanks go to Jason Ranker and Sarah Nelson.

Yet another round of supporters requires acknowledgement. John Donatich, publisher of Basic Books, and William Frucht, became enthusiastic and respectful supporters of this book. Their enthusiasm made me a better writer, and I very much appreciate it. As editor of the book, Bill Frucht was not only a constructive editor but also a nourishing presence. I would like to thank Felicity Tucker and her copy editing staff, as well as the jacket designer, Bradford Foltz, for their excellent work.

Finally, let me thank again, as I did in a previous book, economic historians as a group. I mildly criticize some of them in this book, but I am grateful to all of them. They should be more highly regarded in their academic profession. They provide perspective to a discipline that is more often influenced by ideology or fashion than is admitted.

All of my family and a few key friends are my best advisers. I thank them most.

1

Why Economies Grow

AT A CONFERENCE NOT LONG AGO, AN ECONOMIST PLACED ON the overhead projector a graph all too frequently used when discussing the origins of economic prosperity and growth. It showed a line that rose slowly during the Middle Ages, representing a negligible rate of economic improvement over eight centuries between the years 1000 and 1800. But around 1800, the line shot up at an angle of 45 degrees or so to the present. The Industrial Revolution had begun, and incomes consistently advanced at a rate that was extraordinary by any former historical standard.

The economist then asked the conventional question: Why wasn't technological advance adequate to raise rates of growth before 1800? He assumed, like many and perhaps most historical observers, including many trained economists, that technological advance was the origin of economic growth, and the central and implicitly even the sole cause of the Industrial Revolution. By "technological advance," he apparently meant the great inventions, from spinning wheels and water mills to steam engines and electric dynamos. In other words, there just were not enough great inventions to produce rapid economic growth in the Middle Ages and even the Renaissance until the more or less magical demarcation point around 1800.

Similarly, if asked why the U.S. economy grew so rapidly in the late 1990s, most people today, including many economists, will answer with nearly perfect certainty that it was because of new technology. In particular, of course, they mean information technology generally associated with semiconductors and computers—again, great inventions.

This book argues that such a view of growth is wrong. It tests the conventional wisdom on this and a wide range of matters, using historical, anecdotal, and empirical evidence, as well as economic theory. The central argument is that inventions in and of themselves are not the sole or even leading source of prosperity. Technological innovation is necessary to growth, but it is as much a consequence of economic opportunities as it is their cause, and perhaps even more a follower of economic growth than a leader. Moreover, technological advance does not include just great inventions but also hundreds and often thousands of related innovations. Even the great inventions were more incremental developments than is widely believed, with many contributors and innovators building on what preceded them.

This book argues that the growth of markets through trade, colonization, and domestic expansion was the predominant factor in Western economic development. By "markets" I mean groups of people exchanging goods and services. These markets grew as population and incomes grew. The growth of markets was closely associated with the rapid flow and dissemination of information, which was typically a by-product of expanding markets and immigration. Markets and information are inseparable. Such a view implies that the policies most popular today to support economic growth, including increased savings, deregulation, and other laissez-faire approaches, and even subsidies to research and development, are inadequate. Markets and information, even if the predominant causes of growth, are not sufficient factors for growth. In fact, many factors cause and enhance economic growth, and in turn affect each other. To take a contemporary example, many countries had access to America's market in the decades after World War II, but among developing nations only East Asians were able to take full advantage of it. Aside from the size and growth of markets, the flow of information, and technological advance, these conditions of growth also include the literacy, educational attainment, and health of the population; the distribution of wealth or income-making assets; the availability of financial capital; the development of financial and legal institutions; the abundance of natural resources; the vitality of entrepreneurialism; and peace and political stability. Most of these are necessary conditions for growth, but no one of them is sufficient in itself. All are both cause and consequence.

Still, over the course of modern economic development, which this book takes as starting around the year 1000, some of these factors have been more important than others. To put it differently, some are closer to first movers than others, closer to a true source of prosperity.

If we were to place them on a continuum, with those factors that are more cause than consequence on the left, market size and dissemination of information are furthest left and are closest to first movers or true leaders. In addition, the first of these is the size and expansion of markets for goods and services. The possibility of trading goods in large volume was a major source of growth beginning at least in the Middle Ages. Domestic markets, including internal trade, as well as cross-border trade, provided the possibility to produce goods on a large and efficient scale, creating powerful demand for services, notably communications, transportation, and the retailing and wholesaling services associated with the exchange of goods, and providing incentives to create new products and new techniques. Exchange and trade always entailed a flow of new ideas and information.

The existence of markets in itself implied that private property was acceptable or protected, even if only by the force of owners or traders. But legal institutions, or semilegal ones, including judicial systems, were more the consequence of growing markets and trade than their cause. The early existence of markets does not mean that they were "free markets" in the contemporary sense. Monopoly was common to early markets, as was the forceful control of trade routes. Government or community control was needed to open markets to even the slightest competition and to protect the rights of buyers and sellers. Free markets as we understand them today were largely a late development; they were certainly not the state of nature.

The second factor to the left of our continuum is the availability of information. More precisely, it is the cost and accessibility of information and the ability of a large proportion of people to assimilate it. Markets and trade were long the main conduits of information; they generally went hand in hand. Where markets grew, information was passed on. The frequent migration of workers across Europe was a major source of information about farming and production techniques in early years. Literacy and education eventually raised the value of information because more people could use it and expand on it.

The development of towns and cities was the quintessential example of trade and information coming together. Trade fairs were a central part of the economies of the Middle Ages, but eventually towns and cities usurped them. Both the fairs and the cities were essentially more efficient markets, where goods, services, and information could be exchanged at low cost. Transaction and transportation costs were minimized, as was the cost of communications. Towns and cities were integral to economic growth in Britain and Europe. In general, access to information seems to be closer to a first cause of prosperity than any other factor but the size of markets, and it is typically difficult to separate from the development of markets.

The central importance of markets is expanded on elsewhere in this book. For now it is important to recognize that exchange itself improves economic welfare. One person sells what he or she makes best and buys what someone else makes best. One agricultural region sells what it grows best and buys what another region grows best. Another region may have developed an expertise or skill for geographical reasons and can then import products for which it has no particular skills in exchange. As Adam Smith wrote, "Give me that which I want, and you shall have this which you want. . . . It is in this manner that we obtain from one another the far greater part of these good offices which we stand in need of." The advantages of large markets increase as economies become more sophisticated.

One might suppose that natural resources, from coal, iron ore, and oil to fresh and plentiful forests, are surely first causal factors, to be placed well on the left of our continuum. But this simple assumption is not so clear. To take an obvious example, Arabia had enormous oil reserves for centuries before they were discovered, developed, and put to commercial use. At the other extreme, Japan developed rapidly despite a lack of resources. As economies develop, nations tend to find more resources beneath their surfaces, partly because the economic incentives and available tools and finances to explore and develop them are greater. Even the United States, so rich in initial resources, continued to find more reserves as its economy grew.

Another common argument is that surplus capital (savings) is a first condition for growth. It is assumed that the savings will then be invested, and that capital investment in turn is the engine of growth. This argument dominated thinking in the 1990s. In early economies, however, one could save only if he or she had met the most basic needs for food, shelter, and clothing, and if there was a reasonable future benefit in doing so. The accumulation of savings is generally possible only when economies are already growing, when income is already substantial, and when there are good opportunities (incentives) to utilize these savings as investments. When this happens, capital tends to accumulate or be imported from elsewhere. Thus, savings are not likely to be far left on the spectrum.

What is most misleading about the idea that finance is a central determinant of economic growth is the presumption that if there are adequate or, as some argue is best, excess savings available for investment, they will be usefully invested. This assumption characterized much of early economic thinking, including Adam Smith's. After the fact, investment and savings are equal, but it is controversial to deduce from this that a rise in savings will result in a rise in investment. History strongly suggests the opposite. Savings are important to economic growth but not a first mover. Investment was induced by the opportunity created by growing markets or new products more so than the availability of savings. Much growth, including early America's, was financed by international borrowing to compensate for inadequate savings.

Similarly, some argue that the development of banks and similar financial institutions should be placed to the left on our continuum. But such institutions typically came into being when economies became sufficiently sophisticated to make the intermediation between savings and business necessary. They did not create the conditions for economic growth. Financial institutions became large and influential when the need for them grew—that is, when savings were large and could be productively pooled for investment. Large, innovative, and aggressive financial institutions can contribute enormously to an economy's growth as it matures by actively investing accumulated savings. Diversified investments from a large pool of capital can substantially reduce risks of investing. But financial institutions are classic followers, not leaders, somewhat to the right on our continuum.

An especially common argument these days is that basic economic rights—such as guarantees of private property or legal contracts—were first causes of economic growth. These were integral to economic growth in Western development, but again, they were hardly first movers. Their development, even in their earliest manifestations, was very much the consequence of new and growing economic incentives. The prospects for exchange and trade were an inspiration for the development of economic rights and laws that guaranteed markets, and inchoate markets of adequate efficiency existed before the guarantee of property rights in any contemporary sense. There were clearly some acknowledgments of property, but these were often a function of might, not right. Relatively free markets, as Karl

Polanyi pointed out, were social constructions of government. Nations with widely differing kinds of economic rights than the West's—China, for example—have developed strong economies.

Finally, many observers, notably Joseph Schumpeter, argue that entrepreneurialism is the great source of economic growth. At some point in an economy this is certainly the case, and the argument brings us closer to the true sources of economic growth than does attributing it to technology in general. Entrepreneurs create new products, marketing methods, and managerial systems. But entrepreneurialism is not far to the left on our continuum. It requires a context; it is not a human trait that stands alone. In other words, it requires fairly sophisticated business incentives—a payoff—for the effort. There must already exist an economic system with adequate rewards for risky investment and the development of new ideas. In fact, the most influential sources of entrepreneurialism are large markets and rapid economic growth itself.

The same can be said for the importance of managerial competence and innovation, so forcefully brought to our attention by the historian Alfred Chandler. America's ability to manage and its affinity for size were central to its economic development, but it was a consequence of opportunity, not a first mover of economic growth.

Where does technological advance lie on this spectrum? Technological innovation as pure invention is not even always a necessary condition of economic growth. Innovations in managing resources and production, and in marketing and distribution, have caused growth without serious new invention. Henry Ford's great innovations were much more managerial than technological. Another good example of a cause of growth that requires no serious technological innovation is the discovery of precious metals like gold and silver, which almost invariably creates a surge in demand for goods and services. Yet another is the opening of new markets through exploration, discovery, or military conquest.

Still, sustained growth generally requires technological innovation. But this does not mean that inventions themselves lead to growth. First of all, not all technological advance has economic implications. Electricity clearly had vast benefits for economic development, but arguably the most influential technological advance of the twentieth century, nuclear energy, has had relatively little economic impact.

Second, inventions, from gunpowder to the compass to wind mills, existed for decades and even centuries before they were put to commercial use. But technological advance that matters for economic growth usually, maybe even always, requires large markets that permit economies of scale as well as entrepreneurial incentives. Commercial technological innovation usually becomes more vigorous when economic incentives are higher, and profits on investment are highest when economic growth itself is fastest. The conditions to use and further develop and adapt technology are what matter most, not the inventions themselves.

Ironically, if economic growth is dependent on major inventions alone, as some argue, there is reason to be pessimistic. There are statistical arguments that a major invention will likely appear in the future, if we wait long enough. But this is merely a probabilistic assertion, meaning that there is some probability it will not happen. Moreover, such a major invention will have to be of the kind that affects economic growth in a significant way. This reduces the probability further. If future economic growth is related to a flow of small and moderate rather than major technological innovations, we can rest easier; these are highly likely to occur. But if we must wait for a great and unimaginable new invention to secure our future, I am nervous for the state of humankind.

The sources of growth, then, are many, and they interact with and affect each other. Markets and information are linked. Rapid growth produces more savings, making capital investment easier and less expensive to undertake, just as growing savings helps facilitate growth. A growing economy motivates people to educate themselves and make the public investments in transportation and communications often necessary for further growth, just as more investment in education raises the potential rate of growth. The appropriate economic model for growth is organic, not mechanistic. It is not a simple box into which one places inputs, such as capital and inventions, and out of which emanate rising incomes. It is therefore less given to mathematical modeling than economists would prefer. Ideally, economic behavior is reduced to mathematical equations, not to oversimplify it but to make it more understandable, testable, and predictable. But such restrictions can too easily inhibit speculation about the causes of growth, and indeed make the process more mechanical than it is.

Further, if markets and information remain on our far left as first movers, this does not imply that they require the most attention all the time. If we are to sustain growth we must be concerned with all these factors and emphasize those that are most neglected at any particular time.

Added to this list is one final related factor. It is apparently a human instinct to improve one's material well-being. But we cannot take this for granted, because this basic motivation has often been undermined by despair, humiliation, poverty, and tyranny. The first human material motivation is to acquire adequate food and shelter. The second seems to be security—that is, to ensure that food and shelter will be available well into the future. The third is apparently purer pleasures: good wine, a glass of soda, leisure. (I am not dealing with the clear fact that relieving one's basic hunger is also of course a pleasure.) A fourth is all the complex issues of status and identity.

The instinct to improve oneself materially is necessary for growth, but it is too easily confused, especially in the Anglo-Western world, with individualism and the inevitability of intense competition. It is a mistake to assume that self-interest ineluctably leads to competitiveness and an inherent need to prove individual superiority. People can seek material betterment collectively and noncompetitively, in tribes, religions, and the governments of nation-states. They can also seek it individually and competitively. However it is implemented, economic growth will not occur unless a people has a drive toward material betterment.

This drive becomes a significant source of growth in the modern world as people increasingly believe material improvement is possible. If humans are given to believe that they have the opportunity or power to improve their material well-being, they will expend more effort to do so. During the Middle Ages, people eventually began to believe they could master nature. This complex change in attitude was partly a consequence of material improvement itself. It also eventually required the development of pro-growth institutions, often but not always including the legal protection of the right to private property. I believe faith in material betterment also required the inclusion of a broad proportion of the population. Thus, some degree of inequality is tolerable in many prosperous societies, but some relative equality in both material and social assets, such as literacy, is also a necessity. In earlier societies, this was often achieved through a broad distribution of land. Such societies, including that of nineteenth-century America, were also often broadly literate. Such inclusion is a key to long-term economic growth because more of the population is motivated to improve itself and thereby contribute its talents and, just as important, its energies constructively to the economy. The incorporation of the broad population into an economy has been integral to modern growth in most instances.

There are two final clarifications. First, when discussing a hierarchy of causes of economic growth, we are presuming that an elementary economy exists, which includes at least modest markets; an informal acceptance of private property, even if based on force; and a stable social structure. Too few growth economists make this major assumption clear.

Thus we are not trying to determine the first causes of civilization itself. In a pure sense, there was economic growth even with the first tribes and surely with the first food gatherers. More definitively, there was economic growth when people learned to domesticate crops and animals. The advent of fire and the wheel was equivalent to any so-called macro-invention of the modern age. In such earlier and purer cases, natural resources and geographical advantages were probably closer to first causes of growth than they are in modern economies.

By causes of economic growth, then, I mean those factors that propelled growth after a minimal stratum of economic development had been reached and that already contained at least primitive markets; contractual institutions; private property at some level; and an organized society of cultural, religious, and governing traditions. The causes of growth discussed in this book are mostly related to development in the West and began in the Middle Ages. This is the historical period that is most relevant to our current situation.

Second, I am not trying to determine a model of development for today's extremely poor nations or nations in which market mechanisms have been dissolved by the political state. The basic conditions of growth for such nations are the same as those outlined above, but their priorities may differ. A nation like Russia clearly had to attend to the development of market institutions in the 1990s and rushed toward them too rapidly. Sub-Saharan nations must attend first to extreme poverty, health, and political governance, then address questions of land distribution and other ways to close the gaps in wealth in these nations.

Assessing and ranking the causes of growth requires humility. The case made here rests on historical and contemporary data, example, and anecdote. To the extent that statistical economic tools are helpful, they are cited, but they are generally still too clumsy to draw definitive conclusions based on empirical evidence concerning these large questions. The analysis and conclusions of this book are essentially consistent with economic theory, even when they are at odds with mainstream opinion.

There has been a tendency to focus on only two or three growth factors in recent decades, as if they are universal. These typically include technology, national savings, and lower taxes. The modern practice of economics has a disturbing tendency to seek such universally applicable solutions based on theoretical principles that I believe a disinterested view of history often does not bear out. The theoretical principles, if debatable, are often fine, but even when agreed upon, their applicability is at best relative. This book focuses on the specific causes of growth in the late 1990s in the context of the long, fascinating history of economic growth since the Middle Ages. It takes a decidedly organic view. In the end, we will find that in a world of scarce resources, we must neglect some factors of growth. The ideal would be to optimize as many factors as possible without significantly undermining the others. Where we must choose between and among factors, we must understand what we are giving up.

2

The Invention of
the New Economy

THE LATE 1990s WERE NOT CONGENIAL TO AN ORGANIC VIEW OF economic growth. The belief in technological determinism—that technology was the principal determinant of growth—reached its height in those years. It was accepted with little skepticism by the media; used by Wall Street to promote extraordinary levels of specu- lation in securities; and eventually accepted and advocated in its sim- ple form even by some economists, who were too easily wed to mechanistic views of economic growth and perhaps too eager to par- ticipate in the fashionable conventional wisdom of the time.

Without the widely unquestioned faith in this myth of technology, the so-called new economy would not have been born. The new economy was essentially an invention of the media and Wall Street. As *The Economist* wrote, a "big idea" was necessary to explain the sudden and surprising prosperity of the late 1990s in the United States. A new economy generated by technological transformation was that idea; it fit the rhetorical need, and the thinking about it was characteristically undisciplined. By the late 1990s the *new economy* mostly referred to the development of computer-related information technology.

It is interesting to trace the spread of the idea, for it shows how loosely defined the issues were and provides a case study in the sociology of knowledge in our time. The media were in search of a new economy long before the late 1990s. There was, in fact, a "need" to find a new economy. Americans were confused and disappointed by the economy's poor performance between 1973 and 1995. Few were fully aware of how poorly the economy was performing even as late as the mid-1990s, because on average it kept growing. But it grew at historically slow rates. Incomes stagnated or barely rose; jobs were harder to find than in the past; and spouses went to work in large numbers, remaking the family in America. Americans blamed big government, lost morality, the abandonment of self-reliance, and many other often nostalgic factors for their failure to meet expectations, but the central source of people's confusion, anger, and the search for scapegoats in these years were historically poor economic performance and the resulting slow growth of their own incomes.

The first serious recession of the post-World War II period took place in 1973 and 1974 and was soon followed by unprecedented high levels of inflation and interest rates. In 1982, the worst recession of the postwar era occurred. The economy grew rapidly after the recession but slowed down again by the late 1980s. On average, since 1973, once the fluctuations of the business cycle were taken into account, the economy had grown slowly. People thus longed for a "new" economy, and with every momentary improvement in economic prospects, the press and some authors were ready to oblige.

Business Week, for example, first referred to a new economy in the summer of 1981, after the nation had struggled for years with high oil prices, interest rates, and inflation. "Perhaps at no time since World War II has the performance of the U.S. economy been more mystifying," wrote the magazine. It "is a restructured economy running by new rules . . . creating a new economy that is more resistant to business cycle downturns and able to absorb large increases in employment." Its main characteristic was the growth of services, concluded *Business Week*, not as yet new technologies.

Business Week made this claim in a period in which the economy had temporarily improved, and it was plausible that the extraordinary problems of the 1970s were behind us. But the worst recession of the post-World War II period began only a few months later. As a result, there was little mention again of a new economy until the mid-1980s, after several years of rapid expansion following the 1982 recession. Talk of a new economy then became something of a craze. The personal computer (PC) had been introduced a few years previously. In 1985, *Business Week* devoted a special issue to "the most revolutionary economic change in a century—the emergence of a 'new economy' of services and high technology." The next year, a *U.S. News* cover hailed a "Brave New Economy." *Fortune* put "America's New Economy" on its cover in that year as well.

A number of independent writers, some of them thoughtful but many not, heralded a new economy. For the most part these claims of a new economy were related to the rise of services, which in truth long before had overtaken manufacturing as the largest segment of the economy. Services included banking, retailing, healthcare, transportation, fast food, and entertainment, among other industries. Computerization was still a secondary theme in these analyses. For example, Ronald K. Shelp, a business executive, and Gary W. Hart, the former senator, co-authored an article, "Understanding a New Economy," that was largely about the requirements of a services economy. Its main policy recommendation, even then, was better education and job training in an economy that would require more sophisticated workers due to the rise of services.

The concept of a new economy had credibility when the economy was strong, but it turned out that the return of economic health was a temporary consequence of a normal rebound from the serious recession in 1982 along with the rapid rate of federal, personal, and business borrowing. It was not a new economy. The stock market crash of October 1987 deflated the optimism of the mid-1980s. Still, use of the term "new economy" had become so common that it did not fade away, even in bad times. *Business*

Week's cover in 1988 ironically announced: "The New Economy: Say Hello to the Lean Years."

Growth resumed in 1988, but the economy performed poorly beginning in 1989 and suffered a recession in 1990. The recovery that followed was again slow. Now, the new economy was said to be one that was deindustrializing. For example, Robert Reich, President William Clinton's labor secretary, repeatedly discussed a "new economy," in which good manufacturing jobs were being lost to overseas competitors. For a few years, the new economy meant bad times.

By the mid-1990s, the public was well-primed for a new economy and no doubt longing for an optimistic version of it. An extensive search of newspapers and magazines in the 1980s and early 1990s shows the phrase "new economy" being used to describe the services economy, the information age, deindustrialization, wage stagnation and inequality, deregulation and privatization, lower tax rates, high levels of debt, and of course early computer technology. It was whatever one wanted it to be.

But the rapid growth in the late 1990s, and the spectacular rise of stock prices, gave the concept of a new economy a credibility that was unmatched in earlier years. No major business or financial publication resisted the urge to describe the changing economy as a "new industrial revolution." Men and women who presumably knew something about these matters habitually made grand pronouncements. "This is truly the second industrial revolution, and it will change every aspect of people's lives," said John T. Chambers, the CEO of Cisco Systems. No doubt he read the same articles everyone else did for his information. In particular, Alan Greenspan, the highly regarded chairman of the Federal Reserve, was a voluble advocate of the idea that something fundamental had happened to the U.S. economy that occurs only once or twice a century.

The media seldom defined the new economy, and as shown they changed the meaning to suit the times. *Business Week* was more consistent than most and, by the mid-1990s in any case, claimed that the new economy rested on two factors, globalization and the advance of information technology. *The Washington Post* added deregulation and corporate restructuring to these two in a definition it proposed in 1997. But by 1998 and 1999, the new economy was increasingly associated with only one phenomenon: the Internet (and the analogous private "intranets" of large corporations and other institutions). The abiding belief in technological progress was the source of this faith that invention alone could ensure prosperity. As corroboration, speculators drove the prices of high technology stocks to levels that the economist Robert Shiller showed were on average without historical precedent. There was little room for a broader view of the causes of economic growth in the public discourse. Technology was the source of growth, and further, because technology would always advance, so would economic growth.

What is remarkable about the new economy advocacy was that, even after substantial data revisions that raised reported performance, the numbers themselves in the late 1990s, though strong and welcome, were not vigorous compared to the robust periods of former business cycles. Given the poor rates of growth of the economy since 1973, they certainly suggested an improvement, but compared to similar exuberant periods in the past, such as the 1920s, 1950s, and 1960s, they were actually below average. Growth was also more robust throughout the last third of the 1800s, even at a point when the U.S. economy was already the largest and most productive in the world. There was no reason to assume, based on the rates of growth between 1996 and 2001, that this was an "industrial revolution" without precedent since the rise of the automobile and electricity. Moreover, the rate of growth between 1973 and 2001, even including the rapid growth of the late 1990s, was still historically very slow.

If this was a new economy, there had been many new economies in U.S. history. In the early 1800s, there was a new economy based on cotton, grain, and tobacco exports to industrializing Britain and Europe, where a true new economy—the first major industrial revolution—of textiles, steam power, steel, shipping, and retailing was underway. The American canals, like the British ones, were built by government (in our case, by state governments), which made transporting people and goods more efficient. The government also built new roads. The cotton gin was the significant invention of this period, which, along with the intensive use of slave labor, made the growing and harvesting of cotton continually less expensive.

In the decades before the Civil War, a new economy that manufactured textiles in huge mills in New England, as well as farm equipment, firearms, and other products from iron nails to furniture, was impinging on an agricultural society; the nation's natural waterways were further connected by canals and turnpikes; and affordable sewing machines became common fixtures in households, enabling homemakers to make their first curtains, rugs, linens, and clothing. Railroads also began to take hold, supplementing the waterways and soon overtaking them as efficient modes of transportation. The postal service in the United States was already well-established. A vast free primary school system was developed.

After the Civil War, railroad expansion became frenetic, and the telegraph made instantaneous communications the norm for business. Industrial giants mass-produced oil, steel, and consumer products such as wooden wagons, bicycles, cigarettes and matches, breakfast cereals, frozen meat, canned goods of all kinds, beer, and chewing gum. Large wholesalers and retailers distributed them via rail and steamboat to every corner of the nation, and new highly productive retail chains such as the Atlantic & Pacific Tea Co. (the A&P) sold packaged goods and machine-made clothing conveniently and at low prices. An enormous and efficient continentwide marketplace was thus created.

In the 1920s, the modern consumer economy was underway, led by the widespread purchase of automobiles and exciting new electrical products, such as washing machines, radios, and record players. New government-built sanitation and sewage systems, started in the early 1900s, were now making enormous cities habitable. New roads were paved. Telephones were in wide use by business; X rays, the small pox vaccine, and, later, sulfa drugs saved or improved millions of lives. Aspirin became the drug of choice (it was the "age of aspirin," eventually wrote the playwright Clifford Odets). Powerful new fertilizers, pesticides, and seeds made agriculture radically more productive. Free high schools were built across the nation. In no period in American life, including the 1990s, was change as rapid as in the 1920s, with its ripple effects continuing even into the Great Depression of the 1930s.

In the 1950s and 1960s, free television, jet travel, plastics, powerful big-finned cars, fast-food chains, air conditioning, the widespread use of antibiotics, the discovery of the polio vaccines, and suburbanization remade the economy and the American way of life yet again. Veterans went to college by the hundreds of thousands. A dozen years after World War II, a highway system leading to a network of paved roads connected 90 percent of U.S. homes.

In the late 1990s, the United States again enjoyed a wave of exciting new technologies. We had cable television, inexpensive VCRs, cellular phones, the personal computer, a new highway called the Internet, antidepression medicines, and all kinds of discount and specialty retailers. A higher proportion of Americans than ever before went to college. Observers widely proclaimed that there was never anything like it before. By comparison, the telephone or the car, and surely the railroad or the sewing machine, seemed archaic and ordinary.

So thought every generation of Americans as it looked back on its predecessors. But America has always been a nation of extraordinary change and excitement. And it was usually well aware of it, invariably exaggerating the importance of its own time. "The nineteenth century moved fast and furious, so that one who moved in it felt sometimes giddy, watching it spin," wrote Henry Adams in 1905. Humanity may be historically myopic by nature, but Americans' long mistrust of the lessons of history, to which they were eloquently exhorted by Ralph Waldo Emerson and many others, may have made the nation even more so.

The appearance of new computer-based technology and the rising stock market swept up the nation. The media, Wall Street, Washington, and increasingly some economists claimed that the nation had solved its problems. The soaring stock market confirmed it. In truth, there was arguably less change emanating from this new economy than from its predecessors.

Even after the modest recession of 2001 and 2002, technological determinism remained a powerful idea. It fulfilled many needs. As noted, the media needed the idea of a new economy to make sense of the good times for its readers and viewers. Wall Street analysts and economists needed the new economy to justify unusually high stock prices and promote securities. Alan Greenspan needed the idea to justify stimulating the economy without fear of generating high inflation again. How simple to believe that information technology was an enabling technology, like the railroads or electricity, which created a full-scale industrial revolution that needed little further support. In truth, the impact of the railroads and electricity as sole progenitors of growth was exaggerated as well.

To be sure, there were many skeptics. But even they rarely challenged the central historical tenet that technological advance was the main source of economic growth. When the complex arguments of some sophisticated economists were boiled down, for example, they maintained that because there will always be technological advance, we can simply count on ongoing economic growth. In fact, some anticipated that technological advance would proceed at an ever-faster rate of growth, thus ensuring fast economic growth.

In other instances, talented economists, even while criticizing the assumption that computers were the driving force in a new economy, assumed that America's most rapid economic growth earlier in the century was largely the consequence of the internal combustion engine, the electric dynamo, and a few other key inventions.

Probably most influential, the accomplished economic historian Paul David hypothesized that the rapid growth of the early twentieth century was the consequence in large measure of the adoption of electricity. The nation took a long time to adjust to the introduction of electricity, and David thought it was possible that, for similar rea-

sons, the nation was taking a long time to adjust to information technologies. Eventually, he suggested, it was possible that the U.S.
economy would grow rapidly again as information technology "matured"; that is, as a growing number of companies adopted it and
learned to use it more effectively. Technology, he thus seemed to assume, was the main cause of economic growth, or so this analysis implied. But if the maturing of electrical usage was the key factor of
growth in the early twentieth century, all more or less advanced
economies should have risen at the same rate. Why did electricity
yield it fullest economic potential in the United States and not elsewhere?

Consider how weak the historical argument for such technological
determinism is. In the mid-1800s, for example, the United States
was hardly a leader in advanced technology; Britain and other parts
of Europe were. Yet by the late 1880s, only a generation or so later,
America was the largest and most productive economy in the world.
Most of the initial technologies that spearheaded growth in America
were based on inventions it borrowed from Europe, including the
water mill, the steam engine, the sewing machine and countless textile technologies, the steel furnace, the Bonsack cigarette machine,
and the automobile. The widespread introduction of sanitation in
cities, which contributed so much to growth, was based on the scientific breakthroughs of the Frenchman Louis Pasteur. These technologies blossomed commercially in the United States.

It is widely agreed that the Industrial Revolution started in Britain
in the second half of the 1700s. But there, too, key technologies were
borrowed from other nations and even civilizations. The spinning
wheel, gunpowder, and the compass were China's. The water mill
was known early in Persia and even the Roman Empire. These technologies often lay dormant for centuries, available to any knowledge-
able comer. But they were commercially exploited in one nation at a
particular time and not another. Why? That is the central issue of
economic growth, and it is the question that needs a better answer
than it has generally been given if we are to understand what hap-

pened to the United States in the late 1990s and what is likely to happen in coming years.

Many economists and historians, including those discussed previously in this chapter, are of course aware of the dangers of oversimplification; they know these basic facts. But attributing economic growth to great inventions has become an intellectual convenience that is difficult to discard, as much for the student as for the old intellectual hand. There is a strong temptation to seek a single cause or a great economic turning point to explain economic movements, and great inventions seem to fit the requirements. In economic history, some scholars strongly support the idea that certain macro-inventions were the great sources of economic growth. They see such macro-inventions as creating a stream of influences.

But even those who insist that there are more varied causal factors than invention typically leave the impression that the great inventions were essentially all that mattered. Technological miracles, from the domestication of crops to wind mills to the printing press to the electric dynamo to nuclear energy to the computer, fire our imaginations. It is simply easier to attach history to such hooks, and they easily retain imaginative power over us.

Joseph Schumpeter tried to wean us from dependence on this notion. He warned sarcastically about stressing "the element of invention as much as many writers do." This piece of Schumpetarian disdain, however, was rarely mentioned in the 1990s at the height of new economy advocacy even as Schumpeter's other ideas became popular again. What attracted people to Schumpeter was his praise of the entrepreneur, who created the new products and managerial methods that also stimulated growth.

o   o   o

The principal danger of the mythology of technological preeminence and faith in a new economy is that it misleads us about how to sustain economic growth. In fact, the conclusion of this book is one that not all readers will want to hear. Many of the factors of growth that were neglected in the late 1990s and early 2000s, and indeed since the 1980s, were those that required the support of government and a broader view of the mission of private enterprise. Our future will depend on refocusing our idea of the sources of economic growth.

It would be naïve to believe that intellectual convenience, however, was the only cause of oversimplified attitudes about economic growth in the 1990s. A second sphere of influence was vested financial and political interests, and this is a second battleground for appropriate policy as well. Asserting that technological advance was the main source of economic growth was highly compatible with reduced regulations and lower taxes for corporations. So were assertions that legalizing property rights, a widely popular academic argument, was essentially all that was needed for efficient growth. More vigorous entrepreneurial attitudes were a source of growth in the 1990s, as was some deregulation, and this book argues that a move in this direction, including partial deregulation, was needed. But reliance on these ideas also became zealous in these years. Unfettered private enterprise would in itself solve America's problems, it was argued, because advancing technology, which apparently simply sprang unaided from the human imagination, was essentially all that was required for economies to grow.

The other true necessity for economic development, in this view, was financial capital, by which is meant investable funds. The source of this capital is a nation's savings. Again, lower taxes and less government spending purportedly led to a greater supply of such funds. Once savings were available for investment, technological innovation through entrepreneurial intervention would do its magic. The central policy proposal of the dominating neoclassical economic theories of the period was to raise the nation's savings to make capital available for investment. This was the intellectual foundation for the demands to eliminate America's federal budget deficit: When the government spent more than it received in tax revenues, the borrowing reduced the available capital for business purposes.

Finance matters, of course, but the single-minded focus on it was misleading. One example was the widespread acceptance of the notion that tax increases and reduced federal spending under Presidents Bush and Clinton were major direct causes of the surprising American vigor in the late 1990s. In truth, the restored savings attributable to these policies were almost precisely offset by a reduction in the amount saved by individuals. On balance, there was no increase in national savings and, therefore, there was no independent injection of more funding into the economy in the 1990s.

This is not to say that these policies did not have an important stimulating effect, but their impact was probably largely psychological. They reduced inflationary expectations among investors and arguably also reduced the anticipated funding needs of the federal government. Investors had long forced up interest rates to compensate for what they feared would be a return to higher inflation that would reduce the value of their loans in the future, as well as the great supply for federal debt. Now they acted in the opposite way.

Just as important, investors believed that the Federal Reserve, which controls short-term interest rates, would cut those rates further. Alan Greenspan and his colleagues would recognize that lower budget deficits would enable the Federal Reserve to reduce rates. As a result, investors bid up the prices of bonds, and long-term interest rates at last fell significantly in the mid-1990s. These in turn directly reduced the cost of capital investment and personal mortgage rates, and therefore spurred capital investment, home-buying, and also consumer borrowing against homes. Such home equity refinancings enabled individuals to spend more.

America's own history demonstrates the ambiguities of financial capital as a source of growth. In the nineteenth century, the nation was always short of money. It typically spent more than it earned, invested more than it saved, imported more than it exported, and borrowed unremittingly from overseas investors to make up the difference. Fortunately, European investors were willing to leave their funds in the fast-growing nation. In addition, the nation repeatedly created and re-created a system of credit expansion in the form of a few hundred local banks to support its needs.

But in the nineteenth century, these uncontrollable credit expansions faithfully led to financial panic and deep recession time and again. Enormous trade deficits are not ideal, either, so internal savings eventually do matter. But in themselves, they do not drive growth, especially in the short run. In the late 1990s, the United States again did not meet its own capital needs. Again, it spent more than it earned, invested more than it saved, and imported more than it exported. Once again, it borrowed enormous amounts from willing foreign investors.

Those inclined to the idealized view of financial capital as the fulcrum of economic growth sometimes cite the classical work of Adam Smith, the Scottish economist of the Industrial Revolution. In the seminal *Wealth of Nations*, published in 1776, Smith made clear that the accumulation of a nation's savings for capital investment was critical to economic improvement. He also, I think naïvely, wrote that savings would always be channeled into investment. But it requires a tortured reading of Smith to assume from this that he thought savings were the principal cause of economic growth.

Rather, to Smith, there were several other factors that served as prime causes, and he gave a more rounded view of the sources of economic growth than some ascribe to him. The manufacture of a pin, he found in his well-known observation of local Scottish factories, could be divided into eighteen separate functions, which could radically raise the output of pins in a day's work. To Smith, such a division of labor was not so much a technological advance as it was an organizational and managerial one. Although it depended on new machinery (capital), the division of labor was more importantly a new way of defining and organizing work. Henry Ford's radical moving assembly line of the early 1900s was similarly more an advance in managerial organization than it was a pure technological "invention." The division of labor reached extraordinary productive heights in the late nineteenth and twentieth centuries with the development of both mass production and mass distribution. These generated economies of scale, a central source of economic growth, and higher productivity since the beginning of the Industrial Revolution. The more goods one sold, the lower the cost of production or marketing for each unit sold. No one in Smith's time could have foreseen to what extent labor would be divided and made more productive in the century to come. Enormous economies of scale propelled America's rise in the nineteenth century.

The overwhelming causal factor of growth for Adam Smith, in my reading of him, was in fact the large market discussed previously. The division of labor, and eventually the mass production and distribution of a later century, could only take place in large and growing markets of consumers who had the money and willingness to spend on goods and services and who were readily reached through efficient, low-cost transportation and communications systems.

This was and remains America's decided economic advantage over the rest of the world. In very early societies, when economies and markets were small, people usually had to perform most or even all of their own tasks. They planted seed and harvested their produce; they made their own clothes and built their houses and furniture; they made barrels and with a little expertise, horseshoes, harnesses, and farm tools. Few could become specialists.

When markets grew, however, a society could support expert craftspeople who were able to improve economic efficiency. (High crafts also flourished in ancient wealthy societies because a small number of individuals had control of the vast majority of the wealth and could spend it on such goods.) These early skilled coopers and smiths and toolmakers could make high-quality barrels, horseshoes, and plows more rapidly than could individuals on their own. But such a degree of specialization was economically efficient only as demand for these products grew; a smith in England, for example, could not make a living if only a handful of horseshoes was demanded each year. The artisanal economy could only flourish in a large market. Although they are thought of today as archaic compared to modern versions of the division of labor, specialized crafts were actually early examples of the economic advantages of labor specialization.

"As it is the power of exchanging that gives occasion to the division of labour, so the extent of the division of labour must always be limited by the extent of the market," Smith wrote explicitly and early. "When the market is small, no person can have encouragement to dedicate himself entirely to one employment. . . ." Only with the rapid growth of markets in the 1700s, including thriving exports, did the extensive division of labor make economic sense in new mills, factories, and coal works across Britain. Much larger markets made possible the mass production revolution and economies of scale to come.

○   ○   ○

Why did the economy grow rapidly in the late 1990s? What were the sources of the sudden improvement in productivity? It was not simply the rise of a "new economy" based on maturing information technology. Technological advance was a key source of growth and change, but assertions about the sudden maturing of technology strain credibility. They presume that businesses needed time to purchase and to learn how to adapt to the existing information technologies, and that in 1995 or so they crossed a threshold en masse. Such maturity, it was implied, was simply inevitable.

In fact, many economists have long criticized treating technology as such an abstraction. The Austrian economist Frederick van Hayek long ago correctly criticized economists' references to capital equipment as too general, with their assumptions that such capital was unchanging and always optimal. Other economists criticized the assumptions made by their colleagues that technological advance was "exogenous," which is to say its development was independent of all other economic factors. In past analyses of economic growth, technology was habitually and frustratingly treated as simple "manna from heaven," as a critic noted, inevitably bestowed upon us.

Technological advance manifested itself in specific ways in the late 1990s and was closely dependent on the size and sudden rapid growth of the U.S. market. The most important market effect was a dramatic fall in the price of computer chips, the building block that was critical to the investment in these technologies. Here was a simple and age-old business principle: New technologies were preferable simply because they were much less expensive than older methods, not because they necessarily "changed the way business was done," as the media, Wall Street, and a growing number of new economy gurus suggested. Such a decrease in key costs has happened time and again in the past, in transportation, steel, oil, food, retailing, and communications, for example. As in the past, the fall in computer and chip prices was also highly dependent on enormous economies of scale (as was the fall of other key prices in the past). In other words, these industries depended on a large market for their lower prices.

A second cause of the economic advance in the late 1990s was that the exciting new products were standardized and appealed to a mass market. Far from the niche products that dominated the economy from the 1970s to the mid-1990s, which were also dependent on technological advance, the dominant new products of the late 1990s possessed the characteristics that traditionally helped drive American economic growth: Because they were standardized, they could generate great economies of manufacturing, distribution, and marketing scale. Consider how standardized this era was: MS-DOS, Windows, Apple, the basic PC, the video game box, the networking of Cisco, Word, and so forth. This was not the inevitable consequence of maturing technologies; it was fortuitous. No such good fortune has struck nuclear or solar energy, for example, or as yet, biotechnology.

But also contributing significantly to economic growth was growth itself, prompted by subdued inflation, a shift in the policies of the Federal Reserve, the soaring stock market, consumer and business borrowing, and strong demand for the U.S. dollar. Market expansion created incentives for investment and technological innovation and made full exploitation of economies of scale possible.

There was also a cultural shift that made business and entrepreneurialism acceptable and even glamorous again. This book argues that this tendency has gone too far, but it cannot be denied that a cultural shift in attitudes contributed to economic growth, as did deregulation in some industries. The energies of business were extraordinary in this era. The reinstatement of market values was valuable, to a large degree. But the contributions of the labor force, which accepted slow wage growth, willingly did all manner of work, and energetically re-educated itself, were underestimated. (These factors are discussed in greater detail in Chapter 7.)

Our intellectual purpose is to determine why economies grow. Our ultimate purpose, however, is to determine how to sustain America's economic growth. Some argue that because the nation's standard of living is already high, we need not grow rapidly again to satisfy the nation's needs. But slow growth creates serious problems. First, the financial rewards of slow growth are not distributed as equally or as fairly as are the rewards of fast growth. Many get left behind, and their confidence and ambition are undermined. Second, key services, notably education and healthcare, continue to rise in price faster than typical incomes in a slow-growing economy because they are not given to productivity gains. A rising number of Americans cannot afford them when the economy grows slowly. Third, although savings do not matter in the short run, nor are they a trigger to growth, remaining competitive over time requires the ability to generate sufficient savings, including ample corporate profits. A nation starved of growing incomes will not accomplish this. Fourth, the United States may neglect its government programs and its public investment when personal incomes do not rise rapidly. It is not in America's character to sacrifice too much personal gain for public good. Ultimately, this will reduce economic growth as well.

Implicit in this discussion is that America may not grow as fast as it can. I argue that there have been substantial and important improvements in the rate of growth compared to the slowdown between 1973 and 1995, but that the economy will probably not return to the long-term rate of growth that characterized it since the Civil War unless we undertake a broader approach to enhancing this growth. Even then, it may not grow as rapidly.

Meanwhile, the nation's problems are far from solved. Income inequality is high, male wages have grown little and have fallen for many, our child poverty is the worst in the developed world, and the quality of the public school system is highly unequal as the costs of education rise much faster than typical incomes. Similarly, the cost of healthcare is rising much faster than typical incomes, leaving an enormous proportion of people poorly cared for. Almost nothing significant has been done to accommodate the greatest social revolution of the time, the advent of the two-worker family. Jobs in general are also more uncertain, and healthcare and benefits tied to these jobs are less secure. The new needs of a changing economy require still more education and new institutions to cope with an intensely competitive and riskier economy. The economy is not a stationary target but a moving one. Maximizing the rate of growth is imperative in the face of such problems because it will provide the resources necessary to solve these problems. Without those resources America faces a serious dilemma. It may well have to learn to live with slower economic growth indefinitely for the first time since the Civil War. This will not be easy, especially if the nation is misled by its experts, Wall Street, and the media.

To explore the sources of prosperity, we must focus on productivity, a word that has become widely familiar in the public discourse in the past ten years and is central to a rising standard of living. When we talk about why economies grow, we are essentially talking about why productivity grows. When we talk about how we can raise the standard of living, we are talking about how to make the nation's businesses more productive. We must begin, then, with some basic concepts and definitions.

3

The Importance of
Economic Growth

ONE REASON THAT ECONOMICS CAN BE CONFUSING IS THAT ITS terms are fairly arbitrary and do not always reflect common-sense meanings. Economic growth is an unclear concept to many people, and the word "economy" itself is ambiguous. To many, the economy may mean all the businesses that make products or create jobs in the nation. We say, for example, that America's economy produced 2.5 million new jobs in 2000. Others may think of the economy as the value of the nation's physical assets, such as its land, houses, cars, airplanes, office buildings, and plants and machinery. To a large number of people, the economy is no doubt the nation's financial wealth: its savings, its retirement funds, and the stock market. If the stock market goes up, many seem to believe that means the economy is stronger.

When economists talk about the economy, however, they are referring to the goods and services that are made each year. Goods are tangible, such as cars, food, and clothing, but the meaning of services, which actually constitute most of what we spend our money on, requires further explanation. Retailing, transportation, and banking are key services of the economy. A retailer has goods on its shelves, but its business is running the outlet that enables people to shop. Shopping on the Internet is such a service. An airline has jet planes, but its product is travel. Even banks deal in hard cash, but their products are services such as clearing checks and making loans.

The sum of all goods and services produced and provided by business and government each year is the nation's gross domestic product (GDP).[1] When we deduct the inflation of the prices of these goods and services to derive the actual quantity bought and sold, we call it real GDP. (GDP in this book usually means real GDP.) This is what economists generally mean by the economy, and it is a useful if sometimes limited definition.

One reason this definition of the economy is useful is that it tells us about the growth of incomes in a nation. When GDP grows, more goods and services are made and sold than in the year before, and this generates more income in the form of profits and wages (as well as rental and interest income). Thus, when the economy—that is, GDP—grows faster, so do incomes in general. As businesses make more money selling their products, they often hire more workers, and the rate of unemployment falls. As the availability of surplus workers is reduced, businesses are usually forced to pay higher wages and salaries to most workers. Rents also typically rise as GDP grows because there is greater demand for space. Americans also usually put more money into banks and savings accounts, from which they earn more interest. As GDP rises, Americans on average are therefore generally better off year after year.

A recession occurs when the GDP not merely fails to rise but actually falls. Roughly one-fifth of the time in U.S. history, the amount of goods and services contracted. In such recessions, jobs were typically lost and the rate of unemployment rose; business and career opportunities contracted; and although wages usually did not fall on

(handwritten margin note: WAY TOO BROKRD & ALMOST PURE WRONG EXCEPT AS TO WEALTH)

---

[1]To be precise, these are the final goods and services in the nation, not intermediate goods that businesses buy from each other to make products for consumers, government, and capital investment. If we included in GDP, for example, the parts a car maker buys from its suppliers, it would be doubled counting. The price of the car already includes the value of these parts.

average, they essentially stagnated.[2] In the past, the U.S. economy always recovered from recession and usually recaptured the lost GDP within a few years, and often more quickly. That is, it was soon producing and providing as many goods and services—and therefore, creating as much income—as it had before the recession, and soon it was exceeding previous levels. The longest recession was the Great Depression of the 1930s, which lasted ten years; it was actually composed of two severe depressions, with a short recovery in between. A single business cycle includes recession, in which the quantity of goods and services falls; recovery, during which GDP rises to the level it reached before the recession began; and the expansion that raises GDP to new high levels.

In most years of the nineteenth and twentieth centuries, then, GDP was higher than it ever had been before; in other words, the United States was usually wealthier at any given point in time than it ever had been before. Even GDP per capita—per man, woman, and child—was usually higher than it ever had been before, although the population kept growing.

In fact, ever since the Industrial Revolution of the 1700s, it has not been a dramatic event that GDP was generally higher year after year or that a nation was richer than it ever was before. What increasingly mattered has been the rate of improvement; economies that grew slowly compared to others, such as Britain's in the late 1800s and early 1900s, were left behind. Because of America's fast rate of growth, its annual GDP was already larger by the late 1800s than the annual output of goods and services of its nearest rival, Britain, which had stood as the most powerful economy in the world over the preceding one hundred years. By 1929, the year of the Great Crash, the United States was producing eight times as many goods and services annually as it did in 1870. Part of this growth was

---

[2]In the 1800s, the relationship was often reversed. Nominal wages remained the same, but in recession prices often fell. Thus, real wages, after inflation, often rose during recessions and fell during expansions when prices rose again.

the result of America's rapidly expanding population. But the U.S. economy also produced about three and one-half times per person (GDP per capita) what it produced in 1870, a level that was significantly higher than anywhere in the Old World. America's European rivals started to grow more rapidly than the United States for an extended period of time only after World War II, at which point their GDP per person was lower than America's.

The level of GDP reached in 1929 turned out to be a high point for the next decade. At one point in the 1930s, annual GDP was nearly 50 percent below its 1929 high, and the rate of unemployment exceeded 25 percent for several years. But with the outbreak of World War II, the 1929 GDP level was restored, and in the post-World War II years GDP grew rapidly again. By 1970, the annual production of goods and services had risen some three and one-half times over the 1929 level, and by some thirty times over the one hundred years since the end of the Civil War. Much of this increase was due to population growth, of course, but GDP per capita was more than six times higher in 1970 than it was in 1870.

GDP by no means provides all the information we might like about how well off we are, however. It does not account for the degradation of the environment, for example, or rising traffic congestion, or the labor of spouses in the home. It does not measure the nation's total wealth—its assets, such as land, housing, and stocks—as opposed to the annual volume of goods and services made and provided. Total wealth may actually decline even as GDP rises. For example, when a hurricane seriously damages the coast of Florida, there is no deduction in GDP for losses in destroyed homes and roads. To the contrary, reported GDP usually increases because more money is spent to rebuild the region even though the nation's wealth temporarily declined by the amount of damage.

In addition, GDP does not tell us as much as we would like about what people actually earn. It does not tell us how the nation's total income is distributed among workers, for example. Higher income workers may get most of what the nation produces, as has been the case since the late 1970s. It does not tell us how many hours workers must work to earn their money. It does not tell us whether their jobs are more or less secure.

Nor does GDP tell us much about the impact of new products on how Americans live. The composition of an American budget was much different in 1900 than in 1800 and much different in 2000 than in 1900. If Americans could buy eight times as many products in 1929 as in 1870, this figure did not take into account how much better and exciting those products were. But even if modern products are immeasurably more advanced than earlier ones, we should be careful about assuming that the modern products *improved* lives more than did historical ones. It is the degree of improvement that matters, the rate of change, not the absolute level. A car in 1925 probably had a much larger impact on lives than did inexpensive jet travel or a personal computer in 2000. A new sewing machine in 1850 probably had a greater impact on lives than did a PC. The growth of GDP nevertheless gives us a sense of the dimension of change over time; it tells us that our resources commanded a much greater quantity of goods and services over time. Beginning in the 1960s, the federal government has attempted to adjust GDP for improvements in the quality of products, but comparisons across long periods of time are still dubious.

How well off people are—a comprehensive measure of the standard of living—simply cannot be reduced to a single number. But making many further adjustments to GDP would make it a less useful and more ambiguous measure. Rather, we can supplement GDP with other measures. Throughout most of American history, many of the other aspects of the standard of living that we might be interested in usually improved along with GDP. Incomes generally rose (with many exceptions) for all levels of workers, so inequality was not an issue. The health of the nation deteriorated in the nineteenth century as it industrialized, but by the twentieth century Americans were living far longer and much healthier lives. In the twentieth century, jobs became more secure and hours worked were dramatically reduced. In these senses, rising GDP was a good measure of a broad increase in a rising standard of living; most measures of well-being improved along with it. No doubt these material gains came with costs, such as a damaged environment and new kinds of personal anxieties, but the benefits of economic growth over time were unquestionably extraordinary and widely shared.

○   ○   ○

The general source of this economic growth was rising productivity. Productivity is easy to define. It is the amount of GDP (less government spending) produced for a given amount of work. Economists usually refer to it as the output of goods and services per hour of work.

But even if productivity is simple to define, it is in reality a complex concept. It provides a shorthand answer for why economies grow. But why does productivity grow? To get a better sense of what productivity is, let's consider a farmer in the early nineteenth century. Threshing, a process in harvesting wheat, had been done by hand for hundreds of years by workers pelting the raw wheat with wooden flails to separate the grain from the stalks. On average, a single worker could thresh about seven bushels of wheat per day in the early 1800s on American farms. But affordable mechanical threshers were developed in the early 1800s that rotated around an axle and could be drawn by a team of horses or mules. By mid-century, these machines were able to thresh 100 bushels a day, a nearly fifteenfold increase over the daily output of one worker. This is what is meant by an increase in productivity. More output could be produced per hour of work. (Adam Smith figured that his pin factory produced two hundred or so times more as a result of the division of labor.)

This single increase in productivity could, and usually did, set off a series of other economic events. One might immediately assume that the farmer would fire his extra workers because, with the thresher, he could harvest as much wheat with fewer of them. The replacement of workers with machines has occurred repeatedly in history, beginning at least as early as the Middle Ages (causing labor strife even then), and has become a constant and understandable fear.

Many farmers, however, were more ambitious. They bought more land with their profits and cultivated still more crops because they realized they could make even more profit by doing so. They might have thereby kept workers employed or hired more. To cultivate more land, they would have bought more seed and, perhaps, more horses or mules and more tools and equipment: another plow, a new mechanical reaper, or more pitchforks and fencing wire. They might have also bought a better or bigger wagon to bring crops to market more quickly and over a wider geographical area, thereby enhancing the value of the new equipment by selling a greater quantity of produce.

Some farmers could also have cut the price of the wheat they sold as the cost to thresh each bushel fell. Even though they might earn less per bushel of wheat, they would make more profit overall because they could sell much more. To do so, farmers would have had to be confident that they could sell the additional wheat. The strong, growing market in early America, as well as increases in exports of agricultural commodities, provided such an assurance. This competitive pressure forced other farmers to buy new equipment so they could be more productive and cut prices as well, or they would lose their market.

The benefits of a single farmer's improved productivity spread. If the farmer bought more land with his profits, he put more money into the seller's hands. If he purchased new tools or a wagon, he put additional money into the hands of toolmakers and wagonmakers. These businesspeople thus also earned more profits, which they might have invested in the expansion of their own businesses. Greater sales also increased business for the professional wholesalers who distributed these crops. They might now have invested in larger storage facilities.

Price cuts also saved consumers money, which immediately raised their standard of living by enabling them to spend their cash savings on food or other goods or to save money to buy land or a house, or invest in a business. The manufacturers and distributors of these other goods—say, textiles, iron nails, or sewing machines—might in turn also have invested in more equipment or built new facilities because their sales rose. They might have been able to make their own products more productively through technological advances and further investment. Still more goods and services were sold, more profit earned, and more investment made. GDP grew as a consequence of this chain reaction.

As demand for goods and services rose for all these reasons, businesses typically found that they needed more labor, not less. The farmer competed with the stores and wholesalers and the makers of wagons for unemployed workers. As surplus labor was utilized, the farmers and wagonmakers, food stores, and wholesalers had to increase wages. The higher wages, in turn, were spent on more goods and services and GDP increased.

This is the power of rising productivity. A nation's overall economy can grow even if productivity remains the same because more people may enter the workforce, earn a wage, and raise demand for goods and services. But unless the economy is producing more goods and services for a worker's effort, there will be no additional revenues from which to pay higher wages on average. If someone gets a raise, another will have to take a cut in pay. GDP per capita, the standard of living, will not rise.

We have thus seen that there were two general sources of growth for the economy. The first was the growth of the workforce. As more workers were employed, the economy grew faster. The second was the growth of productivity, or the output per hour of work of all workers. The rate of growth of total GDP equals the sum of the rate of growth of the workforce and the rate of growth of productivity. But only the portion of growth due to gains in productivity is available to raise the nation's living standard. Without productivity gains, any growth in GDP is exactly offset by population growth, and the average income stays the same.

○   ○   ○

Economic historians calculated that productivity for the American economy as a whole, excluding government but including all business goods and services, grew by more than 2 percent per year on average after roughly the end of the Civil War. Because productivity has grown so rapidly in so many industries since the 1800s, America's standard of living is dramatically higher than it was a century and a half ago. Today, a farm's output per hour of work is about twenty times what it was in the mid-1800s.[3] Similar gains were made in manufacturing and services industries across the nation. The development of department stores and retail chains in the late 1800s, just like the development of fast-food restaurants and Internet commerce in the late twentieth century, increased the volume of sales per hour of work. Railroads increased the speed at which cargo could be transported, as did vast oceangoing vessels, jet planes, and computerized mail a century later. Because of the astoundingly efficient economics of television, a subject addressed several times in this book, a consumer company could send an advertising message to a household for a small fraction—literally, fractions of pennies—of what it cost fifty years earlier, thus dramatically reducing the cost of marketing.

The productivity increases in so many industries created a chain reaction of productivity gains, multiplying the value of a productivity

---

[3]Threshing was not the only task in the harvesting of wheat. Many new tools were created, including eventually the tractor, to harvest and prepare the wheat. The U.S. Department of Agriculture estimated that in 1822 it took fifty to sixty hours of labor to accomplish all the tasks necessary to harvest one acre of wheat. By 1890, the average time to harvest an acre of wheat was reduced to only eight to ten hours.

Five to six acres of wheat, then, could be harvested in the time it took to harvest one in 1822. Productivity did not increase equally each year, of course, but to make historical comparisons, we can again compute an annual rate of growth, which as noted earlier is similar to the compound interest earned in a savings account. According to these government estimates, the productivity of harvesting wheat grew by about 2.5 percent a year on average over approximately seventy years.

Besides harvesting their produce, farmers also had to clear and maintain the fields, fence off the property from predators, and market the produce. Productivity improved for some of these functions. Inexpensive wooden-wheeled wagons made distributing goods much more efficient, for example. In some areas, however, productivity did not improve at all, and perhaps even fell. When all activities that required labor hours were taken into account in the production of a year's crops in America, the rate of growth of agricultural productivity was about 1 percent a year on average over the course of the nineteenth century. Thus, American farmers were on average producing about three times more per hour of labor in 1900 than they were in 1800. Agricultural productivity growth at such a rate over so long a period of time was a revolution by any former standard. In the twentieth century, agricultural productivity grew much faster still with the aid of biological and chemical advances that resulted in more efficient feeding of animals, new hybrid seeds, and dramatically improved fertilizers and pesticides.

improvement in any single industry and raising productivity in the economy as a whole.

In general, the rate of growth of wages reflected the rate of growth of productivity in America. Like almost all things economic, average wages in the nineteenth century rose and fell cyclically. But the best evidence to date suggests that American wages rose on average over the entire nineteenth century by about 1 percent per year. That is to say, the average American worker in 1900 was earning about three times what the average worker in 1800 earned, discounted for inflation. In the twentieth century, real wages rose by roughly 2 percent per year.

○   ○   ○

Some readers may consider this only an ideal version of the way markets work. Returning to our farmers, for example, we can easily imagine that they could get together and refuse to cut prices or invest in more equipment. They could hoard their profits as their costs fell, fire workers, and figuratively stay fat and rich. The replacement of workers by machines under such circumstances could cost many jobs on balance and keep wages down.

In truth, the economic model described previously was more subtle than this. It required only a few farmers to be competitive to force other farmers to respond. If only a few (or sometimes even only one) cut their prices, for example, most other farmers would have to cut prices or they would lose market share. They would have to invest in new machinery, train workers, buy other tools, and so forth to keep prices low and maintain their share of the market. Thus, all participants in a market need not be competitive or even rational to force most farmers or other businesses to raise their productivity and create the circle of productivity gains throughout the economy.

Also, entrepreneurial activity coupled with rapid technological advances themselves could undermine the monopolistic hold of even powerful businesses by creating new products to attract consumers away from old producers. The candle, for example, was undone by the kerosene lamp and the kerosene lamp by the electric light bulb. Countless smaller technological advances undermined the hold of some companies over their markets. Today, network television is undermined by cable television, just as network television undermined the old-style cinema and radio, and e-mail today substitutes for letters, phone calls, and fax services.

Nevertheless, history also bears out general concerns about the anticompetitive power of large corporations. Despite the natural efficiencies of markets and the protean nature of technological change, large corporations have often enjoyed monopolistic power that enabled them to keep up prices, keep down wages, or reduce competitive innovation. A handful of large companies in a given industry (oligopolies) frequently colluded to set high prices, hoard profits, keep new products out of the marketplace, suppress wages, and demand long hours from workers in poor conditions.

Thus, other factors were needed to support growth. One was the intercession of government to ensure, as even Adam Smith argued it should, that markets remain competitive and to limit the price-setting and distributional control of companies. Government also enabled labor unions to organize and demand higher wages, thus offsetting the natural power of giant corporate entities, and also adopted regulations to protect workers, including a minimum wage. These measures contributed significantly to the fair distribution of the gains from productivity improvements.

Many other conditions were clearly necessary to produce economic growth, and some of these were efficiently provided by the market. The wheat farmer in the 1830s needed capital to pay for his new machine. A financial system, if an unstable one, was created quickly in America. The farmer also might have needed access to more affordable land, or enough fresh water, to exploit fully the expensive thresher. America had an abundance of such resources. Most important, he needed a large and growing market in which he could sell the far greater quantity of wheat he could now harvest so efficiently. This, America provided uniquely.

The farmer needed good roads to make delivery to a wider geographical area possible, and later canals and then railroads. He needed a pool of labor that was moderately literate and educated so that it could learn, for example, to operate the thresher. He needed political stability and secure property rights. All of these required government investment, subsidy, and legal intervention. Markets alone, especially in the early development of the nation, could not fill such needs, although they provided incentives for other conditions.

In America, all these conditions came together. A large and growing market enabled farmers to sell their produce. Land was fertile and abundant. Other natural resources were plentiful. Roads were built to reach consumers everywhere. Communications systems were established, from the telegraph to newspapers and the postal service. A banking system was created, albeit in fits and starts.

From our secure position in the modern world, we take for granted that people were confident in the usefulness and future benefits of new machines. But the farmer of the early and mid-1800s had little experience with such complex machinery as the thresher, or later the tractor, and was not easily convinced of the benefits of new technology; in fact, a generation passed after the invention of a usable thresher before it was adopted widely on American farms. A sense of optimism about machines and the future itself was thus also a component of growth. The farmer might take the risk of buying the machine if there were already an entrepreneurial spirit in the air. The farmer also had to believe his rights to his profits were protected from war or the rapacious behavior of others. Ideally, property rights were protected by law.

One point must be reemphasized. The invention of the thresher itself was a response to a need. Had there been no obvious demand for a great deal more wheat, the commercial thresher might not have been invented when it was. The heart of technological advance might well be human curiosity and the need to express oneself through creative invention, but economic opportunity—and a culture of opportunity to support it—were integral to it.

From the example of the thresher alone we can make some useful generalizations about the many conditions that sustain economic growth. The conditions for productivity growth in America included the following:

1. Large and expanding markets;
2. Technological advances, such as the thresher;
3. The availability of financial capital;
4. Improving transportation and communications systems to make the delivery of products fast and inexpensive, and the information about technology and the demand for goods widely available;
5. Comparatively high educational and literacy standards, so that knowledge of new methods and available products could spread among producers and consumers;
6. A culture (including religion) that encourages commerce;
7. Natural resources, such as adequate land and water; and
8. A legal and social environment that protects both economic and (I argue in this book) political rights, ensures a competitive economic market, and protects those less advantaged in the marketplace.

Despite having these advantages, America's economic development was sporadic and painful. Entrepreneurs often failed and financial market crashes undermined the best of intentions with uncanny regularity every twenty years or so. In early America, entrepreneurs and land owners could easily find themselves in debtor prisons or in penury when speculative bubbles burst. The fear of panic and bust were ever present.

But it was workers who largely bore the pain of capitalistic change. The plight of farm workers (and eventually small farm owners) as America evolved from an agricultural society into an industrial one was especially difficult. Initially, the number of workers employed by farms grew rapidly, even as productivity rose. Eventually, however, the farms were able to produce more than people could eat, and eventually jobs on the farm dwindled. Farmhands had no choice but to move in tens of thousands to the often ugly, crowded, and invariably mystifying and fearful cities to take jobs, often the most poorly paid ones.

But new jobs there were, and this became a "second frontier" for Americans, replacing the original frontier of vast, cheap, and fertile land. Workers in industry after industry lost jobs to more modern industries. Wooden wagons were replaced partly by bicycles and then by automobiles. The A&P replaced the corner store. The railroads replaced the canals; cars, trucks, and planes eventually reduced the demand for rail transportation. Television and radio news replaced much of the newspaper industry.

But as productivity improved in most manufacturing and service industries, the demand for goods increased so rapidly that once again many more jobs were created than lost. The number of workers in manufacturing in particular rose from hundreds of thousands to millions by the turn of the century. The unemployment rate on average in the late 1800s was about what it is in the contemporary era, but workers both lost and found jobs more readily. Although workers did most of the sacrificing in capitalistic development, average wages nevertheless rose substantially in the second half of the 1800s, and even though they probably became increasingly unequal until the twentieth century, wages significantly rose for all income levels.

○   ○   ○

Over time, the difference between rapidly growing productivity and slow-growing productivity is enormous. The rate of productivity growth of slightly more than 2 percent per year meant that the nation produced twelve times more goods and services per hour of work in 1970 than it did in 1870. This created ample revenues from which to raise wages, support government services, and save. Had productivity grown by a rate of only 1 percent per year, the U.S. economy would have produced only three times what it produced per hour in 1870.

The best evidence to date suggests that U.S. wages rose on average over the entire nineteenth century by about 1 percent per year. That is to say, the average American worker in 1900 was earning about three times what the average worker in 1800 earned, discounted for inflation. In the twentieth century, over the course of which productivity rose still faster, real wages rose by roughly 2 percent per year.

Beginning in 1973, however, there was a decided change in America's prospects. GDP began to grow significantly more slowly than it had since the mid-1800s. Had household labor (the work done by spouses at home) been included in GDP, the slowdown would have appeared even greater. Because spouses went to work in such great numbers in the decades after World War II, their incomes were increasingly included in GDP, as for the most part were the incomes of those they hired to do housework and childcare in their stead. This raised the rate of reported growth compared to earlier periods, when wives mostly stayed at home and their contribution to the economy was not included in GDP. (Some foreign governments compute an estimate of the contribution of household labor, and it is a large percentage of GDP: in fact, as much as 30 or 40 percent.)

Just as fast growth produces a wealthy nation, a slowdown in the rate of growth has severe adverse effects. Revisions in the data over the past twenty-five years have made historical comparisons difficult, but we can generally conclude that since 1973, when the first harsh recession of the post-World War II era struck, productivity has grown about 1 percent per year more slowly than it had on average since the mid-1800s. As a result, GDP was a full 25 percent lower in 1995 than it would have been had the economy grown as rapidly after 1973 as it had on average since the mid-1800s. The income of the typical family would have been approximately $10,000 per year more, an increase of about $200 per week. The annual revenues of the federal government would have been more than $400 billion higher, more than enough to guarantee the future of Social Security and Medicare or to guarantee health insurance for many more Americans and still balance the federal budget. The entire Social Security program cost about $400 billion in 2000, for example. Corporate profits would probably have been another $75 billion per year. I believe such slow growth accounted for a great deal of the disarray and anger in the nation and the repeated claims that America had "lost" what it once had.

Beginning in late 1995, GDP began to grow rapidly again, defying almost all expectations and giving rise to claims that there was a new economy. The great hope in the late 1990s was that the nation had returned to the rates of growth that had formerly made it so prosperous. And the source of this growth was thought to be rising productivity.

The return of growth in late 1995 was a salve to a wounded nation. GDP grew more than a full percentage point faster each year in the late 1990s than in the early 1990s. Wages increased significantly for all levels of workers. Almost everyone seemed to have a job who wanted one. Those under forty were at last buying homes in large proportion again. People were buying new cars again in a volume that was at last more commensurate with the rate of buying in the 1960s. In truth, after nearly a quarter of a century of lagging incomes and slow economic growth, there was more pent-up demand for the material promises of American life than economists had realized. (The proportion of those under forty who owned homes had declined since the 1970s. The number of new cars bought per worker had fallen to extremely low levels in the 1970s, 1980s, and early 1990s.) In 2001, slightly more than half of American families owned a personal computer.

Politically speaking, the United States also breathed more easily. The constant fear of the 1980s and early 1990s that the United States had lost its direction subsided, as did the search for a moral explanation of the country's alleged decline. Americans were less angry at each other and at government. This was a consequence of more rapidly growing productivity.

The historical relationship between rapidly rising productivity and a growing standard of living was reaffirmed in the late 1990s. A slow rate of productivity growth, however, did not seem to be sufficient to raise the standard of living for most Americans, as was evident between 1973 and 1995.

The Industrial Revolution that began in Britain in the 1700s and spread widely is the ultimate example of productivity growth. But the story of productivity starts much earlier.

4

The Causes of
Industrial Revolution

THE INDUSTRIAL REVOLUTIONS OF THE PAST ARE THE GREAT case studies from which we can learn why economies grow. But for almost every assertion about industrial revolution, there seems to be a contrary one. Some serious scholars insist that there was no industrial revolution at all, but rather a series of unrelated events that culminated in a single movement only in the retrospective view of historians. Others believe that these economic transformations were evolutionary rather than revolutionary. This latter point is surely true. But the word "revolution" is still an appropriate description because these economic transformations were pivotal, even if they came together more slowly than the word usually implies. Most historians still agree at least on this: The Industrial Revolution started in Britain in the late 1700s and spread relatively quickly across Europe and North America in the following century, and that it was a threshold that, once passed through, increased a society's wealth far more rapidly and consistently than ever before.

I can find no simple or adequate definition of "industrial revolution," but for our purposes, the Industrial Revolution marks the point at which productivity began to grow consistently. From then on, the standard of living—the GDP per capita—rose steadily, interrupted only temporarily by war or recession. For example, even as Britain's economic advance was eclipsed by rapid economic growth in America, Germany, and other European nations in the late 1800s, its standard of living continued to rise. By contrast, before the British Industrial Revolution, the standard of living of a leading nation or city-state typically declined in absolute terms or at best stagnated when another economy displaced it as a leading economy. The British Industrial Revolution represented a decisive break in the course of human history. It was the beginning of an inexorable rise of productivity.

Many early historians of the Industrial Revolution sought a single explanatory cause for it, or at least a leading catalytic factor. It was only natural, especially in the period in which it was occurring, to believe that the major catalyst was the invention of machines themselves. They were the most tangible and starkest marvels of the new age. This habit has stayed with us. "The history of the English working classes begins in the second half of the eighteenth century with the invention of the steam engine and of machines for spinning and weaving cotton," wrote Friedrich Engels in 1845. "It is well known that these inventions gave rise to the genesis of an industrial revolution." Arnold Toynbee's 1884 *Lectures on the Industrial Revolution in England* is widely cited as among the first analyses of the period. Toynbee wrote that society was "suddenly broken in pieces by the mighty blow of the steam engine and the power loom."

Even the best of scholars continued to think along these lines, usually attributing the Industrial Revolution to single industries, or at least assuming that one industry spearheaded the movement. David Landes, for example, argued that the textile industry was the lead industry of Britain's Industrial Revolution, even as he emphasized the cultural changes that were necessary to make it possible. Carlo Cipolla argued that all aspects of society contributed to the economic awakening, but singled out iron and coal as the leading factors.

However, the improvement of productivity was not the simple consequence of new machinery. First, machinery and mechanization in general were not necessary conditions for economic growth historically. Rudimentary productivity improvements were to be found in the earliest known communities, long before what we think of as mechanization flourished. Roughly 8,000 years ago, for example, after having roamed the earth as hunters and food gatherers for several million years, some tribes began to domesticate animals and grow their own food. To do so, they developed new but simple tools, such as flint sickles, baskets, and mortars and pestles. These latter tools were hardly sufficient causal factors of growth in themselves but rather responses to the needs of domestication to feed a growing population. It is difficult to imagine that someone invented a basket and then decided it would be a grand idea to start domesticating plants that could be carried in it, but we make such assumptions about complex modern tools and machines all the time.

Early tribes also adopted new agricultural techniques apart from the use of tools, including the planting of seeds and harvesting. As early communities ate more consistently and nutritiously, their populations became denser. As they became denser, there was also greater incentive to make agriculture more productive because they consumed more food. New tools were needed, but so were new ways to organize the early society. Hierarchy and bureaucracy emerged.

Long before Adam Smith, labor in such societies was divided and specialized. Among the new skills was writing, the first uses of which were probably for keeping inventories and recording trade. Evidence suggests that the first alphabet was probably developed around 1,500 B.C. in the Fertile Crescent and spread widely over the next thousand years. Writing was a specialized skill that was learned by only a relatively few scribes. No doubt it was widely thought that most people could not learn such intricate skills, much as it was asserted that computer skills in the 1990s might be beyond the grasp of many Americans.

If it were possible to measure the consequences of such managerial and informational innovations, as well as new rudimentary tools, we would find that they raised productivity fairly rapidly by reducing the work time needed to produce a calorie of food intake. The "standard of living" of these societies improved as they produced more food in less labor time.

Several factors, then, were at work, even in such communities, which made them wealthier through improvements in productivity. These included the development of tools and weapons, specialization of labor, new learned skills such as writing, and an internal demand for food. What is also clear is that these improvements required the development of a way of organizing society. Innovation and social organization were inseparable in these early societies, and the same is true for more complex and sophisticated societies. It is entirely possible that economic growth in these early societies was substantial, at least over short periods. The incentives to produce more food led to a variety of nonmechanical innovations that resulted in productivity growth.

If technological invention is not necessary for productivity growth, neither is it sufficient by itself to produce it. Many of the extraordinary devices of the Industrial Revolution were by no means new in the 1700s. Mechanization had captured the imagination of Britain and Europe in general, but mills, spinning wheels, compasses, gunpowder, and other key inventions of the later Industrial Revolution were borrowed from earlier and even ancient civilizations. Around the year 1,000 A.D., an age of advanced tools and machines was launched in Europe that improved the productivity of many of these societies. Why didn't an industrial revolution therefore occur then?

The gains in productivity in the Middle Ages were astonishing by the standards of the day. The first such gains in productivity occurred in agriculture and were based both on new methodologies and increasingly complex tools. The improvements in farming methods included crop rotation so as not to deplete the resources of the land (a practice used in ancient Rome). Sheep, it was discovered, could be gainfully herded to fallow land for their natural fertilizer.

Equally important was a change in the organization of farming. Previously it was dominated by inefficient manors, owned in effect by traveling warlords, and run by their managers, who had little incentive to improve yields. Serfs and peasants had at best small plots of land that could not support further investment. But during the Middle Ages manorial agriculture evolved into family farming, with plots large enough, and incentives great enough, to encourage productivity gains.

But what prompted the vast change in farming organization? The economic historian Meir Kohn points out that the most advanced agricultural methods were adopted near urban centers, because demand for produce was strong. Modern farming methods were also most quickly adopted near the coasts, which had access to trade. Thus, the demand for produce—that is, a strong market— created the incentives to make farming more productive. Kohn claims that the direction of improvement was not from technological inventions such as the heavy plow to family farms to large markets, but the other way around. The demand from markets induced organizational changes in farming that made the adoption and development of technological advances and new farming and husbandry methodologies both desirable and possible. This is an early and important piece of evidence about the influence of markets and the direction of causality.

Demand also created greater incentives to adopt new tools. The heavy plow was developed and widely used, making the clearing and tilling of land more efficient. As the use of such plows spread, farmers adapted powerful animals, particularly horses if they could afford them, to farm work. The nailed horseshoe was another example of an important advance, enabling horses to work longer and faster without injury, as were harnesses that enabled horses to pull plows and wagons with less effort. One reason we know horseshoes were valuable was that ferries charged twice as much to transport a horse with horseshoes across a river as one without them.

The yields on farms increased significantly as a result. Wrote one historian: "The heavy plow, the open fields, the new integration of agriculture and herding, three field rotation, modern horse harnesses, nailed horseshoes . . . had combined into a total system of agrarian exploitation by the year 1100 to provide a zone of peasant prosperity stretching across Northern Europe from the Atlantic to the Dnieper."

The 1100s and 1200s were also the first manufacturing age. "It is an astonishing concept to the modern mind that medieval man was surrounded by machines," wrote the historian Jean Gimpel. "The fact is, machines were not something foreign or remote to the towns-people or the peasant in his fields. The most important was the mill: converting the power of water or wind into work, grinding corn, crushing olives, fulling cloth, tanning leather, making paper and so on. These were the factories of the Middle Ages."

The miraculous sight of water mill after water mill stretching to the horizon in their own day transfixed contemporary observers in Britain. Here was a wealthy society, rich in capital investment. When William the Conqueror sent his surveyors across the land in 1086 to collect taxes, as recorded in the Domesday books, they found more than 5,600 water mills, or one per fifty families.

These mills essentially required fewer hours of work to produce the key manufactured products of the day, notably cloth and food-stuffs. The basic mechanism can be thought of as a motor. The rapidity of the rotation driven by wind or moving water far exceeded what a single worker, or even a team of animals, could accomplish. Early water mills probably generated up to 3.5 horsepower, and eventually as much as 10 horsepower. Windmills, a more modern development, were used where waterpower was less accessible, and technological advances made them increasingly efficient. The windmills generated up to 20 or 30 horsepower, but their use was more limited by the vagaries of weather.

Earlier societies had only animal and basic vegetable (timber, peat, and later charcoal) power. The mills enabled societies to exploit waterpower. The Northern European societies did not invent the mills, nor were they the first to use them. Windmills probably first appeared in Persia in the seventh century. Water mills were used in ancient Rome. But Britain and the Northern European societies were the first to use them to great economic advantage.

Again, it appears that the market, not technology, was the first mover. The earliest use of water mills in the 600s was for grinding grain. These early mills spread because the market for grains was substantial; food was the greatest need of an undeveloped economy. Moreover, grain mill technology could be economical with relatively modest demand. The uses of mills for textiles and metallurgy, the foundation of later manufacturing economies, could not develop yet, because the large markets needed to make the more complex mill technology did not exist yet.

Flanders, which occupied the region that is now southern Belgium and part of northern France, became the continent's leading economy in the twelfth and thirteenth centuries largely by importing raw wool from Britain's great sheepherders, manufacturing it into cloth, and exporting it across Europe and to the Levant. "The economic rise of Flanders in the twelfth and thirteenth centuries is one of the wonder stories of medieval economic history," wrote the historian M. M. Postan and Edward Miller. "Indeed, the earliest casebook example of economic development as now discussed in relation to the so-called undeveloped countries."

Flanders could utilize new technologies because of its dominance of trade. And trade had expanded in this era. Periodic fairs in France served as commercial exchanges and gathering places. This expanded the market but also became a site for the exchange of information in a time when few could afford books. Buyers at the fairs learned about new products, and sellers learned about what consumers wanted. The interchange of ideas inevitably provoked more ideas. Towns and cities themselves were also growing more rapidly and had become central marketplaces for the exchange of goods and ideas. These new urban areas became focal points for markets, information, and ideas.

Other factors influenced Flanders's development. After years of war, it had acquired political independence and a measure of stability. Moreover, there was relative peace in Europe for the first time in centuries, so that societies were not under constant threat of violence or diverted by expensive preparation for battle. Flanders also had a heritage of skilled workers.

Observers of the time mostly focused on the new machines, and observers in our time, when looking back, too often focus on machines as well. In fact, the growth of markets and the exchange of information were the more influential factors of growth. Flanders's access to trade was pivotal in its success.

Economic improvements were by no means limited to Flanders. In fact, Flanders's bright star was eventually dimmed by growing competition from Italian city states, as well as parts of France and Spain. Trade had opened many regions to new opportunity. And historians have developed substantial evidence that economic growth in this period was rapid and that standards of living rose. The value of the goods on which duty was paid in Genoa, for example, rose by four times in only the twenty years between 1274 and 1293. Weavers in Ypres almost doubled the production of cloth between 1306 and 1313. Comments such as the following made in Milan around the turn of the thirteenth century sound much like the romantic claims made 500 years later in early America: "Here any man, if he is healthy nor a good-for-nothing, may earn his living expenses and esteem according to his station." Wrote another Milanese observer: "With a few pence, people felt rich. Men long to have horses and arms." Concluded the economic historian Carlo Cipolla: "The fourteenth century opened with the flag of optimism flying high." Some historians have referred to the economic advances of the 1200s as the "first industrial revolution."

Despite these gains, productivity growth in these economies could not be sustained indefinitely and were insufficient to keep pace with the rising population. As these societies became wealthier, their populations grew rapidly, but neither food nor goods could be produced in sufficient quantity to keep apace of people's needs. Agricultural yields fell as farmers tilled less fertile land to increase the supply of food. Some claimed that climate changes reduced productivity. An insufficient number of new jobs was created to employ surplus workers, and wages fell in such key industries as construction and manufacturing.

Banking crises due to over-lending also helped bring down Florence and other major economies. Personal wealth was dissipated and often entirely lost, and wages typically fell dramatically. Finally, the Black Death descended on Europe in 1348. Some 25 million of the 80 million inhabitants lost their lives to the plague; Florence, for example, may have lost half its population.

In sum, the advances in economy-wide productivity were not yet strong enough to withstand the vagaries of nature. Only because the plague sharply reduced the size of the workforce did wages eventually begin to rise again. Once the turmoil of the first half of the 1300s had passed, the demand for work again outpaced the supply of workers. By 1400, prosperity had returned. In Florence, for example, according to one estimate, real wages were 50 percent higher than they were before the plague. One local Italian writer concluded that at the end of the 1300s, "The people of Placenza live at present in a clean and opulent way and in the houses they now possess implements and tableware of a much better quality than seventy years ago."

○　　　○　　　○

Were machines simply not adequate yet? Looking back, it seems that this was the case. Nature still overpowered people in the mid-1300s, and only nature, by eliminating workers through disease and starvation, was able to restore prosperity. In retrospect, we generally assume that the reasons for this are straightforward. Technology was too primitive. The scientific revolution was still a couple hundred years away. The use of the windmill as a "factory" was a remarkable advance for the times, as were a variety of other tools, but there were too few of these inventions. In other words, technological advance was deeper than modern observers imagine but not broad enough to

sustain productivity growth even as population increased. A chain reaction of productivity gains could not be truly triggered.

But the failure of gains to sustain themselves was not simply a failure of technology. Markets were simply too small to support great innovation and ever greater labor specialization. Transportation was
still only poorly developed and highly restricted, and thus costly, limiting the growth of markets in the process. Large regions remained
impenetrable, which also restricted the development of new agricultural land. Towns and cities were still generally small in this age as
well. Small markets limited opportunities to profit, economies of
scale, and incentives for further innovation and technological advance. Without demand for useful invention deriving from large and
thriving markets, there was less invention. The great inventions to
come almost all required much larger markets to be commerical.

There was also less exchange of information. A major impediment
to growth was that literacy was still relatively limited. The immigration of skilled workers was the principal source of important information. The lack of an efficient printing press was a hindrance to
economic advance. At one point, a book cost as much as two cows. In
the 1400s, a professor's annual salary could buy only four medical
books. Even such innovations as the rotation of crops were generally
passed from farm to farm only if workers from more sophisticated
farms brought the knowledge with them. Too few farmers could read
the exegeses on farming techniques, admirably handwritten by a few
farsighted people.

Meanwhile, the nation-state was not yet the formidable stabilizing
presence it would one day be, and democracy and individualism
were still in their infancy. Government was not yet the healthy influence it would later be. Feudalism remained a formidable obstacle to
innovation. Farming reorganization was still not complete. Then,
too, neither culture nor religion had as yet fully bestowed approbation upon materialism and financial self-aggrandizement; Martin
Luther was yet to make his contribution to the Western world. Humankind still believed it was subservient to nature. Finally, there was

war. The Hundred Years' War began in 1337. Conflict was common and destabilizing in these years.

To consider the inability to grow rapidly a failure of technology is a vast oversimplification. The expanding population in the 1300s overwhelmed productive capacity too quickly. Conditions of growth required a longer time to evolve.

Nevertheless, when productivity did increase in this period, it worked its conventional magic. David Landes has estimated that, with the rise in wages of the 1400s, although the distribution of wealth was often execrable, wages for peasants and workers were three times higher in about 1500 than they were five hundred years previously. Fabulous wealth was temporarily created in Flanders and the Italian city-states, including Venice and Florence, as well as regions of France and Spain.

○   ○   ○

After the Black Death, major technological innovations continued to be made in printing, clock making, arms manufacture, shipping, and navigation, but again they did not result in industrial revolution. Cannon-bearing oceangoing ships shifted the balance of military power in favor of Europe over the Levant, and European nations, their ships first-rate and well-protected, explored and conquered the New World. "The bursting of Europe's oceanic boundaries at the end of the fifteenth century is one of the central events in history," wrote historian Lynn White. "It was made possible by a long and ingenious series of Medieval and Renaissance improvements in shipbuilding and the nautical arts which were entirely empirical." Oceangoing ships and the printing press, some historians argued, together sustained the Renaissance that fully blossomed in the 1400s and 1500s.

Again, however, such single- or dual-cause theories reflect the unquenchable human thirst for simple, explicit, and technological explanations. Much else motivated the technological advances in shipbuilding and navigation, not least the desire of wealthy societies to find new treasures to sell in thriving world markets.

By the Renaissance, Europe was probably wealthier (some, as usual, disagree) than any other region in the world. But, again, despite major inventions, industrial revolution did not take hold. Spain eclipsed Italy in the sixteenth century as Europe's leading economy, due partly to the extraordinary flow of gold from its conquests in the New World. But it did not nurture the educated population and internal investment that would possibly have enabled it to maintain its lead. It imported goods from Holland and England, among other regions, rather than make them itself, concentrating on war and glory instead.

Spain provides yet another argument that industrial revolution was not the ineluctable consequence of technological advance. Growth could be obstructed by social structures, ingrained traditions, and the refusal to recognize the demands of a broad cross-section of the population. An elitist Spain had all these problems. Its ruling class fought wars effectively and bought expensive products from the north. But it did not see the possibilities of developing its own domestic markets, skilled workforce, or manufacturing capabilities. It would be overtaken by more egalitarian societies among whose central social commitments was broadening economic benefits. *＋thus increasing "demand"*

The superiority of Italian city-states in manufacturing had also been increasingly challenged in this period by countries in the north, whose tradition of manufacturing excellence had begun in Flanders, and was revived in the more northern low countries, later to be called The Netherlands. The English also began taking advantage of their sheep-grazing pastures and fulling technologies to export cloth, not merely raw wool. The Italian economies suffered significant declines in the 1600s.

○   ○   ○

As the Italian city-states and Spain declined, The Netherlands, a confederation of several countries including Holland, rose to the leading place among the world's economies and came closest to establishing a modern industrial revolution. Over the course of its long war of rebellion from Spain, The Netherlands had built a strong shipping fleet and consequently controlled the seas and trade, providing itself with a large and growing market and effectively serving as middlemen to the world. Equally important, its internal market was the most developed and efficient of any in the Western world, served by a network of canals. It also adopted sophisticated productive techniques in agriculture as it broke the yoke of feudalism sooner than did most of the rest of the continent. There was a mass immigration of talented workers, artisans, merchants, and financiers from the southern provinces, including Flanders. Several thousand productive windmills were dedicated to manufacturing a wider range of products than in the leading economies of the past, including oil, wood, grains, cloth, paper, and hemp.

The Dutch, then, combined aggressive trade with highly productive shipping, agriculture, and manufacturing in a wide diversity of goods. They intensely exploited sources of energy, mainly wind power and their native peat, for heat and fuel. They also raised entrepreneurship to a craft in itself. Their society was cohesive and well organized, with a vigorous banking sector.

It was an extraordinary achievement. With only 1 million people, The Netherlands became the most powerful economy in the world. At the time, Spain had some 6 million inhabitants and Britain 4.5 million. The Netherlands, according to modern estimates, sustained consistent productivity growth for the entire seventeenth century. Economic historians estimate that the average annual rate of productivity growth over this Dutch Golden Age was 0.3 percent. In other words, by 1700, almost twice as much output was produced in a single hour of work as in 1600. Such estimates are contentious, but a reasonable conclusion is that no other nation had ever equaled this rate of productivity growth for so long a period of time, and the nation's standard of living rose accordingly. "Wages were notoriously high," concluded Carlo Cipolla. In this wealthy environment, painting in particular thrived, and the University of Leyden rose to a pre-eminent place in Europe.

But despite its control of trade, its strong domestic market, its manufacturing base, and its entrepreneurial society, The Netherlands was not the sight of full-fledged industrial revolution. Its productivity growth was not sustained into the 1700s. Dutch historians have long argued about the causes of the nation's famous decline. The Netherlands may have been locked into a set of technologies that were too difficult and expensive to replace with the new coal-fired technologies that would soon help launch Britain on its industrial revolution. It developed railroads later than did Britain, in part because it already had a fine transportation system of canals and barges. Some accused the Dutch of complacency and nostalgia, the indulgence of social elites living off their past glory.

The Dutch did not on average suffer a decline in their standard of living in the 1700s. This stability was itself proof of historical economic progress. In the Middle Ages, stagnation would have been a significant achievement after a long period of growth. But economic advance clearly stopped in The Netherlands, and if GDP per capita remained stable on average, it certainly declined for large pockets of the population. Stagnating economies do not keep all boats above water; many typically suffer. For all the technological, financial, and navigational innovation, its domination of trade, and its sophisticated and entrepreneurial culture, productivity growth in The Netherlands could not be sustained.

Again, a multi-causal argument is probably required to explain the decline. I am not so ambitious as to offer a complete theory here, but one important overlooked factor is that the worldwide market, despite its growth, was not yet large enough to support two rapidly advancing nations. Britain was on the ascent, and where it gained in a still relatively small world market, the Dutch usually lost. More important, the larger Britain developed a thriving domestic market that would in aggregate become richer than Holland's. For all the efficiency and wealth of its internal market, The Netherlands was ultimately at a great disadvantage due to its size. Its domestic market was simply too small to support competitive technologies as Britain—four or five times as large—blossomed. A combination of exports and large domestic demand in Britain supported the enormous economies of scale to come and the major capital investment that true industrial revolution required. The central fact in the decline of The Netherlands, then, was that its domestic market, limited by its population, was too small. Its emphasis on foreign investment and the maintenance of a high currency were symptoms of growing competition, which if not the primary cause of decline, indirectly contributed to it. But its success, given its small size, was miraculous, and a testimony to its trade, its domestic market, and its egalitarian society, which left few people unproductive citizens.

○   ○   ○

In contrast to conventional views about the British Industrial Revolution, which emphasize technological advances in textiles, steam power, and steel, the two major factors for British growth were a growing export market and the simultaneous development of the domestic market. By the 1700s, the British navy had usurped the Dutch navy and created a thriving export market for British manufacturers, as Britain became the world's leading exporter. It also exported people to find natural resources around the world, principally in North America.

As much as anything else, the development of the home market was a consequence of cultural and political attitudes and a reasonable distribution of wealth and political power. Poverty was surely at inexcusable levels by any modern standard, but political attitudes were more democratic than in most other nations. Britain invested aggressively in its canals and later in its railroads. No other domestic market approached its efficiency in these years. The so-called Golden Quadrangle between London, Cardiff, Edinburgh, and Glasgow, comprising some 10 million people, was the wealthiest consumer market in the world in the nineteenth century.

Despite many scholars' attempts to narrow its foundation to a single industry, the most prominent characteristic of the British Industrial Revolution was its breadth of production. Its agricultural productivity was overhauled, in part as a consequence of enclosing formerly divided land (the peasants bore the pain of the reform) to make more efficient use of new methods and machinery. It gained advantages of scale.

Britain's manufacturing prowess advanced on several fronts. It had used mills productively for centuries to produce wool cloth, but cotton was more amenable to mechanization than was wool. Fulling was already advanced, but now bottlenecks were readily perceived and new inventions devised in spinning and weaving, the other important processes in the manufacture of cloth. The spinning jenny, patented in 1770 by James Hargreaves, made it possible to spin up to twenty-four times as much yarn as was formerly done by hand. As a result, the original spinning wheel, descended from China, evolved within a decade from a ubiquitous tool of the early Industrial Revolution to a relic. The power loom invented by Edmund Cartwright in 1787 in turn revolutionized weaving. It took time for the power looms to replace handlooms, but by 1838, David Landes has noted, one man with an inexperienced assistant could produce twenty times the output of a hand worker.

These major inventions obscured the dozens or even hundreds of minor innovations that advanced the cloth-making processes. Many new machines were developed to speed up the cleaning of the fibers, for example. More inexpensively manufactured chemicals such as sulfuric acid were used in finishing and dyeing. Without such innovation, production bottlenecks would have been prohibitive.

Demand drove innovation. "Britain," wrote the economic historian Joel Mokyr, "had no monopoly on invention, but when it was behind, it shamelessly borrowed, imitated, and stole other nation's technological knowledge." And Britain enjoyed the strongest domestic demand in the world, as well as the greatest export demand. When demand could not be met because of a bottleneck, every effort was undertaken to eliminate it, as David Landes has made clear. He called the dialectical relationship, "challenge and response." The challenge was the growing demand, the response was innovation. A different and more aggressive attitude toward technological innovation than in the early industrial surges even of The Netherlands arose, and there can be little doubt that the scale of technological advance—of sheer invention—had reached a larger dimension. Larger scale made it easier to raise productivity and reduce costs per unit of production or distribution.

This advantage of scale included the exploitation of power sources, which had been one of the foundations of industrial advance since the Middle Ages. First it was water and wind power, later peat (The Netherlands) and charcoal (a form of timber). Now, the British turned their coal reserves to great advantage, in part because of a severe timber shortage (some have disputed this). Once the nation mastered the necessary technology, coal powered the steam engine and took the Industrial Revolution to new heights. Contemporary observers noted how investment in such engines required large markets. It simply required large scale to make such investments profitable. It is doubtful that the smaller Dutch economy could have supported the initial development of coal-powered industry, much as it is doubtful that a small economy could have supported the development of the Internet as efficiently as did the United States in the late 1990s.

Coal power, in turn, made the smelting of high-quality iron more productive, and eventually the production of lighter and more plastic steel even more so. This enabled Britain to make efficient machinery, new specialized tools, and durable new construction materials. In the late 1700s, Britain smelted less iron than did France, but by the mid-1800s, the nation was producing 2 million tons per year, more iron than the rest of the world.

The export markets were important to the iron and steel industries, and the development of railroads around the world was a key source of demand. But railroads in Britain also stimulated the steel industry.

Furthermore, to manage all this, British businessmen mastered the factory system. Organization of labor was a key contribution in the Industrial Revolution. It was as important as new machinery.

Despite the complexity and interrelatedness of British industry and innovation, Carlo Cipolla, as noted, claimed that the development of iron and steel was the dominant factor in the British Industrial Revolution. David Landes believed cotton cloth manufacturing was the prime mover of the British Industrial Revolution. More recently, the historian Kenneth Pomeranz has located the key advantage of Europe in its coal resources and access to raw materials in the New World. Joel Mokyr generally claimed that "macro inventions" such as the steam engine were the prime movers of economic growth, not the other way around. The economist Walt Whitman Rostow reflected the early post-World War II conventional wisdom when he hypothesized in the 1960s that economies always "take-off" on the basis of a handful of basic industries, such as steel. He saw these industries as spearheading advance and pulling other industries along with them.

Such "take-off" metaphors are not justified by the facts. As I have noted, there were many major advances and thousands of minor ones that contributed to the highly complex technological economy Britain developed during the Industrial Revolution. The Industrial Revolution depended on the size and efficiency of Britain's domestic and export markets. Also important were the dynamism of Britain's commercial society, its mastery of the factory system, and the availability of natural resources. Finally, Britain's trading capabilities also enabled it to import raw materials. The nation had plentiful sources of coal, but it needed cotton. Whitney's cotton gin, which multiplied the productivity of plantation labor dramatically, coupled with the availability of slave labor, enabled plantations in the American South to export the raw material cheaply to Britain. In 1860, Britain imported 1.4 billion pounds of cotton at 7.5 pence per pound, the same it paid in 1800 when the industry was a small fraction of the size; expanding demand was readily filled.

The British Industrial Revolution, then, was classically organic in its origins, and its causes could not be isolated to a key industry or invention. Each development fed off the other. Textiles depended on cotton imports and on growing domestic and export markets for their goods. The steel industry was both stimulated and enabled by the steam engine and the railroad. All were supplemented by a navy that could control the seas and a banking system that could provide credit. British commercial culture was the most sophisticated in the world. In industrial revolutions, all factors build on each other, and the whole is greater than the sum of its parts. But the large market was the core reason for growth; it provided the incentives without which this revolution could not have taken place. Productivity grew more rapidly in Britain in the late 1700s and early 1800s than anywhere ever before.

○   ○   ○

Economists have tried to fine-tune the GDP and productivity data of the British Industrial Revolution. Some contend that productivity gains were strong throughout the nation's industries. Others contend that strength was largely confined to the leading industries and spread only slowly to others. But rapid productivity gains were clearly made in several major industries simultaneously: cotton, iron and steel, and transportation as well as agriculture. It is highly possible, even likely, that as more research is completed, evidence will show that productivity gains were still more widespread.

According to data compiled from the work of others by the economist Angus Maddison, Britain surpassed the Dutch economy in the level of output per hour of work in the early 1800s. At that point, and for the rest of the century, Britain's productivity grew at an estimated rate of 1.2 percent per year on average compared to the 0.3 percent per year achieved in the Dutch Golden Age of the 1600s. Although it may appear small, this difference is enormous. Growing at a rate of 0.3 percent per year, output per hour of work will rise by about 35 percent over the course of a century. But if output per hour is growing by 1.2 percent per year on average over a century, productivity will rise by nearly 250 percent. Real GDP, which includes the growth of the workforce, probably rose by about 0.9 percent per year during the 1600s in The Netherlands. It rose in Britain at a rate of about 2 percent per year during its period of ascendancy from around 1800 to the late 1800s. (Such rates of growth are underestimated compared to contemporary methods of reporting because they do not take quality improvements into account.)

Did most Britons enjoy the fruits of this productivity advance? There were wrenching changes in life, as skilled artisans lost their livelihoods, factory work became dismal and unsafe, and squalor became a way of life for many in the bulging cities. Some average measures of health declined in the mid-1800s before the introduction of sanitation and public sewers. But incomes continued to grow and reforms were undertaken by government.

Certainly, GDP per capita rose rapidly. To take one example, cotton imports rose fourfold between about 1820 and 1845 alone, an extraordinary rate of increase of 5 percent per year. The population at the time was growing only by about 1 percent per year. Overall, economists estimate that GDP per capita rose from about $1,200 in 1780 to $3,300 in 1890 (in 1985 prices), nearly a threefold increase, although more of the gain came after 1830 than originally believed. But incomes were also widely unequal throughout the nation. Furthermore, some economists believe that in the early years of industrialization, personal consumption fell so that the nation's income could be invested. Changing conditions also exacted a toll. But research by economic historians over the last generation suggests that, despite the wrenching changes, real wages rose, mortality decreased, and literacy spread during these years. In the case of wages, the general consensus among economic historians is that for manual laborers, real wages actually rose in the first half of the 1700s in the decades leading up to the Industrial Revolution, stagnated or fell in the second half, and then began to rise again in the early 1800s.

One contrary finding is that, in the mid-nineteenth century, life-spans, and the average height of the population (stature), two good measures of the level of nutrition and prevalence of disease, had deteriorated (as they did in America). This might not have reflected a fall in incomes for a large number of people so much as the growth of cities mentioned above, where the density of the population made infectious disease widespread. But both of these measures had improved before the period of urbanization and intensification of factory life, and they improved again beginning in the late 1800s and throughout the twentieth century.

We should not conclude from these studies that workers earned a fair wage (a wage that reflected their economic contribution), or what economists call an efficiency wage—that is, a wage high enough to create incentives that would make them work most productively. But in terms of material benefits, life generally improved due to rising productivity. Ironically, the opportunity to earn more provoked discontent among many workers about unfair conditions. Political reform to level and broaden opportunity was a consequence. One consistent fact of history is that reform movements have gained force as economies grew faster, not as they grew poorer. An ironic benefit of economic growth, then, was that it gave the less privileged the wherewithal and motivation to fight for their share, even if the natural forces of the economy did not automatically provide it.

European nations eventually followed Britain's lead: first France, then Germany and Belgium, and later Switzerland and Sweden. Not mere technology but also the attitude that nature could be controlled had spread to lands that had adequate economic and social foundations from which to launch an industrial revolution. These nations undertook their industrial revolutions differently; for example, embracing government more in some places than in others. The peoples of all these other nations enjoyed the fruits of rising productivity, and in some areas the gains were more evenly distributed than in Britain and America. Economists have convincingly shown that average real wages generally rose with increased productivity in these nations, although there were notable periods of stagnation in France, Germany, and Sweden, among others. Health and other measures also improved over time, although with occasional lapses. By the 1800s, world markets were large enough to support the flow of information and knowledge, the innovation, the specialization of labor and mass production, and the capital investment necessary to sustain a dozen or so true industrial revolutions in the world. The largest of these took place in the United States.

5

The Drama of the American Industrial Revolution

THE AMERICAN EXPERIENCE IS THE CLEAREST EXAMPLE OF THE influence of large and growing markets on economic development. As in almost all developing nations, trade was a great source of growth for early America. Agricultural abundance enabled it to export wheat, tobacco, and eventually cotton in enormous volume, and pay for imports of finished goods and other necessities. But America also simultaneously developed a large and dominating domestic market that was unparalleled. It easily fed itself and invested heavily in early manufactures, including mills, new cities, and shipbuilding. It benefited greatly from its natural resources, its navigable rivers, and it moderate climate, and also from its British commercial heritage and its strong sense of egalitarianism.

It was the large continentwide market, I believe, that ultimately made the nation unique. A key to this was broad access to fertile land. Relative self-sufficiency among a high proportion of early Americans created the basis for a large domestic market and a democratic sense of entitlement. It also reinforced the nation's sense of egalitarianism and demands for democracy.

The domestic market for goods and services grew rapidly in America and spread across the nation, as did the retailing and transportation activities to service it. The large market also created incentives for the rapid spread of information. By the 1830s, America had an efficient postal system. By the mid-1800s, it was laying telegraph wire across the nation. The number of its newspapers was astounding. America had a largely literate society even then, and its instinctive desire to educate itself was extraordinary. But education was also driven by commercial opportunity. It was clear even then that educated people did best.

At first, as the economic historian Nathan Rosenberg has illustrated, America's basic technology was mostly borrowed from Britain and the Continent. With the important exception of cotton technology, notably the cotton gin, there were few solely American macro-inventions in the earlier years. But by the mid-nineteenth century, and increasingly after the Civil War, America's Industrial Revolution already had a different character than Britain's or Europe's. The nation was raising mass production and distribution to technical heights that the Old World would not match until after World War II. The main reasons were the size of its domestic, one-language, tariff-free, continentwide marketplace and the efficiency of its transportation and communications systems.

America's transportation system was of paramount concern to the nation. The federal government hesitated at first to take the lead. The New York State government undertook the building of the Erie Canal in 1817 and finished it by 1825. The canal made New York City the nation's major port. The success of commercial trade on the canals of Britain provided a clear lesson. Several other states followed New York's lead. Private turnpikes were also built. Slowly, the federal government also started building important roads.

By the 1830s, the railroads were being built. In the 1830s and 1840s, railroad lines were short, connecting cities such as Boston and Lowell, New York and Philadelphia, and Baltimore and Washington, but they would soon surpass the canals. The great era of canals lasted only two decades. There were already 9,000 miles of railroad track in 1850, compared to only 4,000 miles of canals, and within only a few years, lines were built to connect the east with today's Midwest. "For the first time in history, freight and passengers could be carried overland at a speed faster than that of a horse," wrote the business historian Alfred Chandler. By 1880, America had more than 90,000 miles of railroad track compared to only 16,000 in Britain. In the ensuing decade, it would add another 75,000. It also had more than 300,000 miles of telegraph lines, which were mostly used for business.

Early America shared immediately in the benefits of Britain's Industrial Revolution, finding in exports to the mother country an almost insatiable market for its grains, tobacco, and later, of course, cotton. Economic evidence is persuasive that agricultural productivity was improved through crop rotation, more efficient use of animals, and the planting of high-yield seeds that could be exploited because of growing domestic and international markets. But this evidence also suggests that productivity was optimized only when demand grew rapidly, even in colonial times. More sophisticated machinery, such as the cotton gin and later the thresher and tractor, improved productivity markedly. Always, however, high domestic and export demand for American produce created incentives for innovation and investment.

The currency earned on exports was reinvested in the United States in such early industries as shipbuilding and milling, which were protected by tariffs. Because demand was so great, American business could build large integrated mills, which were especially productive because all operations were placed under one roof. By controlling the flow of work from one worker to the next, managers could minimize bottlenecks and idle time. The integrated mill became a model of advanced labor specialization and the forerunner of the nation's great factories. Lowell, Massachusetts, with its access to waterpower, was the nation's textile capital, and the largest Lowell mills employed several hundred workers each by the 1830s.

Another unique step forward was achieved at the Springfield, Massachusetts, armory before the Civil War. With a fixed contract for firearms from the U.S. army, the managers of the armory perfected a system that standardized the gun's many parts to make them completely interchangeable.

Standardization had been accomplished in woodworking, but not in the metalworking industries, where it was far more difficult. With the interchangeability of parts, work could be increasingly specialized. In the past, a single artisan had assembled an entire firearm and typically fitted all the parts himself. Now each worker could be assigned a section of the firearm, which he passed on to another worker who could fit his section into it. The speed of production was greatly increased. Visiting Britons in the 1850s were stunned by what became known as the "American system of manufacture," which raised productivity dramatically over the next half century and was the basis of mass production.

The growth of the market after the Civil War was the most astonishing factor in America's ascendancy. It was now linked efficiently by the railroads and the telegraph and resulted in an unforeseeable but highly productive extenuation of Adam Smith's early principle. In the abstract, the larger the market, the more specialized labor could be. Also, new sources of power could be fully exploited. Mass production and distribution were the summits of such labor specialization and efficiency of power. They ultimately divided work into the smallest specialties and fully utilized the enormous power generated by steam, oil, and electricity. By the 1890s, the American market was already more than twice as large as Britain's in terms of money spent on goods and services. The market was some four times larger than Germany's.

The importance of economies of scale is generally underestimated in economic theory. It seemed on the face of it that a plant would soon fully exploit cost-cutting possibilities. But the benefits of scale spread well beyond manufacturing to distribution, marketing and advertising, research, and managerial competence. Technology advanced to such a degree, as well, that far larger markets than were once imagined were necessary to generate the most efficiency. Coal power and later electricity would have been largely superfluous in smaller markets. Petroleum refining required huge markets to make it economical. Communications seemed to find no limit to the value of scale, in cinema, radio, and especially television. Efficient electronics manufacturing, notably computer chips, also requires a volume of sales unimaginable to previous generations. A market that was twice as large would be more than twice as advantageous due to the division of labor and economies of scale because costs per unit were lower in large markets than in smaller ones.

Productivity was radically improved in industry after industry, sharply reducing the price of key goods throughout the economy. The distillation of petroleum was made more efficient by the ability to apply intensive heat to it in huge refining plants. Much more petroleum could now be refined quickly, as could similar liquids, as long as there was a market large enough to absorb the production. The costs fell dramatically. The cost of distilling a barrel of kerosene, for example, fell from 6 cents per pound in the late 1860s to 1.5 cents in 1882, a 75 percent reduction. But the full exploitation of such power sources and new technologies was not possible without enormous demand for these products. The processes would not have been economical at slower speeds of production.

Productivity in mechanical industries increased many times. A machine invented by the Briton James Bonsack in 1881, and cleverly imported to America by James Buchanan Duke, could produce by the late 1880s 120,000 cigarettes a day compared to at best 3,000 a day rolled by hand. The Bonsack machine rolled the tobacco onto a moving tape, compressed it, wrapped it in paper, pasted it, and cut it. Labor hours were reduced by 95 percent. Such "continuous-process" machines also revolutionized the production of matches, soap, and film, among other products. Flour mills also adopted continuous-process techniques, which reduced their costs dramatically. The mills raised their production fivefold as a result and cut costs accordingly.

The most significant gains in productivity were made in the metal-making industries, notably steel, and the metalworking industries, which turned out products such as machine tools. But these gains required greater technological innovation, intricate machinery, and more intensive use of heat than in other industries. In steel, the new Bessemer process was introduced to America from Britain around 1870. The open-hearth technique was adopted in the 1880s. By 1890, the large steel establishments, which integrated all the processes of production in one site, were producing 1,000 tons of steel per week, compared to the 70 tons or so produced by a blast furnace in 1870. The cost of steel rails fell from $67.50 per ton in 1880 to $17.63 per ton by about 1900, a stunning reduction in perhaps the key material of the time.

In such a market, a wide range of services, from transportation to retailing to communications, also became highly productive. This is too often overlooked as even economists have gotten into the habit of presuming that services productivity usually rises slowly. The speed of railroads and the size of cars were increased. The early wholesalers of grain, and eventually of sugar, fruit, and furniture, located in cities such as Cincinnati and St. Louis, raised productivity levels by building large centralized storage facilities. Similarly, the first retail chains, such as the Atlantic & Pacific Tea Company, as well as the first department stores, such as Marshall Field, became highly efficient in the 1870s and 1880s through centralization of inventories, billing, and other activities.

Well before the development of a commercial automobile and the widespread use of electricity, then, America's productivity increases were dramatic across a breathtaking range of manufacturing and services industries. These productivity gains were by no means isolated to the building of the railroads of the nineteenth century, as some observers too casually suggest, nor would they be isolated to any one set of industries in the twentieth century or to one or two inventions, such as automobiles or even electricity.

American entrepreneurs were also especially adept at developing new consumer products to stimulate demand. With such a large market, incentives to do so were high. Americans created the breakfast cereals industry to utilize the full productive potential of milling. The Bonsack machine could turn out hundreds of thousands of cigarettes at a time when most Americans who bought tobacco chewed rather than smoked it. James Duke was a particularly innovative and persistent marketer of his new cigarettes. He taught America how to smoke by aggressively marketing and advertising. Similarly, the Singer Company's worldwide domination of the highly popular mechanical sewing machine was more a product of its marketing prowess than its mechanical ingenuity. The number of sewing machines produced rose from 2,200 in 1853 to roughly half a million in 1870.

The young nation raised the commercial culture it had inherited from Britain to a new level, stimulated by a diligent work ethic and a broad, commercially approving religious conversion in the 1800s, known to later historians as the Second Great Awakening (the first occurred a century earlier, and was not commercially oriented). Americans generally believed a good life on earth reflected their faith and religiosity. The wide ownership of land reinforced their individualistic tendencies. The federal government, notably under President Andrew Jackson, aggressively protected access to land, even protecting the rights of squatters. Americans also undid the British laws that restricted the sale of land, such as entails, or that limited the chartering of new companies. They advocated more open competition and access to opportunity. The young democracy also established free primary education that was mandatory for all children.

The American government had a central part in economic growth. Federal and state government protected access to land for individuals, financed the canals and subsidized the railroads, established the mail, built a free primary school system and later a secondary school system as well as subsidizing universities, promoted competition and capital raising through the widespread chartering of companies and the legalization of limited liability, eventually succeeded in stabilizing the financial system, passed a progressive income tax, and created regulations to protect workers.

In sum, the American economy continually changed, and American government adjusted to those changes. These were not invariably satisfactory adjustments. "Internal improvements," such as new federal roads, were widely and powerfully resisted in early America. For too long, companies abused workers. Racial prejudice was tolerated in America and in some regards still is, creating inefficiencies and reducing the productivity of the workforce. All these factors reduced economic growth. But generally, the government did adjust, through public goods, social programs, regulation, and laws against prejudice.

Business adjusted as well. Americans learned to manage size (big business) better than any other nation in the world. This was part of their indigenous innovation, fostered by rapid growth, a huge marketplace, and a commercial orientation, and perfected by professional management. These companies professionalized research and marketing, as well as basic management, in the late 1800s and early 1900s. They created large, trained, and stable workforces as well. Eventually they supplemented their workers' pay with substantial fringe benefits, including pensions and health insurance.

○   ○   ○

America's economy consistently began to grow rapidly in the 1840s, interrupted significantly only by the Civil War. Despite some half dozen severe recessions and several lesser ones in the nineteenth century, by the 1890s America was the largest economy in the world and also the most productive; in other words, output per hour of work was higher than anywhere else. The fastest period of growth was the forty years between 1870 and 1910. Labor productivity grew by more than 2 percent per year, far faster than in Britain, and at a pace that is unadjusted for the kinds of quality improvements that have increased the measures of contemporary performance so significantly. By modern statistical standards, which adjust for quality improvement, growth was perhaps a full percentage point per year faster on average, or 3 percent per year on average.

The most telling piece of evidence about the extraordinary breadth of America's Industrial Revolution in the late 1800s was that prices declined across most industries. Between 1870 and 1910, overall consumer prices fell on average by an estimated 40 percent. This was not caused by a lack of demand for goods but by such strongly growing demand that economies of scale and new power sources (also made commercial by the enormous market) enabled companies to raise the output per hour of work radically in industry after industry. The costs fell significantly for a wide range of goods and services, not just a handful of new or important products. In the language recently readopted for the new economy, "fixed costs" were high but "variable costs" low; the more one sold, the more one amortized the high initial costs.

The events of the twentieth century exceeded even such industrial drama. After strenuous efforts over many years, Henry Ford succeeded in making most of the thousands of parts of a car interchangeable. This required advanced machine tools. He then developed the moving assembly line, first for the production of engines and then entire automobiles. Even these ideas had many antecedents. Until this point, the bicycle was the most complex product for which parts had been made interchangeable; Ford was originally a bicycle mechanic. As for the moving assembly line, meat packers had long used what they called a disassembly line that moved a carcass from one butcher to the next. Wrote the business historian Alfred Chandler: "Labor time expended in making a Model T dropped from 12 hours and 8 minutes to 2 hours and 35 minutes per car" (280). By 1916, the price of the Model T had fallen to $360 from $950 in 1909, and demand for automobiles, aided by the plentiful supply of inexpensive gasoline, rose dramatically.

Electricity was to coal and the steam engine what coal and the steam engine were to waterpower and the mill. Factories and homes were widely electrified between 1910 and 1930. On the one hand, here was an extraordinary source of power that made manufacturing, transportation, and even retailing much more efficient. On the other hand, electrification was a consumer product that not only lit homes, stores, restaurants, and city streets across the nation, but also enabled households to buy and use newly mass-produced and mass-marketed products, from washing machines to electric refrigerators, record players, irons, radios, and telephones. Electrification itself stimulated product innovation just as lower costs of computer power would in the 1990s. Large markets made electricity economical, and its price fell significantly if not dramatically. The importance of dense urban markets was never more apparent. Electricity in rural communities remained very expensive and required government subsidy. American engineers and entrepreneurs learned to transport this energy from the great interior waterways of the nation to the cities. Electricity accounted for 5 percent of power in manufacturing in 1899, 25 percent in 1909, 55 percent in 1919, and 82 percent in 1929. By the early 1930s, almost all urban households had electricity. This was surely rapid change. In just twenty years, electricity in both factories and households rose from restricted usage to almost universal usage.

The automobile spread as rapidly. In 1920, only one in four families owned a car. In just nine years, three out of five families owned one, as the car evolved from a plaything of the rich to a middle-class requirement in less than a decade. In 1920, there were three radio stations; in 1923, there were 500. By the 1930s, half of all Americans got all their news over the radio, there were 80 million admissions to the "talkies" each week, and half of all families owned refrigerators.

o   o   o

Economic historians often call this America's second industrial revolution. In the 1920s, productivity grew by about 5 percent per year, again without including the quality adjustments that raise reported economic performance in the contemporary era. But the key issue is that such rapid growth was not simply due to two macro-inventions, the internal combustion engine and electricity. The automobile and electricity did not result in comparable gains in Europe.

Consider Henry Ford's contribution. A usable internal combustion engine had been invented in Europe a generation earlier, but Ford made it possible to manufacture it on an assembly line—the ultimate specialization of labor. Ford's contribution was less a profound technological advance than a reorganization of labor, requiring a multitude of small technological innovations. Such assembly lines also required an eager labor force to do strenuous, unimaginably boring work, something European workers resisted even for higher wages. This single extraordinary managerial innovation spread to the production of all kinds of other consumer products. The spread of electricity made the factory even more productive, but the entrepreneurial development of inexpensive new consumer products, from washing machines to telephones and radios, in turn, also stimulated the demand for electricity in American homes.

These products were made affordable through the same sort of mass production techniques as those developed by Ford, but they were ultimately dependent on a mass market. The moving assembly line and electricity were overlaid on an economy that was already open to mass production, standardized products, aggressive marketing and advertising, and a material hunger on the part of its citizens. It had the largest, most efficient mass market in the world—by far. Wrote the economist John Schmookler:

> It seems almost obvious, to this writer at least, that the automobile came when it did more because of economic and social changes than because of technological change as such. In the first place, in the automobile, prestige, flexibility, privacy, recreation, and utility are com-

bined in ways which only an individualistic high-per-capita-income society could afford or develop. (The so-called bicycle craze of the 1890s was part of the same phenomenon.) The automobile, after all, did not revolutionize life in low-income India or China. Its effects have been confined primarily to the United States and other industrialized countries, at least roughly in proportion to income. A good case can be made for the contention that among the indispensable conditions for the coming of the automobile age were relatively high levels of income, at least for the middle-income classes, and an individualistic society.

There were also advances in managerial methods in these years, led by the scientific management principles of Frederick Taylor, which reduced the duties of employees to mere bits of work. Big business stressed marketing, research and development, the exploitation of vast economies of scale, and later what became known as economies of scope. These latter occurred when large companies found they could manufacture or market similar products more efficiently through their own organization, taking advantage of their own brand names, distribution channels, and research and development. To take a modern example, Sony was able to introduce the popular Walkman because of its expertise and market penetration in consumer electronics.

The telephone in the 1920s provided America with a vast, efficient, inexpensive network of communications with enormous productivity advantages. The telegraph was a clumsier means of communication, although a great innovation in its day. The rapid spread of the radio set, the average price of which fell from about $130 in 1929 to $10 in 1935, created a new advertising network that was competitive with newspapers and provided another informational outlet to supplement the nation's multitude of newspapers.

The chemical industry also flourished in this period, creating products, including sulfa drugs and then later antibiotics, that made healthcare more productive. The definition of science is more ambiguous than is believed. Advanced science was the source of profound chemical innovations. Chemical companies also produced powerful fertilizers, insecticides, and high-powered seeds, which increased agricultural productivity faster than ever before.

Huge economies of scale were also created by the demand for refined petroleum products, in particular gasoline, as the automobile became ubiquitous. Such refined products were particularly given to mass production. "The large size of the American market had introduced American firms at an early stage to the problems involved in the large-volume production of basic products, such as chlorine, caustic soda, soda ash, sulfuric acid, and superphosphates," wrote economists David Mowery and Nathan Rosenberg. "This ability to deal with a large volume of output . . . was to become a critical feature of the chemical industry in the twentieth century,"

There were critical government-directed improvements as well. Water and sewer systems transformed cities beginning in the early 1900s, enabling them to grow without the debilitating spread of disease. Cities became vital centers of demand and innovation, just as they had been in the Middle Ages in Europe, but on an incomparably vaster scale. Transportation and communications costs were low due to proximity, and ideas generated more ideas geometrically. Americans raised their education level dramatically. In 1910, only 9 percent of seventeen-year-olds received high school diplomas; by the end of the 1930s, more than half did, almost all from public schools. Meanwhile, the government had established the Federal Reserve System in 1912 to provide stability to formerly uncontrolled financial markets. In the 1920s, the government built a vast system of roads to support the new automobiles and the trucking industry.

In the post-World War II period, there were again extraordinary new technologies, which helped raise productivity and made the mass production and distribution economy still more efficient. This amounted, at the least, to another new economy. Remarkable new products were commercialized, such as aluminum and plastic. Jet travel made transportation more productive, as did the supertanker. The polio vaccines were discovered. Perhaps most important, television not only became the dominant cultural product of the century, it also revolutionized mass marketing by making the cost of advertising far lower per family than ever before while presenting a highly potent sales image that deeply reinforced an already materialistic society.

Materialism and the quality of content aside, it was America's particular genius to turn a technological advance such as television into a marketing revolution that affected industry after industry. This was not merely technology at work but the long legacy of a mass production-oriented commercial society. Few if any products in America were more efficient than television programming. The costs to the viewing family for watching otherwise free television were the advertising expenditures imputed in the price of a package of, say, Corn Flakes or the price of a Buick. In the 1990s, all these costs together came to roughly $3 a week for the average family (still less for the median, or typical, family). In other words, for indirect advertising costs of less than 45 cents a day, a family could watch the morning and evening news, *Oprah* and *Seinfeld*, the World Series and the Wimbledon tennis tournament, the Academy Awards, and countless movies (to mention, of course, only a few possibilities). These were the classic "network" effects so widely discussed in the 1990s by advocates of the new economy. The more people who owned a television set, the more value television had, just as the more who subscribed to AOL or a similar service, the more valuable was the Internet.

The marketing efficiencies of television, coupled with mass production efficiencies, made many products extraordinarily inexpensive for consumers because the size of the market was so large. The advertising economies of scale on television greatly expanded the demand for standardized products. A quart of Coca Cola in the 1990s cost far less than a quart of bottled water. This was the result of economies of scale that raised the productivity of manufacturing, refining, distributing, and marketing products significantly.

America's huge market now gave it an incomparable advantage. Advertising and marketing became much more sophisticated. New industries, such as fast food, were born not essentially from technological advance but from entrepreneurial spirit and the economies of scale available in a mass market. The uses of television were maximized.

Moreover, just as the government sent teenagers to high school in the early part of the century, the GI bill enabled millions of war veterans to go to college after World War II. Government subsidy after the Russians launched Sputnik helped tens of thousands to attend college. The nation built a national highway system at great expense, and local communities spent aggressively on roads as well. By the 1950s, 90 percent of all homes were reachable on a paved road, and America's transportation system was never more efficient. Finally, research and development investment by the Defense Department was high and resulted in the development of the Internet, among other products.

In the first twenty-five years following World War II, productivity grew in America by nearly 3 percent per year. Had today's quality adjustments been made, it may well have grown by nearly 4 percent a year. The standard of living doubled (rose by 100 percent) in only twenty-five years. Had today's quality adjustments been made, it would have risen by 150 percent.

○   ○   ○

Thus, America had a "new economy" in virtually every generation, a mini-industrial revolution by another name. To many, computers and related information technology in themselves revitalized growth in the late 1990s. But true industrial revolutions are more complex and broadly based, and highly dependent on large markets and the rapid exchange of information.

Even academic thinking about economic growth began to broaden. Originally, the theoretical instinct was to reduce the causes of growth to a manageable and predictable few. Growth was thought to be essentially a function of capital stock and technological advance. But when economists tried to verify these contentions empirically and statistically, they found that they needed other variables such as economies of scale, managerial innovation, and educational attainment to make sense of how economies grew. For one thing, it became clear that capital investment could only take growth so far.

Over time, technology itself was increasingly acknowledged to be at least in part a consequence of growth and its many interrelated factors, as well as a cause. Case studies of technological change showed that countless important technological improvements were made by individual businesses themselves under the pressure of competition and the drive for more profit. Such "learning-by-doing" and "learning-by-using" were central to America's development.

New theories incorporated this idea, claiming that technology was "endogenous" to a well-functioning economy, not an exogenous creation of lone inventors. In particular, innovation typically spread from one company to another, spurring still further technological discovery and development. For example, the transistor, which was licensed by Bell Laboratories to other companies, produced benefits for the economy far beyond what any single company could earn by developing and exploiting it. So did many advances in agriculture and medicine. The returns on most traditional investment typically decreased over time, but the returns on technological advance could increase for the entire economy as they spread, and they stimulated further technological advances as a result.

These modern growth theories remain incomplete, and the statistical models to support them are ambiguous. In the twentieth century, capital investment in plant and equipment, according to these models, mattered less than it did in the nineteenth century. Other conditions, such as investment in education and job training, the organization of business, scientific discoveries in medicine and chemistry, and more efficient communications, seemed to contribute more to economic growth in the 1900s. In general, total factor productivity, which encompasses some of these factors, rose more rapidly than in the 1800s. Total factor productivity is an attempt to measure how well labor and capital work together. Adding other factors of growth can make the utilization of labor and capital more productive, for example. On the other hand, total factor productivity may understate the contribution of such factors in the nineteenth century because progress in that age could not easily be made without enormous capital investment in new production facilities. Such capital investment might have disguised the contributions of human capital, better management, and new ideas in that era. They were surely important then as well. What modern growth theory does strongly suggest, however, is that the conditions for productivity growth were broader and more interrelated than was believed by scholars only a generation before.

The American Industrial Revolution was easily the most spectacular in history until World War II and the rapid economic growth it generated until the early 1970s. There were major productivity advances in agriculture; dozens of manufacturing industries; and services of all kinds, from retailing to transportation. New forms of power were fully exploited in industry after industry because of the enormous demand for products. To claim that this advance was essentially dependent on only two or three macro-inventions is at best highly oversimplified. Moreover, America's rate of economic advance was not duplicated in any other nation over this period, even those with access to similar inventions and the educated and well-trained workforce to utilize them.

The common characteristic that drove productivity advances in almost all industries was the size of the American markets for goods and services. Because of America's natural abundance of resources, technologies in the United States were also shaped to utilize them. Only after World War II did European nations, as well as Japan, catch up to the U.S. performance. In fact, as they became useful, natural resources such as oil were increasingly discovered and developed around the world. But much of this had to do with the development, in Europe, of newly unified marketplaces and the opening of trade to economies of East Asia, notably Japan, and later several small nations, including Taiwan and South Korea, which grew in part because they could now exploit the U.S. market as if it were their own.

In the 1970s, American productivity growth slowed significantly. As usual, observers typically thought the slowing was due to the exhaustion of technology. But the causes were more complex.

6

The Productivity Slowdown of the Late Twentieth Century

BEGINNING IN THE EARLY 1970s, THE RATE OF PRODUCTIVITY growth fell in the United States by a full percentage point per year from its long-term historical average since the Civil War and by considerably more from the rate of the 1950s and 1960s. It was the longest such persistent slowdown since the Civil War. The productivity slowdown deeply affected the confidence and political temperament of the nation as incomes stagnated, unemployment rose, and federal budget deficits grew because tax revenues grew at historically slow rates. But economists could not agree, and still do not agree, on why the unprecedented slowdown in productivity growth occurred.

There was a growing sense, however, that the great old technologies of America's second industrial revolution, based on electricity as the main source of power and, to a lesser extent, on the internal combustion engine, had at last been fully exploited. Something had to come along to replace them, went one set of conventional arguments, and during the transition, the economy would grow slowly.

Also, corporate profitability had fallen, as did levels of capital investment. Many blamed the nation's low savings rate and high federal budget deficits for the lack of necessary capital to finance investment. Others argued that the government had become too intrusive, disrupting the normal workings of free markets. More savings and less government were the new conventional policy prescriptions of the era.

These reactions were predictable. Short-term policies, such as fiscal stimulus or controlling the money supply, apparently did not work in this environment. Persistent slow productivity growth seemed to be a chronic issue, and economists returned to simple theoretical conventions for answers. Technology and capital investment were the classical theoretical causes of growth.

But economic history contains different lessons. Technology and savings are usually not among the first movers of economic growth. In fact, like the rapid growth that preceded it, the slowdown was not due to slow technological advance or low savings rates. The most persistent of the true causes of the slowdown was a change in the nature of the market. This was largely misunderstood. The large mass marketplace, which had long given the nation a unique advantage, was now fragmented by sophisticated competition from abroad and by consumer demand for less standardized and higher quality products. No longer did it so purely perform the Smithian function previously described: an ever-growing marketplace that supported the division of labor and mass production. During the twenty years between the mid-1970s and the mid-1990s, new products were developed and marketed, often with the help of new information technology, that were targeted more for streamlined niche markets than for standardized mass markets. Adjusting to the fragmented markets was difficult for American business. The intense foreign competition and more particular demands of consumers initially reduced profitability, capital spending, and returns on investment, and they might yet retard productivity growth in the future. Meeting the needs of niche markets was not as given to efficiencies as providing standardized products to mass markets.

The fragmenting of markets was probably the most important single factor in retarding productivity growth, but there were other, more conventional, influences as well, including high inflation, a periodically high U.S. dollar, and effective foreign competition. This period began with the sudden raising of the price of oil in 1973 by the Organization of Petroleum Exporting Countries (OPEC). The cartel tripled oil prices from $3 to $9 a barrel. In 1974, it raised prices by another $3 a barrel to $12 barrel and in 1978 to $18 a barrel.

This sixfold increase in the price of oil had a severe impact on the economy, much the opposite of what had happened when key costs had fallen in the past. The prices of oil and its many products, from kerosene to gasoline, fell by at least 75 percent in the last quarter century of the 1800s, providing stimulus for the economy. Over time, American business had become highly dependent on inexpensive imported oil, and the rising cost was a shock to the stability of the economy, acting like a large tax increase that reduced the purchasing power of both consumers and business. In addition, there was a worldwide shortage of crops in these years, leading to unusual increases in agricultural prices, which also acted like a tax increase.

The OPEC oil price hike reduced purchasing power so rapidly that the economy fell into a recession in 1973 from which it did not recover until 1975. A recession was likely in any case. Such price increases could probably have been absorbed in other times, and indeed were in the 1950s. But profitability (profits divided by capital) had been falling for years, and inflation was already a concern, especially as America spent tens of billions of dollars to fight the war in Vietnam. The price increases helped produce the worst recession yet of the post-World War II period, as the unemployment rate soared. Furthermore, the high oil prices filtered throughout the economy, and as business costs rose in industry after industry, companies raised their prices. When economic growth resumed in 1975, prices rose rapidly. Interest rates rose as well. Lenders would not provide loans at low interest rates if the value of the money they received in the future would be eroded by inflation.

Inflation also took on a life of its own. Typically, higher prices restrain buying. But now, both consumers and business bought more as prices rose, in anticipation that prices would be significantly higher in coming months and years. The demand placed further pressure on supply. Such inflationary expectations pushed prices even higher.

Higher inflation thus affected the economy in several ways. The high costs of oil and other raw materials and business supplies made many business methods and processes inefficient. High interest rates reduced capital spending on new equipment and new businesses. Another consequence of high rates was low stock prices, which also inhibited capital spending. Higher prices also reduced consumer spending power in general. The level of inflation averaged 12 to 14 percent in the late 1970s and early 1980s. Mortgage rates reached 20 percent; the interest on a typical car loan was 22 percent; and the cost of commercial paper, a major source of short-term loans to business, reached 15 percent per year. The three recessions between 1973 and 1982 raised unemployment to its highest level since the Great Depression. The rate averaged 8 percent in this period compared to less than 5 percent in the 1960s. Even when the economy was expanding, wages after inflation rose slowly, and corporate profits were generally weak, impeding capital investment. Profitability fell by 20 percent. Meanwhile, stock prices on average had yet to return to the highs first attained in the late 1960s.

Inflation gradually fell in the 1980s, yet slow productivity growth persisted. One reason was that the nation's central bank, under Paul Volcker, maintained fairly restrictive policies, keeping interest rates relatively high. Even so, there should have been a gradual improvement in productivity growth because interest rates, although historically high, fell consistently in the 1980s. But there was no such gradual improvement, once the ups and downs of the business cycle were taken into account.

As the nation was dealing with inflation, a faltering economy, and low profitability, foreign producers of a variety of consumer goods and business equipment also attracted American customers away from domestic manufacturers. They largely achieved this through new managerial techniques, which involved the use of computers. To some extent, but to a lesser one than was widely believed, they also took advantage of lower wages in their nations.

The Japanese excelled in consumer electronics products, such as transistor radios, stereo players, calculators, television sets, and VCRs. They also of course excelled at making lower-priced but high-quality automobiles. The European manufacturers excelled at making high-quality consumer and business products.

American consumers were demanding more diversity in their choices and higher quality in general. Standardization was no longer satisfactory. The goal now was not simply to sell the same products to as many people as possible but to make products that appealed to segments of the marketplace. The number of new products introduced each year expanded dramatically. Basic new car models alone increased from 30 to 150 during this period. These new demands shifted to services as well. In 1973 there were 300 mutual funds; today there are 7,000. Banks now offer many more products, airlines provide many more flights, and retailers offer many more choices.

Thus, although foreign competition took market share from domestic companies, it also was a catalyst in the fragmenting of all sorts of domestic markets noted previously. This was a major historical shift. The fragmentation did not mean that productivity no longer rose for the economy as a whole. But as we shall see, even as new managerial and competitive techniques were introduced, fragmentation made it more difficult to raise productivity in many industries. Making a greater variety of products meant more fixed costs for development, production, and service operations, and usually more human input. New products required invention, design, testing, and constantly new marketing and sales campaigns.

Five factors stand out as sources of slow growth. Some were temporary, others more durable. The most important, market fragmentation, may yet prove the most lasting. These factors are summarized in the following sections.

Inflation and the Response to It

Inflation rose to high and debilitating levels in the 1970s, and created considerable uncertainty in the economy. The battle against inflation would last another fifteen years and dampen economic and productivity growth in the process. By the late 1970s, the Federal Reserve, under its chairman, Paul Volcker, had adopted stringent policies to deal with what seemed like runaway inflation and high nominal interest rates. He and his colleagues deliberately pushed up interest rates to slow demand for goods and services. At one point, the Federal Reserve raised its target federal funds rates to 14 percent. The policies eventually took hold with the steep recession in 1982. Although the inflationary spiral was clearly broken, the Federal Reserve maintained fairly tight policies under Volcker, and later Alan Greenspan, until the mid-1990s. Meanwhile, bond investors, not fully confident that inflation was permanently reduced, continued to demand relatively high interest rates on bonds. Inflationary expectations remained strong until the mid-1990s.

The Fed's policies were complicated by sharp tax cuts sponsored by President Ronald Reagan. These resulted in rapidly rising federal deficits and enormous issuance of Treasury securities, placing upward pressure on rates as well, or so it was thought by investors. Ultimately federal debt rose from $1 trillion to $5 trillion, equal to about half of GDP. While nominal rates fell rapidly during the recession, real rates fell more slowly. Real rates are nominal rates less inflation, and represent a truer cost of borrowing or value of interest received. The high real rates, even as they fell, were a dampening presence in the economy over this period. They generally restrained capital investment, and probably continued to suppress stock prices because investors could earn such a good return by owning fixed-income investments. The real interest rate of the thirty-year Treasury bond rose from a point at which it was actually negative in 1980 (inflation exceeded interest rates) to well over 7 percent in the mid-1980s. Real interest rates, however, declined gradually throughout the rest of the decade, and helped generate higher manufacturing profits by the late 1980s.

A recovering economy and strong fiscal stimulus due to tax cuts and deficit spending, along with high interest rates, also helped cause the value of the dollar to rise against other currencies in the late 1970s and the first half of the 1980s. Investors preferred to place their money in high-interest paying but secure U.S. government and corporate bonds, as well as in the rising stock market. But a high dollar damaged the nation's manufacturers by making their exports expensive to foreign buyers. The profitability of manufacturing in America was reduced by the falling demand. However, this retarding effect, too, was temporary, because the dollar began to fall again in the late 1980s. Still, despite falling real rates and a declining dollar in the late 1980s, productivity growth continued to be slow.

Lost Market Share to International Competition

Foreign competition rapidly reduced the market share of American corporations in many industries in these years. This was costly for the American economy. Many economists dispute this point, claiming that U.S. companies now exported products in which they had a competitive advantage and imported those in which other nations had advantages. This principle went back at least as far as Adam Smith and was more formally developed by the early nineteenth-century economist and stock broker, David Ricardo. One nation may be better at growing grapes and producing wine, another at growing wheat. It pays for them to trade with each other, each selling what it makes best.

But America kept buying more from overseas than it was selling. The loss of companies and whole industries, such as consumer electronics and textile, to foreign competition was especially significant. The high dollar made foreign entry into U.S. markets even easier, because import prices to American consumers were low. America's imports rose from 4 percent of consumption and business spending in the 1960s to more than 10 percent in the mid-1980s, and its trade balance fell into chronic deficit (imports consistently exceeded exports). Manufacturers' exports fell sharply as a percent of their already weak sales. In the 1980s, the number of manufacturing jobs in America declined for the first time in its history.

Some observers argued that over time American business would shift into industries in which it had a greater competitive advantage, all the while attracting overseas investment. But the trade deficit simply grew larger in the 1990s. Theoretically, at some point, it should have reversed. The weakened manufacturing sector also affected the services businesses that were its suppliers. Such competition had a persistent effect on American corporations, even as they responded by restructuring themselves and adopting more productive methods. The high dollar of the 1990s, even though it attracted capital to the United States, remained a dampening influence on productivity growth.

Growing Demand for Labor-Intensive Services

A third factor contributing to slow growth was the growing demand for certain services that were especially labor intensive. As we have seen, many services in America have been highly productive since the 1800s. Consider the railroads, the retail chains such as the A&P, or, in contemporary times, television or fast-food chains.

But other industries are, by their nature, resistant to rapid productivity increases. The rapidly growing demand for housing, education, and healthcare, in particular, as well as elder care and childcare, placed a burden on the rate of productivity growth. All of these items consume an increasing share of a typical family's budget. The cost of tuition at a public university alone has doubled on average as a proportion of family income. The cost of healthcare and drugs is a significantly larger proportion of a family budget. Even more important, there was a growing demand for business services, such as consulting and financial services. This was a response to global competition and fragmenting markets, which place a priority on more innovative products. The demand for labor-intensive services would probably persist.

The Lack of Investment in Public Goods

A fourth factor was the failure of government to provide adequate public goods to support economic growth. For example, it became clear by the 1980s that a college education was a growing necessity. The difference between the earnings of a worker with a college degree and one with only a high school diploma kept widening in the 1980s and 1990s. Yet there was only a modest increase in subsidies for attending college even as tuitions rose far more rapidly than incomes. Even as more students went to college, they increasingly took longer to graduate, in part in order to work, and borrowed more from parents and grandparents. On average, college graduates have twice as much debt today, adjusted for inflation, as they had in 1970. Still, the pay gap between college and high school graduates did not close, which suggested that too few students were going to college.

Similarly, there was inadequate support for improvement in education, in training more teachers, and in equalizing the quality of education in poorer neighborhoods. Education at primary and secondary levels is largely funded locally. The quality of teachers in inner city and rural schools is inferior to the quality of those in richer suburban regions. The pay gap with college graduates may also have reflected the poor quality of high school education. The point is not merely that educational quality was declining in some areas, but that a changing economy required that it be improved more rapidly.

Also, government provided little significant childcare support for two-worker families even as they became the nation's norm. (Welfare reform in 1996 did provide more funds for childcare, but the quality of the new services was difficult to measure.) This made it more difficult for spouses to become fully productive members of the workforce.

The federal government's investment in transportation infrastructure also faltered. In the 1990s, it was approximately half the share of GDP that it was in the 1970s, resulting in less efficient road transportation, public transit, and airports. Rising bottlenecks clearly reduced productivity. (See chapter 9.)

The Age of Consumer Choice

The fifth and probably the most durable and important contributor to slow-growing productivity was the fragmenting of markets. Changing technologies, new managerial methods, more intense global and domestic competition, and the consumer's satiation with standardized products all contributed to an "age of consumer choice." In this period, business learned to tailor products to niche markets and introduce new products at a much faster rate than in the past. Consumers expected more variety and higher quality. The growing intensity of competition as markets globalized meant that all kinds of businesses were now dedicated to satiating the ever-demanding consumer, including those that could take advantage of low wages.

The standardized products of the past, which created enormous economies of scale, were replaced by a wide range of more narrowly targeted products. Some economists believed new computerized and managerial techniques would make even such fragmented markets highly productive. This is a central source of confusion. On average, businesses learned to reach smaller markets more productively than they had in the past. But this did not mean that productivity would rise as rapidly as it once did. They could not in the aggregate improve productivity as rapidly as when the age of mass production and standardization was at an earlier stage of development.

One way to think of what happened in this era was that an age of consumer choice required far more innovation than in the past, and innovation required the creativity of people. Even if computers were everywhere, and they did change our lives, the need for creativity was a new impediment to productivity growth that could not be entirely overcome by computer technology or managerial innovation.

Ironically, the 1970s represented a return to a crafts economy of sorts, increasingly dependent again on the efforts of people rather than on mass production machines. The trend that began two hundred years earlier, with the division of labor made possible by the standardization of products for a large market of middle-class people who essentially wanted the same low-priced products, was now partially reversed. But the new craftspeople were not weavers, fullers, or smiths. They included technologists as well as designers, marketers, sales people, financiers, communicators, and business managers of all kinds.

○   ○   ○

The more popular view of the slowdown, however, remained the technological one. The contention was that the superseding of an old technology, electricity, with a new one, computers, or more precisely chip technology, was a central cause of slower productivity growth between the mid-1970s and the mid-1990s. The most influential research in this area was conducted by the economic historian Paul David.

One problem with this thesis was that technologies were always being reinvented or replaced in America, and that did not affect the rate of growth in a way comparable to the slowdown of the late twentieth century. Paul David did find that around the turn of the century there was a marked slowdown in productivity growth in America that he believed could be attributed to the high costs and sluggish process of replacing steam-based and water-powered processes with electrical ones. But first, the slowdown around 1900 was neither as deep nor as prolonged as the one after 1973. Second, it was entirely different in detail. Around 1900, the rate of productivity growth in manufacturing slowed markedly, but services productivity kept growing strongly. In the 1980s and 1990s, manufacturing productivity continued to grow fairly rapidly, but nonmanufacturing productivity, including for traditional services as well as construction, utilities, and mining, slowed down and at times even halted. If the replacement of one technology with another was the issue, why were services affected so much more than manufacturing?

A third problem with the David thesis is that it has no predictive value. Just because a new technology takes a long time to develop, it does not mean that every important technological advance will ultimately have a major impact on the economy. There is ample evidence that most major inventions took a long time to become commercially useful. How could it be otherwise? Every invention required significant refinements, some of which were as difficult to make as the initial invention itself. But most inventions never become commercially useful, and computer technology's ultimate impact is by no means guaranteed. The scripts of many hit movies were once rejected. But we do not conclude that, because a script is at first rejected, it will assuredly become a hit.

In my view, the David thesis, which is so widely cited today, presented an oversimplified view of the way technology affects economies, ignored too many other determinants of growth, and has as noted no predictive ability.

Still, it is possible that even if historical analogy is inappropriate, information technologies were the main reason for the rapid economic growth of the second half of the 1990s. Why didn't they stimulate productivity growth earlier? The economist Daniel Sichel proposed one plausible explanation for slow growth through the mid-1990s. His computations showed that, although investment in computers and related information technology such as semiconductors and software increased rapidly after the 1970s, much of it was made merely to replace obsolescent computer equipment and software. So rapidly was information technology outdated that it required constant replacement to keep up, but the net investment in these new technologies— the capital stock—did not accrue rapidly enough to affect the economy as a whole. On balance, the stock of information technology was too small a proportion of America's plant and equipment to matter very much. Only in the late 1990s did Sichel and a colleague, Stephen Oliner, find that the rate of investment rose rapidly enough to raise the stock of capital in new technologies significantly enough to affect productivity. And that is when productivity did indeed start rising rapidly again in the economy as a whole.

One important problem with the Sichel analysis is that many technologies had had substantial impacts on productivity in the past even though they were a small part of total investment. No doubt, for example, the printing press of the 1400s and 1500s was a significant but far from large part of the capital stock of economies in the Renaissance, but its impact was immeasurably greater than its cost. Similarly, the television industry was a small part of America's total capital stock, but it changed the economy significantly by dominating the attention of a nation, on the one hand, and by radically reducing marketing costs and the commercial reach of standardized consumer products, on the other.

There are other examples. Twentieth-century science in general had a large impact on productivity through the development of more efficient fuels, new chemicals, and more effective medicine, among other impacts, but it was made possible by a relatively few research dollars compared to the size of the economy. Air conditioning, based on the invention of Freon, made possible the residential development of Florida and the Southwest. Changes in the organization of labor, such as the scientific management of the early 1900s or the moving assembly line itself, profoundly affected productivity growth as well, but they required minimal capital outlays.

Thus the mere size of the capital stock is not necessarily a decisive factor in economic growth. A small capital stock could well have helped produce rapid productivity growth. But even if it is not necessarily true that size of investment matters, it is still *possible* that it matters. As businesses and consumers use more computers, they may eventually raise total productivity. The computer clearly increased the productivity of tasks in many industries. For example, it once took airlines three weeks to calculate the consequences of a modest increase in their fares, but in the computerized age, it takes less than an hour. Cash windows at banks have replaced multitudes of clerks. Accounting and billing across America are now computerized even in small businesses, as are the keeping of inventories and the filing of records. A semiconductor chip is now in our cars, our refrigerators, and our television sets, enabling them to do things they never did before, and perhaps raising their usefulness. Consumer products, in fact, account for the sale of about 20 percent of all chips per year.

But the question is whether these new capabilities mattered very much to productivity. Several interesting books written in the 1990s offered counter-arguments, in which the authors claimed that much of the work done by computers was superfluous or even created unnecessary or unproductive work. Word processing might speed up writing a first draft, for example, but it did not make novels or magazines any better while it seemed to increase the amount written; paper was supposed to be reduced if not eliminated by computers, but the use of paper doubled per capita. Computers enabled many workers to stay at home, but office space in cities and suburbs was never in greater demand, and software companies and new Internet companies clustered together in Silicon Valley or lower Manhattan. In other words, geographic proximity still seemed to matter. Computers made it easier to search for legal precedents, but they did not produce more skilled lawyers, and they certainly did not reduce caseloads in the nation's overloaded courtrooms. To the contrary, one consequence was that legal briefs were longer than ever before.

Finally, the Sichel analysis, as useful as it is, does not tell us anything about exactly why capital investment is either high or low. Capital investment in high technology before the mid-1990s may have been low for a variety of reasons, such as that it was too expensive or not yet valuable enough to business. Capital investment in high technology may have been undertaken because the technology became very inexpensive in the late 1990s, an argument made in the next chapter and one that Sichel has been among the first to acknowledge is possible. This does not necessarily mean that the way business is done was changed permanently, as new economy advocates usually suggest. As for the future, the trends of the recent past are a less useful guide than many think. The returns on high technology investment may simply fall to normal levels in coming years as businesses run out of new applications.

The Age of Consumer Choice: A Change in Markets?

The most significant impact computers had on productivity before the mid-1990s was to help produce the age of consumer choice mentioned previously. The low level of capital stock in computers suggests that they were only a component of this process, and that new managerial, marketing, and financing methods were as or more important. This would be entirely consistent with historical patterns of economic development.

New computer techniques enabled innovative companies to retain or win market share by the constant introduction of new and better products, as well as better control of inventories. But new products required more human input as well. It was people who had to design, market, sell, finance, and manage the greater diversity, and this need kept productivity gains modest.

Discussion with corporate executives bears this out. They typically say that they must now introduce products more frequently, but they cannot amortize these costs over as long a period as in the past. The shorter life cycles of products means constantly higher start-up costs, which usually are more labor intensive.

This issue explains much of the weak productivity experience, especially stagnant productivity growth in so many services industries. The age of consumer choice more or less began with Japanese car manufacturers, led by Toyota. They learned how to make a wider variety of durable automobiles by linking new managerial methods with computerized information and inventory systems, as well as with computer-aided designing and manufacturing. Probably more important at this time, Toyota adopted new managerial practices that forced workers to take more responsibility. In fact, analyses of the production methods in this period rarely mentioned information technology, although it played a central role.

These managerial methods and new information technology reduced the average hours of work required to manufacture a vehicle at Toyota from ninety-seven in 1974 to sixty-six just three years later. The Japanese manufacturers were able to design, develop, and market new cars more rapidly, and make a profit selling far fewer of them than could the Detroit manufacturers, who were still wed to mass manufacturing of standardized cars. Ultimately, new models took only eighteen months from the drawing board to the production line at the major Japanese automakers, compared to three or four years for American automobile companies in the 1960s and 1970s. In the mid-1950s, there were only thirty basic models of cars made in the world, excluding frills and modest design variations. By the 1980s, there were more than 100, and by the 1990s more than 200, and there were thousands of variations in total.

American companies were skeptical of and even derisive about Japanese companies such as Toyota. But eventually they began to emulate the leaders. Meanwhile, European manufacturers found profitable niches in low-priced automobiles, such as the Volkswagen, and luxury automobiles, such as the BMW, Mercedes Benz, and Volvo.

American business had grown mighty and dominant by selling as many standardized products as possible to reduce production, distribution, and marketing costs per unit. Such economies of scale brought dramatic productivity gains. But with the new methods, the driving force in business became new and higher-quality products. The new approach spread from one manufacturing industry to another and across national boundaries.

Less widely recognized but still more important, the approach—eventually to be called a "new paradigm"—also spread to services. In fact, services in general bore the brunt of the demands of an age of consumer choice. A range of services industries adopted computer-based methods even more aggressively to increase flexibility and introduce new products more quickly. Such retailers as Toys-R-Us were among the most successful users of computers. Wal-Mart, through aggressive computer use, is one of the most productive services giants in the world. But the largest investments in information technology were typically made in services such as finance and insurance, which offered increasingly specialized products for ever finer market segments. Reaching these markets efficiently called for new production, marketing, and finance methods. The number of new products in services industries increased even faster than in manufacturing, making it difficult to improve productivity.

Long before the advent of the personal computer or the Internet, then, computers had enabled business to adopt new strategies to win market share. Once some companies began to do this, all who wanted to compete effectively had to do the same. Flexible production and fragmented markets replaced mass production and mass distribution. An age of consumer choice replaced an age of standardization and could be seen in the breadth of new products available to consumers.

In the mid-1950s, only five cars accounted for 80 percent of sales in the United States, and a single model might sell nearly 1 million units. Now, with lean and flexible production methods, car manufacturers could make a profit by selling 50,000 units or less. But new products multiplied in almost all industries. In 1970, approximately 1,000 new food products, from snacks to dairy products, were introduced in America, a level of innovation that was already impressive. But by the mid-1990s, some 15,000 new food products of all kinds were introduced each year. There was a proliferation of new electronics products, from miniature stereos to the Walkman and VCRs, and eventually to the cellular phone and the PC. There were new healthcare products and new appliances. Nike introduced a new model of running shoes every six weeks. The Gap, the popular retailer and manufacturer, completely changed its inventory every six weeks.

The services sector expanded even more dramatically. Countless new air routes were introduced at affordable prices once prices were deregulated. Multiplex movie theaters offered a dozen or more movies at a single stop. Major retailers like Wal-Mart adapted the computer to innovative use, especially in the efficient control of inventory and supply. They could thus offer a far wider range of products and replace low inventories rapidly, and some companies sold products at significant discounts. By the 1990s, "superstores" could specialize in selling books, sports equipment, home supplies, and office supplies in large part because computers enabled them to carry large inventories. Soon grocers opened giant stores as well. The vast, inexpensive, and computerized furniture stores of IKEA spread across the nation. There were also new food specialty chains, such as Starbucks and Au Bon Pain.

Similarly, in the early 1970s, there were a few hundred mutual funds. By the 1990s, there were twenty times as many, offering investors a wide range of specialized products to meet various needs. Computers were critical to accounting for the rapid, enormous flow of money as well as to communicating with hundreds of thousands of customers in a single day. Banks and insurance companies similarly multiplied the products they offered.

In this age of multiple consumer products, such key services as marketing and advertising became all the more significant. Companies had to spend money to differentiate their products. Advertising expenditures grew about twice as fast as GDP, and marketing became ever-present in our lives, from insignias covering athletes' clothing and billboards draped across athletic stadiums and rock concerts to product placements in movies and mail boxes stuffed with catalogs.

The age of choice was encapsulated best in the programming offered by cable television, whose technological advance was also dependent on the semiconductor. *TV Guide* in 1970 listed seven television channels in the New York metropolitan area. *The New York Times* television section in 1999 listed approximately ninety.

A rough estimate is that the new computerized and managerial methods, stimulated in addition by rising competitiveness around the world, had so changed the American economic landscape that by 1995 there were some five to ten times as many products in many and perhaps most categories than there were in the early 1970s, and a large number of entirely new categories as well.

The age of choice that began in the 1970s arrived just in time because, by the late 1960s there were signs that American consumers were satiated with the standardized goods of more than a century of mass production. Economists generally attributed the falling profitability of American corporations in the late 1960s and early 1970s to rising wages, but another factor may have been lack of interest among consumers in the standardized and lower-quality products offered by American businesses. In 1976, the economist Tibor Scitovksy published an influential book called *The Joyless Economy*, in which he expressed dismay at the monotony of American products. Like many before him, Scitovsky suggested that continuing material consumption was not a path to contentment. But Scitovsky, who was dubious about material fulfillment in general, underestimated the innovative capabilities of global and domestic business. Earlier in the century, simply owning a car or a washing machine was extraordinary to an aspiring middle class, no matter that it was just like everyone else's. By the 1960s, a much wealthier nation of consumers clearly wanted more choice and distinction, and by the time of the publication of Scitovsky's book, they were beginning to get it.

Keeping foreign competition out of America would not have helped prevent a slowdown, and it would have deprived consumers of a great deal of, as economists put it, satisfaction: in other words, more products of higher qulaity at lower prices. Had the Japanese and others not introduced exciting new products, it is likely consumers would have bought standardized American products at a slower rate, and growth would have declined. Scitovsky would still argue that material fulfillment is evanescent, but at least now more variety fills some of these fleeting moments.

Thus, a new economy of some kind was well underway for fifteen or twenty years, but it was much less productive than the media and

Wall Street realized. Anything associated with computers was presumed to have only the most positive impact on productivity. However, this was not the case before the late 1990s.

In this period, America's vast marketplace was the trying ground for countless new and differentiated products from Japan and Europe, as well as from the start-up Asian economies, such as South Korean and Taiwan. Productivity grew at historically slow rates in the United States. But in this age of choice, productivity growth also slowed markedly in Japan and Europe. If the new techniques were so productive, why didn't productivity in these other nations grow more rapidly as their exports expanded? As mentioned previously, conceiving, developing, financing, marketing, and making new products required creative human input in the business process—and on balance more hours of work than otherwise would have been needed. Shorter business cycles required more start-up expenses, new equipment, new or differently trained workers, new organizational and managerial procedures, new marketing campaigns, and sometimes new financing techniques. Much of this productivity slowdown appeared in services, not manufacturing. Labor-intensive services were after all the sources of creativity in the economy, from consulting to marketing, finance, design, and retailing.

Once again, it is useful to think of this transformation as a return to a modern version of the old crafts or artisanal economy. In the past, U.S. productivity depended largely on the size of operations, the factory system, scientific and centralized management, access to capital, natural resources, and the domination of distribution. The huge American market was the nation's unique advantage. But in the age of choice, many more independent decisions were required at lower levels of employment. The new crafts were management, finance, marketing, sales, design, teaching, writing and editing, and computer and engineering specialties. The advantage of the large American market was at least temporarily diluted.

A good example of how advanced technology can have a paradoxical effect on productivity is the television industry. In the 1960s, network television was highly efficient. Three networks reached 90 percent of all families every night of the week. Because this market was so large—more than 100 million households by the 1990s—television networks could afford to invest heavily in programming. This was mass distribution and standardization of a kind unimagined by any economists before the advent of television (although the success of the radio a generation earlier intimated it). Companies such as Microsoft and various Internet providers were by no means the first to understand that providing their services free to customers meant more, not less, potential revenue; the television networks provided their programming for free from the beginning. (When observers are aghast that Americans watch so many hours of network television they usually overlook that it is free, which is probably the single most important cultural fact in American life.) The efficiencies of television radically altered the economics of marketing in America and helped raise productivity across many industries in the process.

With the maturation of cable television, these basic economics changed. Where there were once five or six stations at most in a large single market, and only three nationwide networks, there were now at least a few dozen cable outlets and usually more, offering a wide range of programming. Now the three networks together reached on average only 50 percent of the audience, and the cable outlets divided up the rest of the market.

Reaching 90 percent of the audience required more creative input than was the case when only three networks and a handful of local stations dominated each market. Movie channels such as HBO, USA, and Showtime showed original movies; sports channels provided twenty-four-hour coverage of a wide range of events; new news channels covered the world; and entertainment channels developed new nightly programming. All these required additional personnel. Thousands of independent television producers, often with complete staffs, appeared to create the new products.

At the same time, marketers could no longer reach 90 percent of America simply by advertising on the three networks. Now, to get the same coverage, they had to advertise on a variety of different cable channels as well, and supplement this more than in the past with print ads and direct mail. Also, the cable networks were often stealing away the more affluent viewers, leaving the networks with households that had less money to spend on advertised products. According to one consulting study by McKinsey & Company, and countless anecdotes, marketing costs rose significantly in this period.

There were advantages to the new media environment. Sellers of products could now direct their appeals to specific groups of customers: the young, the wealthy, the fashionable, housewives, or working men. They could target markets to sell products of narrower appeal. But there was a price paid for such targeting in lost efficiency. In general, new technologies made production in the entertainment industry more labor-intensive as new producers, writers, and other creative and administrative personnel were needed to supplement an industry that was once fairly centralized.

The efficiency of making each program probably improved. Special effects became better and less expensive. Fewer people were hired per production, especially as union contracts were rewritten. Cameras were lighter and more efficient. Tape was much less expensive than film, and easier to edit. But regardless of the improved productivity of a given program, many more programs were now needed than in the past to reach 90 percent of the audience. In sum, the number of people working in television increased faster compared to revenues than it had in earlier years.

o   o   o

The entertainment media epitomize an economy that, overall, could not reduce its labor intensity as fast as it once did because the number and variety of products were multiplying in industry after industry, culminating in our age of choice. Consider banking. Computerization eliminated many clerical tasks, and banks were able to reduce their workforce in these areas. But now banks had to compete for the consumer's attention in other quite costly areas that required more sophisticated personnel. They offered financial advice, sold mutual funds, specialized in retirement investing, and provided personal service to a large proportion of their customers. Although they no longer competed on the basis of the services they computerized, because their competitors were equally good at it, they now had to innovate continuously to keep the customer's attention. In addition, they had to market these new services aggressively, and to do so they vastly increased the outlay and the number of personnel (including contracting these services out to independent providers). Productivity did not increase substantially until the late 1990s.

Similarly, United Parcel Service computerized its transportation and package delivery system, eliminating rote tasks and, one might think, reducing the demands on personnel. But this only increased the complexity of tasks assigned to trucking operators because the computerization of elementary tasks intensified competition, particularly as volume increased. UPS personnel were now picking up packages at the door on little notice, for example. More decisions were moved down to the level of the driver. As one economist told me, slightly facetiously, in the past all these delivery people had to do was to be proficient at double parking. Now, they had to know how to operate portable computerized systems, organize and maintain extremely demanding delivery schedules, and deal in a friendly and presentable way with customers. They are among the nation's new crafts workers.

If almost everyone agreed that increased innovation was a characteristic of the new economic transformation, few considered its true costs. In *New Rules for the New Economy*, Kevin Kelly insisted that plentiful amounts of down time—what was waste only in the "old" economy— were necessary for the creative ideas of the new economy. Kelly was right that the new economy required a lot of creative down time. But he and many others were wrong in thinking that the new business ideas that were generated would somehow compensate for the extra time spent. In this economy, a great deal of labor time was needed simply to meet consumers' more complex and demanding needs.

If product differentiation retarded productivity growth, however, why did manufacturing productivity grow rapidly after the mid-

1980s? In fact, at a rate of growth of roughly 2.5 percent a year, manufacturing productivity grew almost as fast as it had in the 1950s and 1960s.

This rapid growth reflected two new factors. First, manufacturers contracted out an increasing number of their creative, labor-intensive tasks to the service sector. They hired consultants to install and manage their information technologies, reorganize them, perform engineering and design services, market their products, and perform financial tasks. In addition, they increasingly hired temporary workers, which according to some estimates increased their productivity in aggregate by several tenths of 1 percent in the late 1990s. In the government data, these consulting and temporary workers appeared in the services sectors, thus slowing reported productivity in that sector while raising it for manufacturing. Large service companies also contracted work out, of course, but this did not shift the productivity because it all remained in the services sector.

Second, the rise of productivity among manufacturers also reflected triage. Since the 1970s, the sales of U.S. manufactured items grew slowly, in large part due to competition from abroad. In fact, they grew more slowly than the overall economy, which itself was growing unusually slowly. In manufacturing, only the fittest—that is to say, the most productive—survived foreign competition. Companies and entire industries, such as textiles or electronics assembly, were either shut down or moved to lower-wage nations. Many plants were moved overseas. The average productivity growth of companies that remained in the United States was therefore necessarily high. In sum, manufacturing productivity grew about as rapidly as it had in the 1950s and 1960s, but output itself grew much more slowly, and productivity grew more slowly on average than it did overseas.[1]

---

[1]There is also a widely overlooked possibility of measurement error. Large manufacturers pressured parts and components suppliers to accept much of the burden of competition by meeting far tougher quality, delivery, and product specification demands. Productivity may well have risen slowly or stagnated in such companies, but because sampling methods are not as accurate for the smaller companies, their poor performance may have been underestimated.

The burden of the age of choice fell specifically on many services. This is, to reemphasize, why the Paul David thesis does not stand. A broad technological transformation, if it was the main cause of slow productivity growth, should have affected manufacturing more. The services sector of the economy expanded rapidly in this period. Some believed this was the natural result of a maturing economy in which consumers, satiated with manufactured goods, now wanted more services. (They also increasingly tended to buy their goods from foreign manufacturers.) But the greater increase in the demand for services in the past twenty-five years came less from consumers than from businesses themselves. They required consultants, managers, designers, and marketers. They devised new financial techniques, such as leasing, and complex trading, which also required outside expertise. Much of this was in response to the new economy of innovation that required new products, organizational methods, marketing campaigns, and financial creativity—and intensified both global and domestic competition in the process. Business also needed outside expert assistance in adapting new technology, notably computers, to their needs. These kinds of services were more labor-intensive than the key services of the past, such as transportation and retailing, and their productivity was difficult to improve.

Research by the economists Anthony Carnevale and Stephen Rose shows that the great rise in jobs came in just such "office" activities in this period, not in the high-technology areas of the economy. Services productivity overall grew at a rate of less than 1 percent per year between 1973 and 1995, and rose only slightly faster in the late 1990s. In the late 1990s, productivity at last grew more rapidly in retailing and finance. But in some services industries, it actually fell.

○   ○   ○

Some economists concede that fragmenting markets may have impeded productivity growth. But, they argue, if productivity was restrained to provide more consumer choice and higher quality products, then these benefits should be taken into account in reporting output and income. In other words, consumers were better off due to the increased variety and quality of products than the GDP data reflect. If GDP was understated, then both incomes and productivity actually grew faster than reported.

But the improved quality and choice probably brought no greater increase in consumer well-being than the unmeasured improvements of more standardized eras. The first standardized products had far greater impact on consumers than do new products today. We may have twenty-five new beers to buy this year, for example, but did that raise consumer satisfaction as much as the first mass-produced, cheap bottle of beer in the 1800s? Didn't television have a greater impact than VCRs? Didn't the automobile have a greater impact than the PC? The telephone than e-mail? The issue is not which is the greater invention, but how much it changed and improved lives compared to what came before it. E-mail may in some ways be more potent than telephone communications, but before telephones there were no instantaneous voice or house-to-house communications at all. Before the telegraph, there were homing pigeons, semaphore, and the Pony Express.

Also, the variety and quality of new products increased satisfaction only for those who could afford to buy them. The major growth for autos, for example, was for higher-end vehicles, such as SUVs. New health procedures were expensive and unavailable to those without good health insurance. Antidepressant drugs were considered an unmeasured quality gain by some economists, but they were mostly bought by the well-off. The rise in the Internet was restricted to those families that had a PC, slightly more than half. Only 60 percent of households had cable television. There were exceptions, such as inexpensive VCRs and microwave ovens. There was more variety in less expensive goods. But most of the increased variety was for more expensive fare, such as Gap clothing and Starbucks coffee. Thus, any such adjustments are misleading for the standard of living in general;

quality and choice probably benefited better-off Americans more than other Americans.

Finally, critics of the measurement agencies failed to point out how quality often deteriorated in these years. Traffic increased, for example, making cars less valuable. Surveys of consumer satisfaction generally showed a decline. Complaints about services were widespread in such industries as airlines and retailing. Had adjustments been made for such factors, productivity growth might have appeared slower than it was reported to be.

The variety of new products of the age of choice was, in fact, necessary to induce consumers to buy, but they were not necessarily of greater additional benefit than the fewer but more significant new standardized products of the past. If GDP and productivity should be ratcheted up further to reflect more consumer choice, the adjustments should probably be still greater in the earlier data. Thus, it is almost undeniable that the economy grew at historically slow rates over the past quarter century. In all likelihood, the increased consumer satisfaction derived from greater choice and new products beginning in the 1970s was about equal to the increased satisfaction derived from fewer but more fundamental new products in earlier times. In my view, the unmeasured increased satisfaction was arguably less than in most past eras of change. Consumer utility—or satisfaction—probably rose no faster than in the past, and perhaps more slowly. Certainly, sophisticated measures of American happiness declined in these decades. The Bureau of Labor Statistics now made large adjustments to the data for quality improvements that were rarely made before the 1980s, and never made before the 1960s. If GDP and productivity were understated due to rising consumer choice, they were only understated marginally and not nearly as much as in the past.

○　　　○　　　○

Some of the factors that contributed to slow productivity growth between 1973 and 1995 appeared temporary. In particular, the battle against inflation looked as if it had been won by the 1990s, and interest rates were much lower. American business adjusted to the initial thrust of foreign competition and became competitive in many industries. Profitability in general had been restored almost to the levels of the early 1960s. Some observers, such as historian Robert Brenner, make a strong case that these were the elements that at last led to rapid growth in the 1990s. Brenner argues that new profitable technological possibilities existed all along, but corporate America was impeded from taking advantage of them.

But these conditions already had been corrected in the late 1980s, yet slow productivity persisted. Other factors continued to affect productivity growth, and these seemed long-term, perhaps permanent. The growing importance of labor-intensive services such as healthcare and elder care and the lack of investment in public goods are two examples of this. The most important may have been the fragmenting of the market and the ongoing demand for consumer choice. Global competition would intensify competition for niche markets. The widening inequality of income also raised new issues. In the past a fairly homogenous market of consumers created large demand for standardized middle-class goods, but inequality reinforced the age of consumer choice.

One issue persistently undermined much of the conventional analyses. Why did the economy start to grow suddenly in 1996 if technology or improved corporate finances were the main source of growth? At the least, there should have been gradual improvement. But there was none. What happened, then, to enable the nation suddenly to grow rapidly in the late 1990s? As always, several important factors were involved, all of which depended on America's large marketplace and had precedents in earlier periods of growth.

7

Why We Grew
Rapidly Again

IN THE LATE 1990s, PRODUCTIVITY GREW AT NEARLY 2.5 PERCENT per year, and GDP itself grew by more than 4.0 percent per year. The return of productivity growth to a fairly high rate was the primary evidence for a new economy. No one forecast the sudden surge in growth, but it is no surprise that once it arrived, many observers insisted that the economy had gone through a permanent transition in the mid-1990s and that productivity might now grow at 2.5 percent per year indefinitely. In other words, the nation had crossed the threshold to permanent prosperity again.

But the durability of American prosperity will not be determined merely by extrapolating past rates of growth, as many do. Future productivity growth will depend on whether the factors that caused the rapid growth of the 1990s are durable. Were the factors that retarded productivity growth after 1973 at last corrected?

In truth, the causes of rapid economic growth in the 1990s were entirely consistent with past surges. They involved lower prices of key costs, exciting new standardized products that generated economies of scale, and the rapid growth of the market. But, again, economists and other observers resorted to conventional analyses that were abstract or irrelevant but fit accepted theoretical models of economic behavior.

I will first show why these conventional explanations do not fit the events, then discuss the more direct causes of rapid growth in the late 1990s. A prominent conventional argument, as we have seen, was that the financial condition of the nation's private sector improved, aided by the restructuring of business, the suppression of wages, and new government policies.

Businesses clearly had improved their profitability by the late 1980s. They pared operations, closed high-cost operations, held down wages and other labor costs, and for a while at least paid off debt. Profits rose rapidly. Also, government reduced business taxes; eliminated or minimized regulations in many areas; brought down the value of the anticompetitive dollar in the late 1980s; and at last, with the easing of inflation, helped reduce interest rates. But even if higher profits, lower taxes, deregulation, and lower interest rates contributed to economic growth, they were not the determining factors because they led to no immediate or even gradual increase in capital investment or productivity growth. These took another ten years to occur.

The recovery of manufacturing profitability actually began with the fall of the U.S. dollar beginning in 1985 after its long, debilitating rise since the late 1970s. The rise of the dollar in the first Reagan administration undermined the profitability of manufacturing by making exports more expensive and substitutable imports at home cheaper. The Reagan administration at last engineered a decline in the dollar with the cooperation of its major trading partners at meetings at New York's Plaza Hotel in 1985, which became known as the Plaza Accord. Exports became competitive again, and manufacturing prices rose.

Real interest rates had also fallen substantially by the late 1980s, even if they remained historically high, helping to raise profits and also to lift the value of stock prices. The market crash in 1987 was a shock to the financial system, but so rapidly did the Federal Reserve inject liquidity, as did other central banks, that expansion quickly resumed again.

The other important factor that contributed to profitability was the slow growth of wages. Robert Brenner points out that real hourly wages rose by only 0.15 percent per year between 1986 and 1993 in the United States, compared to nearly 3 percent in Japan and Europe. In fact, wages on average had fallen after inflation since 1973. According to the Bureau of Labor Statistics, U.S. manufacturing workers by 1995 earned $17.19 an hour on average, Japanese workers earned $23.82, and German workers $31.58. These subdued wages contributed substantially to rising manufacturing profits.

One other factor helped business: the sharp cut in business taxes initiated by the Reagan administration in 1981. The proportion of business profits paid in taxes fell from around 45 percent to 25 percent by the mid-1980s. Also under the Reagan administration, as noted, regulations in many industries were reduced or eliminated.

The failure of capital investment to rise over this period of profit growth, however, casts serious doubt on the thesis that these financial improvements and market-oriented government policies accounted for the rapid growth that started in 1996. Despite the improved profitability, and falling interest rates, American manufacturers simply did not raise their investment in plant, equipment, and product ideas in these years. A high proportion of available financing was directed to mergers and takeovers, in large part because stock prices were still low and debt financing was widely available. The alleged benefit of the takeover movement was that the nation's businesses became lean as tough-minded acquirers took over companies. Jobs were shed rapidly; high-cost businesses were closed, and others were moved overseas. But the nation increased its actual manufacturing capital stock only at a rate of about 2 percent per year, no faster than in the 1970s, and considerably slower than in the 1960s. Meantime, levels of private debt increased rapidly to finance the takeovers themselves. And manufacturing sales continued to grow slowly as well—in fact, slower than the rest of the economy.

If improved profits were the source of economic expansion, why didn't they have a beneficial impact on capital investment among manufacturers for another eight or ten years and result in products that would increase the rate of growth of sales?

Similarly, the rate of productivity growth in manufacturing did not rise above its 1980s rate at all until the mid-1990s. In fact, manufacturing productivity had been rising handsomely in the 1980s at about the same rate as in the 1960s. This was, as noted, in part because low productivity businesses and entire industries were either being closed or sent overseas. Thus manufacturing sales overall grew slowly, and the industries that remained inevitably had more robust productivity growth. But only in the mid-1990s did manufacturing begin to produce rapidly rising productivity. Sales grew robustly as well.

When capital investment did at last rise in the mid-1990s, many claimed it was the cause of the rising rate of productivity growth. It was more likely the other way around. Increased opportunity for productivity gains, due to falling computer power prices and exciting new products, led to capital investment.

So much attention is devoted to manufacturing here because fluctuations in profits and productivity in this sector are large and affect the entire economy. In 1999, for example, the rise in manufacturing profits accounted for half of all increased profits. But sales in nonmanufacturing industries, including all services, from retailing to transportation to finance, as well as construction and utilities, account for more than 80 percent of the economy, and their plight was starker still. Profitability in these industries was dismal in the late 1980s, despite stagnating wages and lower inflation. Partly due to the low wages, but also because of the new need for human input, as described previously, these industries hired millions of workers in this period, more than compensating for a decline in manufacturing workers in the nation as a whole. This placed a lid on productivity growth because these industries remained very labor intensive. Also, several labor-intensive services industries grew especially rapidly, including education and healthcare. Reduced taxes and interest rates, stagnating wages, and deregulation did not produce rising capital spending in these nonmanufacturing industries until the mid-1990s.

Because the conditions for improved profitability did not lead to higher capital spending or productivity growth until the mid-1990s, many observers thought that information technology must have suddenly matured at this time. But this argument is strained. The spread of information technology, it was argued, was broad and deep enough at last that it affected the economy as a whole. One piece of evidence in support was the rapid increase in investment in information technology in the late 1990s, which as economists Dan Sichel and Stephen Oliner found, added significantly to the stock of high-technology equipment. But why did such investment suddenly occur? After all, manufacturing had been profitable for years before capital investment levels improved. Computers were already "everywhere."

Advocates for a technological revolution generally claim, first, that information technology had at last spread sufficiently among corporations, and, second, that enough companies had at last learned how to exploit them fully. Also, they point out, the adoption of such technologies always required the development of many ancillary activities, such as new business organizations and transformations of workforces. Enough employees also had to be trained in the new technologies.

Again, however, it is not clear why these improvements did not produce a gradual acceleration of capital spending and productivity growth rather than a surge in the latter half of the 1990s. Some hypothesized that computer use had reached a critical mass, like uranium in a chain reaction, in which the entire economy would now profit significantly but before which there would be almost no benefit at all. The analogy suggested that businesses across the nation would suddenly profit as more of them used computers because they interconnected with each other in direct and indirect ways. In communications, there were clear examples. The more people who subscribed to an Internet service, the more efficient and productive that service could be. A single product, with fixed costs, could reach more people. It is possible that as more companies became productive with the use of computers, they made it more efficient for other companies to do business with them. For example, the demand for supplies or consulting services might increase.

But the analogy to a chain reaction that suddenly "explodes" in increased productivity does not hold up empirically. When a business invests in high technology, its productivity should theoretically improve no matter what happens at other companies. Some companies should have learned how to use this technology before others, thus raising their productivity. Productivity gains that depend on the interconnectedness of computer use among companies are an additional potential source of growth, but they too should have probably shown gradual improvement before the sudden burst of productivity growth. In fact, some economists, misreading the economic data, claimed there was a gradual improvement, and used it as proof of their contention. But after data revisions, there was no such gradation, and the claims were simply dropped.

The true causes of rapid economic growth were more down to earth. The advocates of a new economy could have argued more constructively if they acknowledged that high technology's main benefits were often simply to reduce costs, just as with past technologies. This, however, made a dull story. The new-economy advocates instead continually discussed information technology as something entirely new, a new way of doing business. They emphasized faster speed of processes and the small size of components and final products. These were not new, either. Nothing was so important to the mass production of steel, oil, and autos one hundred years ago as increasing the speed of production. The so-called weightless economy became a fashionable idea, because information was substanceless. But the GDP had become less weighty since the late 1800s, when services already had become an increasing proportion of the nation's sales. Natural resources were a much smaller part of the GDP, for example, than they had been in the past.

Claims for a network society were a favorite. We could all now communicate easily with each other in an infinite number of combinations. Telephones were limited to one-to-one communication. Television was limited to communication from one programmer to many viewers. The Internet could allow any number of us to reach any number of others. The forgotten question was, how did we find each other?

In truth, the economic expansion of the second half of the 1990s had to do with the same sorts of factors that always caused major periods of growth. First, computer costs fell precipitously in the second half of the 1990s. Second, new products were developed that were broadly useful and popular, in part stimulated by the reduced cost of computer power. Lower costs and new products stimulated capital investment. These exciting new computer-based products, such Windows or AOL, were, importantly, standardized and yielded enormous economies of scale to the makers of equipment and software and the providers of some mass-marketed services. After two decades of fragmentation, the mass market returned, correcting a fundamental cause of the productivity slowdown. The third contributor to renewed growth was the death of inflation, which enabled interest rates to fall and freed the Federal Reserve by 1996 from maintaining overly tight monetary policies. The foundation of financial improvements was laid earlier with the suppression of wages and new attitudes toward business and entrepreneurialism, but it did not bear fruit until the coming together of these other events in the late 1990s.

The fourth factor, the rapid expansion of the demand for goods and services, was related to the third. This rapid increase in spending, supported by government policies and a soaring stock market, had an independent impact on the nation's capacity to produce wealth, as it always had in the past. It made the rapid fall in computer power prices possible. It also made possible productivity gains in noncomputer businesses. But it was also supported by a rapid expansion of private debt to record levels, an inflow of foreign investment due to confidence that the level of the U.S. dollar would remain high, and insupportably high stock prices. All of these presented problems for future growth.

These four factors are explored in greater detail in the following sections. They reversed some but not all of the causes of slow growth described in chapter 6.

The Fall in the Price of Computer Power

The main way in which technological advance influenced the economy in the 1990s was the rapid fall in the cost of computer power. In 1999, computer power, according to federal estimates, cost approximately 10 percent of what it did in 1990, and by far the largest part of that gain came in the last half of the decade; computer power fell in price by more than 30 percent per year from 1996 to 2000 compared to 15 percent per year before that. Prices of some key computer chips and other key components fell much faster. There is controversy about exactly how fast the actual price of computing power fell; some of the change could well be an artifact of government accounting practices. It was not that microprocessor prices, the main component of computers, literally fell, but that the capacity of these chips increased dramatically while the prices essentially remained the same. Semiconductor chips were the driving force behind not only computers but also telecommunications equipment; machine tools; and many of the innovations made in consumer products, from cars and refrigerators to cell phones. The federal government translated the capacity increases into price decreases for the purpose of estimating GDP.

This decline in the cost of computer power was analogous to, but more pronounced than, the rapid fall in the prices of power (kerosene, petroleum, and electricity), steel, machinery, food and transportation that launched earlier new economies.

The price of few other key components of business ever fell as rapidly in so short a time as computer power. The cost of books fell by as much as the cost of computers after the invention of moveable type, but it took a couple of generations. The cost of transportation fell rapidly in the 1800s with the building of the canals and then the railroads, but neither as rapidly nor by as much as computer power. The cost of steel, of oil and its important by-products, and of transportation, to take major examples, all roughly fell by 75 percent and possibly somewhat more in the late 1800s over the course of a couple of decades. The cost of power, with the introduction of electricity, fell as well, but not by as much. The costs of certain goods that were subject to mechanization, such as cigarettes, fell in price as dramatically as computer power, but these latter were not central to the economy. The advantages of new mass retailing methods helped reduce costs of products by probably 50 to 75 percent as well over two decades. But the cost of computer power fell by 98 or 99 percent after 1980, if the government estimates are correct.

The lower prices of computer components, notably the chip itself, allowed enormous innovation in software and applications, which made possible many exciting new business and consumer products. This cost reduction and subsequent innovation were not the inevitable consequence of a "maturing technology." The price reduction could not have occurred without a huge and growing marketplace to support it. (There were many specialized types of computer chips that required enormous markets within markets to make their production efficient.) The abstract idea of technological advance, which conjures up images of great inventors with a single brilliant innovation, is misleading. Rapid price reductions depended on old-fashioned economies of scale. And even with economies of scale in the past, few central costs of business fell as rapidly as did the cost of computer power.

As products dependent on computer power became less expensive, there was less magic than imagined about why companies bought them. In the 1980s and early 1990s, computerized equipment and methodologies were not economical enough to replace much machinery and equipment or many-labor intensive processes. Now, they could. This was not what the new economy advocates, including Alan Greenspan, were claiming. They had romantic visions in their heads of how computerization changed the way business was done. This was at best minimally true. The lower prices also accounted for innovative new products in areas such as complex machine tools and telecommunications equipment.

Successful New Standardized Products

On the surface, the economy that took hold in the late 1990s was stimulated by the hot, ever-cheaper products that were the result, it seemed on the face of it, of entrepreneurial imagination and inventive genius. But it was the lower price of computer power and the bulging demand for standardized products, creating enormous economies of scale, that were the key catalysts for exciting new products in the late 1990s. The sales of PCs and printers, hand-held computers, cellular phones, software, and Internet services of all kinds, the most important of which was e-mail, grew at extraordinary rates, and in turn created more demand for related products. Both the sale of PCs and capital investment in information technology grew by more than 30 percent per year in the late 1990s. These were the sewing machines, telephones, automobiles, and television sets of earlier eras. The price of highly powerful PCs fell to much less than $1,000 by 1999.

These products had an important characteristic that was largely ignored. They were highly standardized and became the mass products of their time. This was in stark and beneficial contrast to the previous two decades, in which companies sought to fill narrow market niches with differentiated products. Yet the new products of this age were so complex that they enabled more customization. They made it possible for a desktop business customer to tailor Cisco's networking to its own needs. A PC customer could use the computer to write at home, do the bills, or communicate over the Internet. The products themselves contained differentiation that customers wanted, but could be produced with growing economies of scale because they were standardized, despite their complexity. The large majority of software sold, for example, was prepackaged. This was testimony to the integrated circuit microprocessor, which was widely usable in all kinds of applications. But it could be fully exploited only in large markets.

These standardized products generated new economies of scale for their producers, who usually came to dominate their markets and thus assured themselves an ever-greater volume of sales. The more they sold, the lower the unit costs and the higher the efficiency in making them. Windows dominated the market in operating systems, Intel's Pentium in personal computer chips, Cisco and Oracle in business-related computer systems, Hewlett Packard in printers, and AOL and Yahoo! in providing Internet access.

By the late 1990s, America had entered a new (possibly temporary) age of standardization and mass production. It was new because it marked a decided change from the increasingly fragmented marketplace of the previous two decades. The product revolution that took hold in the late 1990s was, thus, astonishing in the *old* American sense. Everyone seemed to want essentially the same products for the first time since the 1950s and 1960s, when consumers all generally bought the same cars and watched only CBS and NBC on television, and being upscale still meant buying Proctor & Gamble mass-market products. Economies of scale were the heart of success of companies such as Intel, Microsoft, Cisco Systems, Dell Computer, Apple, Oracle, and AOL, just as they were once the heart of success for Singer Sewing Machine, Standard Oil, U.S. Steel, General Motors, Sears, the A&P, McDonald's, and AT&T during a century of rapid economic development.

Consider the market share of America's major new companies in the late 1990s. Cisco Systems, which made routers for the Internet, had 80 percent of its market. Intel sold 90 percent of the computer chips in America. The basic personal computer, manufactured by a handful of major companies, was essentially standardized, and companies generated large economies of scale making them. Hewlett Packard made 50 percent of the nation's printers. AOL had more than 44 percent of Internet subscribers. Microsoft's Windows NT had 50 percent of all workstations. The MS Word word-processing program had 90 percent of the market.

In October 2000, *Business Week* wrote:

> Chances are, every company moving online will buy a piece of hardware or software from one of . . . four giants. Cisco makes the routers that do the heavy lifting—shuttling a corporation's data to and from the Net. Sun sells the Web servers that produce millions of Web pages. EMC is the storage king that holds the sea of ones and zeroes that make up digital information. And Oracle makes the database and e-commerce software that enables companies to digitize catalogs, process transactions, and move business online.

There was also a marked increase in productivity in some service industries, notably wholesale and retail trade and finance. Again, economies of scale were the source. Wal-Mart, in particular, learned to pare costs to a minimum, and meet consumer needs, by adopting enormous coordinated purchasing and marketing operations across its markets. Other retailers at last emulated Wal-Mart. The boom in demand for financial services also resulted in growing productivity in the late 1990s.

Preliminary data suggest that there was greater concentration of business in the late 1990s. Since the 1970s, as markets fragmented, large companies had dominated a smaller proportion of the market. But in the 1990s this began to change. The Commerce Department reported that the concentration stopped falling in the early 1990s and began to rise by the late 1990s. It was in many ways a return of the old economy.

Subdued Inflation

In the past decade, consumer price inflation has fallen by more than half, from 5.5 percent in the early 1990s to about 2.5 percent in 2001. This enabled the Federal Reserve to adopt looser monetary policies beginning in 1996, when it cut its target rates aggressively. Investors became willing to buy bonds at lower interest rates because they were confident inflation would not erode the value of future dollars.

Mortgage interest rates fell from 10 to 7 percent during this period, corporate bond rates fell from 9.3 to 7.1 percent, and rates on three-month Treasury bills fell from 7.5 to 3.5 percent. As a result, both capital and consumer spending were stimulated. Lower interest rates also helped stimulate the rising stock market as well.

Alan Greenspan probably should have eased rates earlier. Even though the Clinton tax increases were passed, promising a reduced federal deficit and less pressure on inflation and interest rates, Greenspan and the Federal Reserve raised interest rates by a full 3 percentage points in 1994 and 1995. By 1996, after cutting the rates substantially when the economy had slowed, Greenspan was willing to let rates stay low. Even as the GDP grew more rapidly, he and his colleagues avoided restricting the economy as the Fed had done two years before. Greenspan discussed the possibilities of higher productivity growth due to information technology, but mostly, in my view, he simply watched the inflation data and the bond markets. Greenspan could see no discernible sign of rising inflation.

As I review Greenspan's record, I believe he largely took his cue from the bond market. When bond traders showed confidence that inflation had been subdued by buying in 1996 even at lower interest rates, as they had not done in 1994, Greenspan and the Federal Reserve adopted looser, growth-oriented policies.

What also helped propel growth, however, were the emergency infusions of liquidity by the Fed to minimize the consequences of financial failures in Asia in 1997, and of the failure of the large hedge fund, Long Term Capital Management, in 1998 (as well as the default on foreign debt by Russia). These efforts kept interest rates down and the stock market up, and generally restored rapid growth to the U.S. economy, a fact all too often forgotten.

Meanwhile, private borrowing by both business and consumers, supported by record stock prices, fed the demand for goods and services. It was a "virtuous circle." As the economy grew, it reduced the federal deficit and eventually produced substantial budget surpluses between 1998 and 2000. The surpluses calmed bond traders, and thus the Federal Reserve. Interest rates fell, supporting higher stock prices and more borrowing. The lack of federal stimulus, as the budget deficit fell, was more than compensated for by private spending supported by borrowing and high stock prices. The surging demand for imports was financed by the international flow of capital into American stocks and business in general. A high U.S. dollar kept import prices down, stifling inflation still more, while attracting investment.

New economy advocates, and Greenspan himself, attributed subdued inflation to the maturing information technology. But the long battle against inflation had fully defeated inflationary expectations, and growing demand resulted in enormous economies of scale for makers of computer equipment, chips, and software. The economies of scale accelerated the ongoing decline in computer power prices, as well as in other new industries. Lower computer prices stimulated capital investment and the spread of the Internet. Meanwhile, the high dollar kept import prices low. This wasn't a matter of a critical mass of computer usage and knowledge being reached. It was a classic case of new technologies stoked by rapidly growing demand and a rash of exciting standardized products at ever lower prices. It was the classic circle of economic growth, with many factors contributing, but growing demand probably remaining the first among equals.

A Rapidly Growing Market

The market for goods and services thus burst forth in the late 1990s. What was not well understood or fully acknowledged was that rapid growth of demand itself led to greater economic efficiency. The rapid increases in consumer spending enabled businesses to run full out, utilizing their workers and capital equipment as efficiently as possible and making economies of scale more advantageous for most businesses. The growing demand made new products more profitable and allowed increasing differentiation among them, enabling such products to reach an efficient scale more quickly. Bulging consumer demand for goods and services also did what the economist John Maynard Keynes had once said it would. It increased incentives for businesses to invest in new plant and equipment, enabling them to absorb efficient new equipment and to refine managerial methods.

The growing demand for consumer products was especially important in raising the profitability of wholesaling and retailing in these years. Wal-Mart in particular was a leader in the adoption of new technologies for inventory control and "supply chain" management. But as the large and growing market made these technologies profitable, other companies followed Wal-Mart's lead. A high volume of sales was critical to these improvements, as were the sales of higher value goods to better-off customers, which generated more dollars per sale. High stock prices also made financial companies more productive in this period for the same reasons: They raised both the volume of transactions and dollar value of each one.

Rapidly growing demand across the board contributed to increased productivity throughout the country. Without this growing demand, productivity increases would have been fairly isolated to the makers of computer products, not their users. These makers of computer equipment, along with the retailers mentioned previously, and finance companies, were the principal sources of productivity growth in these years. The evidence suggests that there was modest growth of productivity among the users of computers, but much of it was dependent on rapid cyclical growth.

Cultural and Political Changes?

Earlier changes in cultural and political conditions also helped the economy blossom in these later years, but they were not the key catalysts of growth. A favorable cultural disposition to profits and entrepreneurialism helped improve profits of manufacturers in particular in the 1980s. For three-quarters of a century, business had been criticized for its excesses, often for good reason, a trend that reached its height in the 1960s. The share of profits in the economy was historically low in these years, and the nation's youth looked at business largely with derision.

This attitude was reversed in the 1980s. Profits and entrepreneurialism became prestigious again and attracted more talent to business. The new political attitude also enabled government to reduce business taxes and deregulate. At the same time, however, there was a broad acceptance of lower wages and job insecurity, even among laborers themselves. Unionization declined, the number of temporary workers increased rapidly, and resistance to large layoffs all but disappeared. Jack Welch, chairman of General Electric, became the most admired CEO in the nation as he laid off tens of thousands of workers. To some degree, this was beneficial. Wages as a proportion of GDP were unusually high in the 1970s. Labor contracts may well have been restrictive. Many extolled America's new so-called flexible work force and attributed slower growth in Europe to a less malleable labor market.

But the movement went too far. Incomes became highly unequal. Average wages did not rise even during the era's economic expansions. Workers compensated for stagnating incomes by working longer, having spouses go to work, and borrowing much more. Without borrowing, the rising inequality of income would have weakened the economy as a whole because it would have depressed purchasing power and undermined the advantages of America's enormous market. Workers were probably also increasingly dissatisfied, but their anger was channeled at government, not work. Many workers had fewer resources to educate their children, for example, but they resisted higher property taxes for pre-collegiate education. Never before had American wages fallen below the levels paid in other developed nations.

Had wages increased rapidly rather than fallen, business might have invested more aggressively in equipment and new methods to reduce wage costs, bringing more sustainable long-term growth. Individuals would not have added so much debt to their finances and would have had more purchasing power to support future growth. They would also have had more capacity to save, reducing the nation's dependence on international capital, and they would have had more resources to educate themselves.

Some observers also argued that the many sources of capital in America made entrepreneurship easier than elsewhere. The volume of venture capital soared in the late 1990s, and new companies raised money on Wall Street in amounts that exceeded $300 billion per year. In the 1980s, however, when Japan and Europe were prospering and America floundering, the opposite arguments were being made. The American model, wed to low-quality standardized products and impersonal banking, was then said to be failing.

The problem with attributing the boom to new financial "institutions" is timing. Venture capital soared in the very late 1990s. If it was the source of America's predominance, it would have been a more significant volume earlier. In fact, it amounted to no more than 10 percent of R&D spending until near the very end of the high-technology boom. Similarly, initial offerings to raise money for start-ups, no matter the source, soared at the end of the 1990s. Quite obviously, as Robert Brenner points out, these new sources of funding were a response to the rising stock market, not the source of its vitality or of the economy's rise. It was too much, too late.

In some respects, the new sources of growth reversed the problems of the previous two decades. In particular, markets generated enormous economies of scale once again, and standardized products ruled the market. Also, government policies were growth oriented, and rapidly increasing demand led to still more productivity growth; rapid growth is a cause of growth as markets expand. But how durable are these changes?

8

The Challenges to Prosperity

THE SOURCES OF GROWTH OUTLINED IN CHAPTER 7 PROVIDE A way to analyze future prospects. But they do not provide strong, unambiguous grounds for optimism. Can we count on computer prices to continue to fall as fast? Similarly, can we count on a continuing stream of exciting new standardized products that attract mass demand and generate economies of scale? Is inflation truly defeated, and will the Federal Reserve remain oriented toward stimulating growth? Given their high levels of debt and a weak stock market, can consumers and business keep spending? Will the dollar stay relatively high without ultimately reducing the strength of manufacturing industries, whose exports are now so expensive around the world?

Many technologists are convinced that the costs of computer power can fall consistently for the indefinite future. But they are not sure of the pace of that price reduction. Intel, for example, aggressively accelerated the introduction of new computer chips in the late 1990s, and it is not clear that it will be able to keep up the pace. Moreover, it is also not clear that business and consumers truly require much more computer power. Some economists believe that many are saturated already. Weighing the odds, it is not impossible that computer power prices will fall as rapidly as they have in recent years, but neither is it probable.

If the pace of falling costs slackens, this may well affect the second source of growth, product innovation. We can never be confident that entrepreneurs will continue to introduce products as exciting as those they did in the second half of the 1990s. To the extent that these products depended on rapidly falling costs, it is even more difficult to be completely confident that similar new products will be introduced in coming years. Fragmenting may again overtake markets as consumers continue to demand choice.

There is at least one counter-argument to this concern. The reduction in power prices already made and the new products already introduced may not be fully exploited. Some 60 percent of American businesses have invested in high technology, but not all of these have invested substantially. It is difficult to determine whether this is a high or low figure. Some of course argue that this number suggests we are only halfway through the process of investment in this area. But we may be nearer to saturation than is believed. Similarly, somewhat more than half of the households own a PC. Is this near saturation? The stronger case for productivity growth in coming years is that existing gains have not yet been fully exploited rather than that new breakthroughs are forthcoming. But even this suggests that our present surge may last only a few more years.

Faith in technological innovation for many observers remains the main reason for optimism about long-term growth. A popularly cited possibility is that Internet connections will increase in speed and carrying capacity so rapidly that the PC will become a television set, VCR, and information processor all in one.

But what will that accomplish? The over-promotion of Internet retailers—the dot-coms—is by now bitterly documented. What we have learned from history is that it is the conditions that foster commercially useful technological growth that matter. Technological advance cannot be counted on to proceed on its own or serve as an exogenous

engine of growth. A key challenge, then, is how to create these conditions. Also, a conventional argument is that it is vital to raise national
savings to make finance capital available for investment. Another
source of growth, many economists argue, is keeping wages low and
labor markets flexible.

My reading of history, however, suggests that the foremost requirement for technological advance is to enable the market—the
demand for goods and services—to continue to expand rapidly. This
was one of the causes of growth in the 1990s. Of all the factors cited
that can contribute to the strength of market demand, the defeat of
inflation is probably the most durable. Even if it rises somewhat, the
Federal Reserve will probably not return to the severely tight conditions of the past. The dampening impact of the fight on inflation,
which retarded growth for so much of the 1980s and 1990s, should
mostly be behind us.

As for a low paid workforce, one of the consequences of the cultural shift of the 1980s, those advantages may have passed. Low
wages could seriously undermine the demand for goods and services
because there is little room to expand hours worked, increase the
number of spouses at work, or raise the level of borrowing. All these
compensated for low wages and job insecurity in the 1990s.

The Internet

Given these challenges, can the Internet alone support ongoing
growth? New means of communication have often been central to
economic growth in the past, both because they entailed direct investment on their own and also because they affected businesses and
the general spread of knowledge and ideas. Printing was a thriving
industry in the 1500s in Florence, for example, and the price of
books had fallen precipitously compared to their pre-Gutenberg levels. We have had many communications revolutions since, including
the railroads' and steamships' carrying the mail and newspapers in

the 1830s and 1840s, the telegraph in the mid-1800s, the telephone in the early 1900s, the radio in the 1920s and 1930s, and television in the 1950s.

It is by no means obvious that the Internet will exceed or even equal in importance these innovations. So far, actual commerce over the Internet has been almost trivial. During the boom of the 1990s, consumer sales over the Internet amounted to no more than 2 or 3 percent of all sales. The sale of hard goods was especially limited. Information products, such as airline travel or new publications, were more exploitable on the Internet. As appendages to existing marketing operations of major companies, such as The Gap or *The New York Times*, e-commerce probably had value. But few companies had developed it as a major profit center by 2001. There were only a handful of stand-alone e-commerce successes.

The value of corporate intranets is more difficult to assess. They speed orders, help coordinate sales and production and especially inventories, process bills, improve the communication of product information, and are an inexpensive source of rapid corporate communications for all employees.

It is hard to know how large an improvement this is. Has inventory management been helped significantly more by the Internet than by initial Japanese just-in-time inventory methods of the 1970s and 1980s, which were widely adopted across industry? Individual companies report large savings on personnel. But some of these savings are suspect. Rarely do they include the cost of the capital investment in the new high-technology equipment or the considerable cost of maintenance.

E-mail communication itself can perform tasks that telephone and written communication could not. It is instantaneous, can be distributed widely, and does not require that a recipient receive a message in real time. It is also inexpensive compared to long-distance telephone. On the other hand, telephone conversations, to take an example, do not require typing, the spoken word is fast, and they allow for much more informal dialogue and interplay. Thus, e-mail is a new dimension of communications, but it is not the leap that telephone was over the telegraph, for example, or than the telegraph was over semaphore or the homing pigeon.

The Internet also permits easy access to information on subjects ranging from technical research to airline travel. This expansion of the availability of information must benefit the economy, just as new sources of information did in the past, but such benefit is hard to quantify. We were a well-informed age long before the Internet. The term "information economy" was commonly used in the 1970s.

In my view, the greater value of the Internet and intranets is to create price, quality, and distribution competition among potential suppliers. It can create an auction in all kinds of consumer and business products and reach a wide geographical range. The commercial success of eBay, the Internet auction house, is an example of this. A little-known tile maker in Ravenna, Italy, may now have to compete for customers with a tile maker in San Diego.

The central benefit that new economy advocates attribute to the Internet, however, is that it is a network unlike all others. This idea, we can safely conclude, is highly exaggerated. The advocates note that, whereas a television program can reach hundreds of millions of viewers (the Superbowl and the Soccer World Cup reach billions), television cannot fragment the market efficiently. Theoretically, with the Internet, any individual can reach any number of other individuals with similar interests. The model of the potential market is not, as it is in traditional networks, X times N, where X might be the number of TV stations and N the number of all potential viewers. That is the model for the ultimate mass market. The Internet, by contrast, we are told, is the ultimate niche market. We can each reach any number of others. It is N raised to the Nth, a much larger universe of possibilities.

Although it is theoretically possible for anyone to reach specialized niches around the world, however, it is, practically speaking, almost impossible. It costs enormous money to attract people's attention so that they can take advantage of your product or service. As a result, the greatest irony of the Internet is that it fosters still greater economies of scale, not many more niches. The essence of mass production was that it required high fixed costs: a factory, for example, or a big advertising campaign. But once those fixed costs are met, the cost of every additional unit produced was extremely low.

The Internet makes it possible to reduce the marginal cost of reaching a new recipient to zero. But the greatest advantage goes to whoever can afford to do the most marketing or invest in the highest advertising budget. Product awareness becomes more important than ever before. The N to the Nth model thus falters, at least as an economic model. In politics or technical research, where like-minded or highly motivated people may know how to find each other, it may well be valuable.

Far from encouraging commercial niche markets, the Internet's main commercial influence is to encourage mass markets. It may actually reduce choice over time. It may be the ultimate X times N model. At this point, it is likely that the Internet will continue to contribute to economic growth in the future. New advances to make it much faster will spread its use. But it is unlikely that it alone can sustain rapid productivity growth. The printing press, the telephone, and television were parts of much broader changes when they were introduced. A new economy cannot be based on the Internet alone, but at this stage, it provides the most hope for ongoing technological revolution.

Other Challenges to Growth

The optimistic case for economic growth, then, is based on three assertions. First, the technological revolution is ongoing and potent, and computer prices in particular will continue to fall rapidly. Second, inflation is permanently under control, enabling the Federal Reserve to maintain pro-growth policies. Third, the workforce will remain comparatively low paid and flexible.

The first condition is by no means certain. The second condition is a true cause for optimism, but there is a possibility that inflation will return. The third condition has probably run its course.

But there are also new problems and constraints that did not exist in the mid-1990s. In particular, the financial condition of the nation is a concern. Both corporate debt and personal debt now stand at record proportions of income. Nonfinancial corporate debt rose from about 3.5 percent of sales in the mid-1990s to a record of nearly 10 percent of sales in 2000. Household debt stood at a record level of nearly 100 percent of disposable income. Meanwhile, profitability has generally fallen for American corporations from its high in the mid-1990s, implying that returns on capital are falling.

The stock market complicates the future further. High stock prices encouraged borrowing and spending in the late 1990s, but they do not appear supportable even at the levels of early 2002. Any fall in stock prices could undermine demand for goods and services, as well as capital investment. A fall in prices might also reduce the value of the dollar, as capital flees to more attractive investments. The balance of payments deficit, largely composed of the excess of exports over imports, rose to a higher proportion of GDP in the late 1990s than it had been in the mid-1980s. A falling dollar will relieve pressure on manufacturers and enhance exports, but it could also stimulate inflation as import prices rise and cause the Federal Reserve to raise rates and bond investors to demand higher interest rates to compensate for future inflation. Because Americans save so little on average, a smaller flow of capital to U.S. markets can have damaging results.

The financial conditions in 2002 were thus simply not as conducive to growth as they were in the mid-1990s when debt was still relatively low, profitability was high, stock prices were at least somewhat reasonably priced, the dollar was comparatively low, and the balance of payments was not in severe deficit.

As we look ahead, however, there are still greater challenges to long-term growth. First, the age of consumer choice that began in the 1970s has not ended. Fragmented markets and demanding consumers, briefly checked by falling computer prices and exciting mass market products in the late 1990s, will probably remain future constraints on growth. International competitors will rush to fill niche markets, especially as production spreads around the world. Consumers will remain particularly choosy.

Second, the uniqueness of America's domestic marketplace is being newly challenged. In Europe, the Common Market has continued to extend itself, and the adoption of a new single currency in 2002 makes its markets more like America's than ever before. Moreover, this market could be expanded to many other nations to become significantly larger than the American market. The two most populous nations in the world—China and India—are now growing rapidly and attracting high volumes of investment. If they continue to grow, their markets may readily compete with the American marketplace. Russia and its former satellite nations might also adequately develop. In addition to large populations, these nations enjoy high levels of education. The East Asian nations are also discussing regional agreements to help unify their markets.

Such development may help America grow over time by providing new strong export markets. But American hegemony would be challenged, as would the dominance of the U.S. dollar. Demand for the dollar as the safest currency in the world helped it attract investment even as its domestic savings rate plunged. This considerable advantage could be undermined. Strong international markets would also produce strong regional companies that can compete more readily with American companies.

Third, the demand for inherently labor-intensive services, notably healthcare and education, will increase strongly. These services, not new cars or VCRs, are now the basis of a middle-class life. Their prices will rise faster than other prices because of this labor intensity.

Fourth, and least well recognized, the nation no longer adapts to change the way it once did. America has long neglected public investment, including infrastructure, transportation, childcare, and education, in large part because of more than twenty years of straitened financial conditions. In similar periods in its history, even before the Civil War, America developed new institutions, policies, and corporate practices to address changes brought on by economic evolution. This time it is not. It has not adequately addressed the problems of a new economy that is more insecure and unstable and produced unequal wages; has demanded higher levels of personal investment, especially education; has relied on archaic systems for delivering key services, including healthcare and childcare; and has undermined the confidence in economic and political rights for so many who trailed behind the one-fifth or so of Americans who did well.

These areas of neglect affect the vigor of the market. Inequality of incomes has led to inequalities of skills and education. It has also fragmented the market, as a vast middle market for standardized products has been replaced by an elite market of higher income consumers who demand high-quality and more expensive goods and services, who exist alongside a broad middle whose buying power, without substantial borrowing, is too weak to sustain healthy growth. America in the past always included the broadest slice of its population in the benefits of its economy, as a democracy should. It in turn had highly capable and educated workers. Leaving out a few made the United States a richer nation. Now, we hardly think about such issues. Leaving out many makes us a poorer nation. Where once the nation typically looked forward, now its political leaders invariably look back.

These challenges have to be met directly. There is a constructive agenda that can enable the nation to grow as rapidly as possible. The advocates of the new economy did their greatest disservice to the nation by implying that the agenda had already been adequately met. This is far from the truth.

9

Making America Grow:
Challenges and Principles

A NEW AGENDA FOR PRODUCTIVITY GROWTH IN AMERICA IS necessary because the agendas of the past two decades were at best partial and unbalanced. This is largely because they evolved from incorrect premises concerning the dominating role of capital investment or technological advance and did not take into account the strength of markets, the neglect of public investment, and the new needs of a changing economy. A new agenda should be based on two vital principles. First, a strong market for goods and services is a leading cause of economic growth in general, as is the information that flows in that market. Market growth is itself a major cause of both capital investment and technological advance. Second, economic growth is organic and involves many interrelated factors. A reasonable agenda should address those factors that have been most neglected, including the new needs created by a changing economy. In recent decades, these have included education, infrastructure, childcare, and equal access to new communications media, as well as the strength of America's domestic market itself.

The Myth of Unprecedented Prosperity

Many believe America had solved its problems in the 1990s. Why worry about changing the agenda? Before we move on to a new agenda, then, let's dispose of two myths about the successes of the 1990s. First, that decade's economic growth was not the triumph it was widely held to be. To be sure, during those years not only did the rate of growth increase, but the rate of unemployment fell more rapidly than expected, corporate profits as a proportion of GDP reached new high levels, and wages rose substantially for all income levels. No economist forecast the extent of these gains. Finally, stock prices rose especially rapidly until early 2000, becoming the barometer of the economy's health for much of the nation. Again, no forecaster anticipated the extent of the market rise. It would have been a wildly far-fetched claim.

But by most measures of income and wealth, the new prosperity of the late 1990s did not compensate for the damage done by the slow growth of earlier decades. Family incomes were only modestly higher in 2001 than they were in 1989, discounted for inflation. In previous periods, family incomes had grown by approximately 25 percent per decade. The rate of unemployment was low in the 1990s, but it was lower in the 1960s. The economy created jobs, but not as fast as it had even in the 1980s. Many measures of average wages had not risen above 1973 levels, yet they had grown by an average 2 percent per year for the first three-quarters of the century. A high proportion of male workers—more than half of those in their fifties—were no better off after inflation than they had been ten or twenty years earlier. This last point was a remarkable and little recognized fact. Average wages measure how, for example, the wages of thirty-year-olds today compared to thirty-year-olds twenty years ago. Today's thirty-year-olds are not doing as well by many measures. But even in a slow-growth environment, one would expect that workers will make more money as they grow older and more experienced. Yet according to Census Bureau data, half of male workers who are fifty or so today earn less, discounted for inflation, than they did when they were thirty. This probably never happened before in American history over such a long period of time. It was worst for workers with only high school diplomas.

New products improved people's lives, of course. Many observers cited the advent of VCRs, fast food, color TVs, and fancy sneakers as indications that even low-income individuals were better off. America always produced such products, however, but incomes also rose rapidly for most income groups at the same time. This was no longer the case. Even as families could afford VCRs and new food items, they could not buy nearly the same amount of education, healthcare, drugs, housing, or public transportation as they could a quarter century earlier because the prices of these key goods and services rose much faster than typical incomes. Moreover, for family incomes to increase during these years, both spouses typically had to work, yet the nation did not supply adequate childcare to support these changing needs. The improved economic conditions of the late 1990s also did not reverse the rising inequality of incomes in the nation. Consumers generally "kept up with the Joneses" only by borrowing against their homes and credit cards.

Even the growth rate of the late 1990s, though faster than it had been since 1973, was not unusually robust. Wall Street, the Clinton administration, Congress, and the media nevertheless claimed that the nation had never been as prosperous. It was a preposterous assertion, but it reflected the euphoric times. Rising stock prices seemed to influence all thinking. The expectations of the nation had been driven so low over two decades of slow growth that five years of strong job markets lifted all spirits (amply aided by the growing capacity of everyone, even the poor, to borrow).

The annual rate of growth of 4 percent between 1995 and 2001, as well as the rate of productivity growth of roughly 2.5 percent over the period, had often been exceeded over five-year periods in the past, including in the 1920s and the 1960s. Had the 1920s and 1960s data been adjusted for quality improvements, they would have been even stronger. In fact, an annual growth rate of 2.5 percent under modern data gathering methods was at best equal to the annual long-term rate of productivity growth since the Civil War. More likely, it was below the average.

Even if those five years of growth represented a new trend, then, we had not launched on an unprecedentedly prosperous period. When one adds factors such as the widening inequality of incomes; the longer hours worked by families; and the rapidly rising costs of education, healthcare, and drugs, claims of prosperity made by both Republicans and Democrats over this period are callous and perhaps even deliberately deceitful.

Most economists, at least in the pre-euphoric days before the invention of the new economy, agreed that a long-term trend of productivity growth is probably better approximated by the average growth over an entire business cycle than by the rate of growth during the best years of that cycle. The rapid growth in the second half of the 1990s raised the annual rate of productivity growth for the entire business cycle, which began in 1991, to almost 2 percent. On balance, this meant that over the course of that cycle, productivity grew approximately 0.5 percent per year faster than in the 1970s and 1980s. Observers were mistaken to assume that this 2 percent rate of growth was a return to America's long-term rate of productivity, because the historical data had not been adjusted upward for quality improvements of products and other factors, as they had been since the 1970s. Nevertheless, a 0.5 percent increase in the annual rate of growth was significant over time, representing a partial return to prosperity and suggesting that the improvement may have been a long-term trend.[1]

---

[1]This rate of growth was raised by revisions to the data made in the late 1990s and early 2000s. Before these revisions, the rate of productivity growth between 1973 and 1995 was reported to be 1 percent a year. The cycle of the 1990s, in which productivity rose on average by a revised 2 percent, rather than about 1.5 percent, began after the recession that bottomed out in 1990. By comparison, over the cycle of the 1980s, which began in 1979 and ended in 1990, productivity grew by a revised 1.45 percent per year. Over the cycle that began in 1973 and ended in 1979, productivity grew by approximately 1.55 percent per year. The data revisions reflected changes in the methodology to account for consumers' tendency to switch to cheaper products as inflation rises, quality improvements that had been neglected, and the inclusion of computer software as output.

Such a 0.5 percent increase in the annual productivity growth rate, if sustained, would mean that incomes over twenty years would be roughly 12 percent higher than they otherwise would have been. It would mean another $5,000 per year in the typical family's income and another $150 billion per year in federal tax revenue. If productivity growth can be raised still further, it would add significantly more to incomes over time. A 1 percentage point improvement, which would restore productivity growth to its long-term historical rate, would add $10,000 per year to income in twenty years and $300 billion per year to federal tax revenue.

These adjustments were arguably justified, but still controversial, especially to the degree that they were adopted. For example, when consumers switched from buying, say, apples, because they rose in price, to pears, because they fell, they paid less than was reported by earlier methodologies, which had assumed they were still buying apples. But they also did not buy the piece of fruit they originally wanted. Thus, we could argue that their standard of living was partially reduced. As the quality of cars improved, one got more car for the money. Thus, this should be reflected in GDP for all products for which such quality improvements are obvious. The quality of cars had long been adjusted for by the BLS, but sectors such as electronics and healthcare were neglected.

In another area, the purchases of software had long been considered an expense for business, not an investment. Such business expenses were not included as output or directly in measures of productivity because they were already included in the price of the finished product. But now the enormous purchases of software were considered an investment, and they did raise output and productivity. The problem is that software becomes obsolete much faster than computers or than traditional plant or equipment. Thus, at best, its contribution to income is considerably less than that of other investments.

Finally, adjustments made to the prices of computers and chips were highly controversial. The federal government adjusted the costs of these investments down dramatically from their actual levels to account for increases in power and flexibility. But it is not clear that the buyers of these high-technology products fully utilized all their capacity.

Academic critics proposed a long list of similar adjustments. These critics persistently ignored reductions in quality, as reflected for example in consumer surveys of dissatisfaction, or rising levels of traffic, to take only two examples. Such quality declines reduced productivity. The quality adjustments made are by nature subjective, yet the academic criticism was unusually biased toward claims that GDP and productivity data were understated. In 2002, a National Academy of Sciences study provided a much needed corrective to the conventional claims of academia. It is possible that the data have been adjusted too aggressively.

The Myth of the Best Path to Growth

The second myth is that the nation achieved its growth in an ideal manner, and the policies taken to get there were the best it could have done. As Americans were told, and seemed to believe, that they had solved their economic problems, people like Alan Greenspan and Treasury Secretary Robert Rubin became among America's most popular public figures. Had the 0.5 percent improvement been produced without creating concomitant problems for the future, these accolades would have been more justified. In other words, had the 1990s growth rate been reached without enormous increases in private debt, without overly speculative gains in the stock market, and without a high U.S. dollar that led to record trade deficits as a proportion of GDP and further debt to international investors, there would be grounds for saying the right solutions had been found. But, in fact, these excesses contributed significantly to the more rapid growth. It could well be, considering the scandal over deceitful accounting at Enron, WorldCom, and Arthur Andersen, that even widely misleading accounting contributed to growth by stoking speculation and investment. These factors now present serious impediments to future growth.

Moreover, the growth of the late 1990s depended on factors that may not be repeatable. Stock prices, which supported consumption, will not rise as rapidly as they did in the late 1990s. The PC and the Internet will not again match their surging growth. Foreign investment may be more difficult to attract. The nation will also have to contend with serious new challenges: an age of consumer choice; highly effective global competition; growing unified regional markets around the world; the rapidly rising costs of housing, education, and healthcare; an aging population; and new demands, such as nationwide childcare for working spouses, new levels of educational sophistication, and expensive new drugs (see table 9.1).

Because the nation was simply not adequately dealing with its old problems or new requirements in the 1990s, euphoric pronounce-

Table 9.1 Major Economic Challenges in the Future: A Summary

High Levels of Private Debt

A High Dollar and Trade Deficit

Stagnating Stock Prices

Consumer Demands for Choice and Quality

Intense Global Competition

The Development of Large Markets in Other Regions

Rising Costs of Key Services: Education and Healthcare

Environmental Deterioration

Aging Population

High Quality Childcare for Working Families

More Educationally Demanding Work

Growing Job Insecurity

ments about American prosperity were damaging. That there were achievements in the 1990s cannot be ignored, including the rise of vigorous entrepreneurialism, leaner production and distribution methods, and, most important, the diminution of inflation. Much of what happened in the 1990s must be retained.

But, to summarize, the rate of growth could have been higher. The policies that created large imbalances in finances are now burdens on the future. The damage to incomes of earlier decades was not corrected. And many of the conditions necessary to sustain future growth were not addressed.

○   ○   ○

Contrary to what is generally thought, the devil is not in the details of a national agenda but in its general principles. As stated at the outset of this chapter, a new agenda should take into account two principles. First, the growth of markets is a priority. Second, many of the other traditional conditions of growth have been neglected. Experts should argue about the intricacies of specific policies. What is important is to get the broad philosophy and key objectives right. The consensus has been wrong about these for too long.

Such an agenda, especially an emphasis on the growth of markets, directly contradicts what are now the two leading points of view. The first and most influential model of economic growth assumes that capital investment is the major cause of growth and the principal stimulant of capital investment is high national savings (which keeps interest rates low). Thus, growth is, up to a point, a function of national savings.

According to this model, government spending should be restrained to avoid absorbing the nation's savings. High inflation is also to be avoided, principally because it raises interest rates (and also can weaken the currency, which can lead to still more inflation). Further, there should be minimal interference from government regulation or organized labor in the setting of wages; they will automatically find their appropriate level. Even minimum wage laws are a violation of this principle, as are Social Security and unemployment insurance, because they presumably raise labor costs above the most efficient level and thus reduce profits available for investment. Similarly, government regulation should be minimized. Prices will be set in the market that will lead to the most productive allocation of investment.

The other popular point of view, which is that technological advance is the primary source of economic growth, suggests that the nation's primary task should be to encourage investment in technological research and education. According to this view, the cost of capital may matter, but what matters more are profitable opportunities created by technological innovation. Technological opportunity is thus the principal stimulant of capital investment, and when the capital investment occurs, productivity growth results. Some economists who advocate this point of view argue that government has an important part in subsidizing such research and education. For example, they frequently point out that the Internet was developed by the U.S. Defense Department.

Both of these accounts of growth are so limited as to be misleading and false. First, the stimulants to capital investment are complex and varied, but they are not dominated by the availability of finance capital. Narrow allegiance to this policy results in weak domestic markets that can only be supplemented by a high level of borrowing, as well as in neglected public investment. Similarly, technological advance is by no means only or even largely the consequence of devoting more funds to research. Believing that it is, and neglecting other causes, will diminish technological advance.

Back to the Market

Any reasonable review of history would recognize the role of a growing market as a stimulant both to capital investment and technological advance. A rapidly growing market in the future will allow the nation to stimulate capital investment and technological advance without resorting to unsustainable levels of borrowing and creating unsustainable trade deficits. In the *Wealth of Nations*, Adam Smith made an especially revealing observation: "As the operations of each workman are gradually reduced to a greater degree of simplicity, a variety of new machines came to be invented for facilitating and abridging these operations." Smith was reflecting a certain mechanical attitude that pervaded Britain and Europe and the roots of which are difficult to determine.

Thus, the demand for more products encouraged entrepreneurs to divide labor into increasingly simple tasks. Once that was done, as Smith postulates, it became clear that machines could be developed to complete these simple operations more quickly than humans. Machines did not do complex tasks; they did simple ones rapidly. To Smith, the division of labor preceded and induced the development of commercially usable technology. The growing market, in turn, preceded the need for the division of labor. Smith implied that an entrepreneur was at the center of such decisions, but he did not explicitly define such a role. His insight was greater in this matter, however, than that of later influential economists, such as David Ricardo and Karl Marx, who did not even implicitly credit the role of the entrepreneur. As Joseph Schumpeter correctly reminded the world, this tendency to abstraction among economists led to misleading conclusions, among them that technology arises almost at random and mostly as a result of adventitiously and unpredictably brilliant innovators. Commercially usable technology is more often the result of explicit decisions made by entrepreneurs, and if the process by which they make them is ignored, a full accounting of growth is impossible. That process almost invariably begins with an assessment of the market.

Taking a more "Smithian" view, the history of economic growth makes more sense. Agriculture was most productive near ports or big cities, where produce could be traded easily. Water mills, long known to humankind, were adapted to meet the needs of a growing marketplace, first in grains because they were the primary needs of the market. More sophisticated mills were developed as demand grew sufficiently large to make the capital costs of such "factories" bearable. Coal could be used most efficiently as a power source for the steam engine in Britain than anywhere else because both its domestic and export markets were so large. It would have been far harder to develop coal early and fully as a source of fuel in the Netherlands, with only 1 million people. Why was America the leader in modern assembly line production? In large part, it had the most to gain because it could sell so many cars, or radios, or washing machines.

The opposite point of view is usually represented by Say's Law. Doesn't supply create its own demand? The early nineteenth-century French economist, Jean-Baptiste Say, asserted that supply must constitute demand because a business making a capital investment to expand production will pay workers for their labor, will pay other companies for their machines, and will pay bankers interest on their loans. Where else would the money come from to buy products if not from those who supply them? After all, a market is really the sum of consumer incomes that are spent on goods and services. They can only earn those incomes by working for or owning the "suppliers" of those goods and services.

Arguments about Say's Law can be technical. John Maynard Keynes's major work, *The Theory of Employment, Interest and Money,* is a complex refutation of this mainstream idea. In recent years, Say's Law, if in more sophisticated form, has again been the foundation of much mainstream thought. But by examining Say's Law more closely, we strengthen the case for the importance of markets. The law is not adequate in explaining economic growth or serving as a principle of an American agenda. Yet it, or assumptions like it, are the basis of conventional wisdom about how to make economies grow. This conventional wisdom is "supply-side" oriented. To improve growth, economists generally emphasize raising the "supply" of savings, technology, or education, but they rarely consider the impact of demand. Say's Law assumes that if supply is enhanced, demand will follow automatically.

In its simple form, however, Say's Law is hardly more than an identity, much like the incontrovertible fact that investment must equal savings and savings must equal investment (or you better import capital). Such identities tell us little or nothing about cause and effect. For example, do savings cause more investment or does more investment, by creating more growth and income, create more total savings? Similarly, does demand call forth investment, or does investment create the income to support demand? If we think of a small village with no access to the outside world, it is difficult to understand how Say's Law holds true. Say's Law essentially ignores how business decisions are actually made. Like so much economic theory that follows it, it allows no place for the decision-maker or the entrepreneur. Why do entrepreneurs invest? To put it simply, do they conclude that if they build a factory they will supply the incomes needed for consumers to buy their products? Entrepreneurs usually invest when they perceive there is a market for a new good or a cheaper one.

Would an investor build a major steam power plant for a small village? The economic historian Joel Mokyr quotes an eighteenth-century partner of the great steam engine inventor, James Watt, as follows: "It is not worth my while to manufacture [your engine] for three counties only; but I find it very worth my while to make it for the whole world."

Say's Law argues that the market is secondary, but this was not generally the case historically. Increased savings or investment did not separate successful economies from unsuccessful ones. Domestic markets and trade had more to do with separating successful economies from others. Even the estimable Mokyr, a supply-oriented economic historian who believes technological advance is the main cause of growth, acknowledges the point when he writes his own history of the Industrial Revolution. Mokyr concedes: "Some minimum level of demand was necessary to cover the fixed costs of development and construction. . . . [I]n the eighteenth century the British market was large enough to cover the costs of invention."

In a small market, in fact, the steam engine would not have been profitable. But Mokyr's comments understate the case. Entrepreneurs do not invest, or even hire workers, if they can merely cover their fixed costs. The potential reward has to be greater than simply meeting fixed costs to justify the risk because many such undertakings would fail. There must be a possibility for large profits, so there must be a large market and preferably one that can grow still larger. Far more than a "minimum level" of demand is necessary to provoke such decisions.

Economies of scale also complicate the issues. If there are economies of scale, the more one sells, the lower will be the unit costs. The same investment may provide a profit in one market but may provide a much larger profit in a larger market. Larger markets can therefore grow faster per person than smaller markets, and will stimulate more investment.

To take a simple illustration, let us say we can make one hundred units of a product for a cost of $1 each. If we sell them for $2 each, we make a profit of $100. Sales equal $200, and costs equal $100. But selling two hundred units may reduce the cost of each made to just $.75 because of economies of scale; the cost of plant and equipment is spread over more sales. If we sell two hundred units for $2 each, we make a profit of $250. Sales equal $400 and costs equal $150 because the cost per unit has fallen dramatically. The market is twice as large, but because of economies of scale, our profits are two and one-half times greater.

The large market thus has enormous stimulative power when economies of scale apply. When America's market was twice as large as Britain's around 1890, the advantage due to economies of scale was much larger still. An entrepreneur will judge the level of investment according to such market criteria. A market of 10 million consumers might well stimulate two and one-half times as much investment as a market of 5 million consumers.

In fact, conventional economic theory has long underestimated the value of economies of scale. Some economists assume that scale does not matter after a certain rather low volume of sales. But large scale has turned out to be far more potent than was originally thought, and certainly more so than Adam Smith could have imagined. Detroit auto makers were at their most efficient when they could sell 1 million Chevrolets of a single kind in the 1950s. Selling a mere 100,000 or fewer of a single model, as the Japanese learned to do efficiently in the 1970s, would have vastly raised costs to Detroit. In contemporary electronics industries, vast scale is critical. Computer chips would not have fallen in price nearly as rapidly if they could not be sold in the millions, or even billions. The same is true of the PC and Internet services. But more important, economies of scale go well beyond the manufacturing process to distribution, marketing, and research. There is enormous difference in the economies of television between reaching 1 million viewers versus 25 million viewers. Imagine an economist claiming that the size of the market did not matter after a million or so viewers; the major television networks would be out of business.

Wal-Mart is productive in retailing because of its enormous reach. A chain of twenty stores could not be as productive. Huge markets are also necessary to justify adequate spending in research, large human resources departments, job training, and television advertising, to name a few. It is not an accident that successful business managers, such as Jack Welch of General Electric, demanded that their operations be the first or second largest in their industries.

It is the potential for a large and growing market, with means to earn incomes, that stimulates growth. A large population matters. But more precisely, large, socially functioning populations with some income-producing capacity were the first conditions for the Industrial Revolution to take place. Without such internal and external markets, even great inventions scarcely mattered, and fewer would have been created.

As Mokyr has stated:

Another factor in Britain's head start in technology at the beginning of the Industrial Revolution was that Britain alone among the large European economies constituted a comparatively unified market in which goods and people moved easily. Compared to the European Continent, Britain had excellent internal transportation. Coastal shipping, canals, and roads provided it with a network unequalled by any Continental nation, with the possible exception of the Netherlands. Transport in Britain was itself becoming a specialists' occupation, run by professionals. . . . Moreover, Britain was politically unified and cohesive. No tolls were charged on rivers and no tariffs were levied when crossing man-made lines (unlike France, for example, where before the Revolution internal tariffs were levied on goods moving within the country). (244)

Jumping forward in history, David Mowery and Nathan Rosenberg have made the following observations about the contribution of a large market to America's technological development:

The trajectory of American 20th century technology was traced along paths that were shaped not only by an abundance of natural resources but also by a large population that was already affluent by contemporary European standards before the First World War and enjoyed a more equal household income distribution . . . the less pronounced divisions of social class created a large market for standardized, homogenous products, as is apparent in the speed with which America came to dominate the world automobile industry. . . . The U.S. market was sufficiently large that American firms, whether in automobiles or chemicals, were better able than European competitors to take maximum advantage of economies of scale during the pre-1945 period. Since World War II, an important factor in improved European and Japanese economic performance has been the revival of world trade, which has reduced the penalties associated with small domestic markets. Nevertheless, both the semiconductor and computer industries derived significant competitive advantage from the large U.S. domestic market during the postwar period.

From the water mill to the steam engine to the personal computer to the Internet, large markets were decisive factors in the advance of technology.

The final point to be made about Say's Law is the more common criticism, made by John Maynard Keynes and others. Again, these are fairly technical arguments, but they can be reduced to understandable essentials. Even as an identity, Say's Law falters because the economy does not adjust as efficiently to changes in supply as theory suggests. In advanced economies, where money is the common means of exchange (rather than barter), Say's Law does not hold because money is often hoarded, not spent. For example, if consumers do not find products they want, they may simply spend less and hoard their money. They may hoard money also in times of uncertainty. Advocates of Say's Law argue that such hoarded money will flow into capital investment as interest rates fall. Adam Smith also believed savings would be almost automatically invested. This view is self-contradictory: Without prospects to sell goods, companies are unlikely to invest. This was Keynes's main point, and a basis for his view that demand must occasionally be supported, even if government budget deficits are created.

Similarly, wages do not change fast enough to adjust costs and prices to fluctuating supply and demand. They usually do not fall at all. If there is more supply than needed, costs will not fall fast enough to allow businesses to cut prices and attract more sales. It may also be the case that supply does not result in sufficient demand because wages are repressed for any of a variety of reasons. This, in my view, is exactly what happened in recent years.

For these reasons, Say's Law also fails to explain adequately the Industrial Revolution. The three great modern economies—The Netherlands, Britain, and the United States—all were characterized by strong, internally efficient domestic markets. Each was in its time the most efficient and powerful domestic market in the world, and each usurped the supremacy of the other. If supply, and the savings that made investment possible, were the key factors, why were they usurped? If supply truly created its own demand, the failures of The Netherlands and Britain are difficult to explain. Why did The Netherlands lose its immense advantage to Britain? Why did Britain lose its advantage to America? Both of these nations had immense savings and sophisticated banking systems, and therefore the capacity to increase supply. The argument here is that it was the ever-larger markets, first of The Netherlands, then of Britain, and then of the United States, that led the way to economic supremacy. Capital investment is surely a contributor to growth. Supply creates some of its own demand, but it is not a first mover in the sense that large markets are. There can indeed often be too much savings and too much supply.

In sum, Say's Law, and similar assumptions, are dangerously misleading and founder on the simple empirical facts. Savings will not automatically translate into productive capital investment. The vitality of markets matters. Say's Law ignores the role of the entrepreneur, who will usually build only if there is a potential market. It does not fully allow for economies of scale, where returns rise as markets grow larger.[2] It does not adequately take into account the stickiness of wages, on the one the hand, or the ability to suppress wages occasionally, on the other, among other market failures.

Proponents of Say's Law generally argue that markets always will reach a stable point where supply and demand will balance at the highest level of production and lowest level of unemployment. One should not underestimate the theoretical power of this argument. Its pioneer in an important sense was David Ricardo. More sophisticated theorists followed later in the nineteenth century. The central claim is that prices and wages adjust in such a way as to attract capital investment to where it can be used most productively. This is a strong argument for mostly free markets (and free trade). Prices are extraordinary signals across an economy. In international trade, nations will make what they are best at and abandon what others are better at. The same is true in domestic markets. This is why even local exchange is so valuable.

But markets also fail in serious ways. Wages can be suppressed, capital investment can be discouraged, public investment can be neglected, and information between buyer and seller or employer and employee can be unbalanced. Opponents to Say's Law argue that in the practical world, for the reasons mentioned previously, markets are not perfectly efficient at making optimal adjustments. Supply

---

[2]Technically, advocates will claim that Say's Law can take economies of scale into account, but only in the narrow, tautological interpretation of it. The same investment might yield greater returns in a large market than a small one; supply, it will be argued, will simply create greater demand in one market than another. But a large market, given economies of scale, will clearly stimulate more investment than a smaller one. Say's Law tells us nothing about the causes of investment. An equal amount of savings in a small market will result in less investment than the same amount of savings in a larger market.

does not fully get translated into buying power, or over-supply does not result in rapid price decreases. Economies can stabilize significantly below the optimal level of production or unemployment.

Thus, both domestic and international markets should be encouraged to grow rapidly to support the general Smithian principle of the division of labor and its related principle, economies of scale. Ricardian principles also suggest that growth will improve through exchange.

Yet in recent decades, only international trade and capital flows have been emphasized, and the domestic market has been neglected. Mainstream economists generally believe that domestic markets are operating near their optimal level because there are few barriers to free exchange of goods and services. Thus, when wages fell in the United States they were seeking a natural market level that reflected the true contribution of the worker to the nation's product. Profits allegedly rose to their optimal level, and therefore so did capital investment. According to this view, the domestic market needed little help except in the direction of less government interference. It was as strong as it could be.

On the other hand, according to this view, international trade still contained potential for expansion because it was explicitly inhibited by tariffs, quotas, and less formal trade barriers. Attempts to add further requirements, such as worker rights or minimum wages, to free trade agreements would allegedly undermine the efficiency of markets. The principles of growth can be best served by removing trade barriers.

The argument of this book is driven by Smithian principles of division of labor and economies of scale. It is the domestic U.S. market, not international markets, that has been most neglected. In the United States, the domestic market has been weakened by tight Federal Reserve policies, the overvalued dollar, and high interest rates caused by powerful bond investors with incorrect inflationary expectations. Unequal incomes have undermined the middle markets, where standardized products usually flourish. The market has suffered from highly unequal education, poor public childcare, and unequal access to healthcare. Labor markets can generally be inefficient due to an imbalance of information between employer and employee. High levels of unemployment for more than twenty years also raised fears among employees that weakened their willingness to demand higher wages. Active attempts to undermine organized labor also weakened wages. Finally, a cultural attitude swept the nation that placed both government and workers in disfavor. All these weakened domestic demand.

The growth of the external market did not compensate for this. Moreover, free trade, and free movements in capital and currencies, also led to serious distortions. It raised the value of the U.S. dollar to levels that placed manufacturing—and, most important, capital investment in future manufacturing—in jeopardy because the strong dollar undermined exports. This was high irony; few things meant more to advocates of free trade than capital investment. Furthermore, as manufacturers invested less than they otherwise would have in new products, Americans bought far more from abroad than at home and required foreign funds to finance these purchases, placing more upward pressure on the dollar as foreign sellers placed their money in dollar-denominated investments. The dollar was also the only reserve currency in the world; investors flocked to dollar-denominated investments as a safe haven. Soaring stock prices also attracted foreign investment. On balance, an overvalued dollar further undermined the internal market in the United States by limiting the expansion of manufacturing businesses. Observers said this was more than compensated for because funds were imported for investment. But, if the dollar was overvalued, these funds were misallocated to businesses that gained from a high dollar, such as certain service businesses dependent on low-cost imports, rather than to manufacturers.

The new agenda proposal is not single-mindedly devoted to expanding the market, but a healthy market is central to its success. It alone can create balanced long-term growth. Ignoring it has resulted in a lopsided economy, laden with debt, neglected manufacturing, and a high dollar. If this argument is right, the nation must emphasize the health and vitality of its domestic market. But it must also address the other neglected sources of growth, which arise both from the conventional needs of the past and the new needs of a changing economy and society. History provides us with clear lessons. We have ignored them for a variety of complex reasons, but we can no longer afford to do so.

10

Making America Grow:
An Agenda

HOW, THEN, DO THE CAUSES OF GROWTH SHAPE AN AGENDA FOR America? First, we must recognize the weakness of the conventional policies. The capital investment model of growth, which argues for the primacy of savings, did not work. Savings never increased substantially in the United States even with the 1993 Clinton tax increase. Federal budget deficits were offset by reduced personal savings. Thus, more savings could not have been the cause of more growth. Interest rates fell in the second half of the 1990s largely because bond investors, and then the Federal Reserve, came to believe that inflation was defeated and were therefore willing to buy bonds at higher prices, or that reduced deficits meant a slower rate of economic growth and less demand for funds. Corporate profits were also helped by slow-growing, even stagnating wages, more layoffs, and more low paid and expendable temporary workers.

Moreover, although the emphasis on reduced government spending and low wages had some benefits, whether psychological or real, it also did damage. Tight federal budgets meant the nation neglected other important conditions of growth, including education, transportation infrastructure, and healthcare. Low wages, in turn, brought high levels of borrowing, reduced savings, and less personal investment in human capital. The domestic market was never as vigorous as it could have been. Inequality of incomes widened over this period of slow growth, as lax labor markets enabled businesses to pay less where demand was least.

Many economists concede that the conventional policy recommendations for increasing savings never did increase them. But they nevertheless insist that the key to growth is higher levels of national savings, and the way to get there is by restraining federal spending. Some also encourage the use of tax subsidies for savings, such as 401(k) plans. It is in fact much more likely that national savings will increase only if the economy continues to grow rapidly. Profits are a key component of savings. Modest federal deficits are not dangerous if they are used to support needed public investment, which will raise the growth rate over time.

A New Agenda

Four propositions are critical to a new agenda: it must emphasize the growth of internal markets, promote equality, invest in public goods, and respond constructively to change.

1. **Growing internal markets are critical.** As amply discussed, vigorous, growing markets are a major source of productivity growth because they stimulate capital investment and technological advance. The development and spread of communications is vital to the expansion of such markets and often concomitant with it.
2. **Inequality is unproductive.** Inequality in America has reached untenable proportions. Inequality of income undermines growth because it weakens the demand for goods and services, as well as most Americans' ability to save. Families in the 95th percentile of income earned 3.15 times what the typical family earned in 2000, compared to 2.59 times in 1979. The gap between richer and poorer families rose still faster. Inequality of income also under-

mines people's ability to invest in themselves through education and healthcare. Both of these are vital to economic growth. The inequality of education and healthcare in America is now stark. Such inequality probably also undermines the optimism of Americans and their faith in the fairness of the economic system. This may result not in political dissent but in simple apathy.

3. **There is a strong case for public investment.** The economic basis for public investment is widely accepted by most main-stream economists. Markets cannot solve all problems of scarcity because some goods—public goods—produce benefits well beyond the businesses or individuals that invest in them. Education is a good example. An individual will benefit from her or his education, but so will society at large, because it makes the workforce more productive, more creative, and more com-petent in using the products available to it. Businesses and indi-viduals will only invest to the extent the payoff helps them indi-vidually, not society at large. A society that neglects public investment deprives itself of key benefits, many of which are critical to future growth. Therefore, society must supplement such investments if it wants to maximize the nation's potential to grow. Classic public goods also include transportation and com-munications infrastructure, research and development, and childcare. They have been neglected in the past quarter century.

4. **Economic change cannot be ignored; nostalgia can be un-productive.** Economies change, and always have. They create new demands on their constituencies that are sometimes best met by government. The early American economy needed new forms of transportation, higher literacy and numerical skills, protections for the ownership of land, and the freedom to com-pete. In the late 1800s, it was clear that workers needed more protection from abuse, the nation needed a more stable finan-cial system and currency, and municipalities needed public health and sanitation systems. In the 1900s, the nation needed still higher education, including high schools and later colleges, better roads and highways, improved public health, laws to pro-

tect civil rights, unemployment insurance, and financial protection in old age. The contemporary economy presents new demands, including childcare, still more education, protection against the loss of job security, better transportation infrastructure, and protection against the health and security threats of globalization. Unlike in the past, however, Americans do not now answer the call of change; they look backward, not forward.

With these four propositions, we can build an agenda that will maintain and invigorate growth. Strong internal markets should be maintained through pro-growth economic policies, regulations, and subsidies. The victory against inflation should diminish at least the tendency of the Federal Reserve to err on the side of suppressing rapid growth. Bond investors seem for now to accept the victory over inflation, but they may have to be convinced further in the future. Markets can also be strengthened through policies that encourage wages to rise and reasonable equality in income and benefits.

The main areas of neglect in the economy include education, healthcare, childcare, and transportation and communications infrastructure. The costs of education and healthcare will continue to rise rapidly. Inequality in access to both education and healthcare is extreme. Seriously increased public investment is warranted in these areas. Evidence of inefficiencies in transportation is ample. Again, public investment is warranted.

The new demands of a transformed economy are also clear. They include the needs of two-worker families, better and more accessible education for youth and adults, access to new communications media, and ways to mitigate risk for a permanently less secure labor force. Attending to these needs will enhance growth while also reasserting humane and inclusive policies that will motivate a broader cross-section of Americans to participate fully and more productively in the workforce.

Each of the areas discussed in the following sections must be addressed directly by the nation. How they are addressed specifically will be a matter of debate, but here I propose some basic policy ideas.

Strong Markets

Federal Reserve Policy

Federal Reserve policy must be dedicated to supporting reasonable growth, not simply controlling low inflation. Moreover, the Fed should recognize that rapid economic growth can foster low inflation by creating incentives for capital investment and therefore higher productivity. With higher productivity businesses can raise wages without raising prices. The Fed, for example, probably pushed up rates too quickly in 1993.

Fiscal Policy

Reasonable budget deficits should not be feared. They are still necessary to fight recession, and if undertaken to support public investment, they are productive. But deficits cannot be taken carelessly or indefinitely. Undue fear of deficits will inhibit growth; but repetition of irresponsible tax cuts or unproductive government spending will be harmful.

Equalizing Incomes

Growth by definition means that the market for goods and services will keep expanding. It provides the incentives for capital investment and technological advance. It also is self-reinforcing because it keeps the demand for labor strong and keeps pressure on wages to rise. This central economic principle was de-emphasized in the inflationary 1970s, 1980s, and early 1990s. It was, ironically, generally regarded as a social good that wages be kept down because this contributed to growing profits and reduced pressure on corporations to raise prices. But wage suppression is not a basis for long-term economic growth. By the same token, the economic vitality of much of the rest of the world will keep competition intense and will thus exert constant pressure on business costs, including wages. A balance must be sought between maintaining competitiveness and supporting an internal market through higher wages. There is no simple return to an earlier era when America paid easily the highest wages in the world. The pendulum swung too far the other way in the 1970s and 1980s, but it cannot swing the full way back.

A series of government policies to strengthen markets by raising wages for lower-end workers is now necessary. In the 1970s the top 10 percent of families earned 28 percent of the nation's income; by 2001 this group earned 40 percent. Progressive income taxes should be restored. As for direct regulation, there should be further increases in the nation's federal and state minimum wage laws. Job subsidy programs for low-wage workers have also been more successful than is generally believed. They should be explored and discussed. Similarly, the right to organize labor has been widely undermined in recent years. A more balanced approach between wages and profits is now necessary.

Restoring Security

The rights of workers to corporate benefits, including pensions and healthcare, should be reasserted or taken over by the government. If the objective is to keep markets flexible, the federal government should enhance the portability of these benefits and raise requirements rather than imposing new costs on business. Direct contribution pensions have reduced the cost of retirement benefits to corporations but have failed to provide adequate pensions for middle- and low-income workers. This must be addressed. In addition, too few poorer workers have even minimal healthcare benefits.

At the same time, jobs are less secure. Temporary workers should be given corporate benefits after working a minimum number of hours with a firm. The drive toward flexibility has been costly to workers and to the strength of the internal market.

Most important, as job dislocation becomes a way of life in a changed economy, the government should establish relocation policies that provide for assistance, income, and substantial training of workers. These can be done as subsidies to private corporations or through public institutions.

A New Cultural Attitude

The nation and its media lionized the wealthy in the 1980s and 1990s. But this attitude became damaging when it encouraged lower wages and high levels of layoffs. The volume of layoffs constantly reached new highs in the 1990s. Chief executive officers of the largest companies earned 419 times the average wage of production workers in 1999, compared to 93 times in 1988 and 25 times in the 1960s. The average company's performance in America, even if superior, could not justify such a differential. General regard for working people must be restored. The nation went through a similar period after the Civil War, and it was reversed in the Progressive Era under Theodore Roosevelt and Woodrow Wilson. But leadership is unlikely to come from the corporate sector. Rather, as always, it must come from the people.

Communications and Information

Television, radio, inexpensive cinema, and the telephone were ultimately democratizing breakthroughs in communications. It remains to be seen whether the Internet, cable television, the cellular phone, and the $100 million blockbuster movie are relatively elitist forms of new communications. Only 45 percent of Americans subscribe to an e-mail service, and only 53 percent of families have a personal computer at home. As networks reduce their commitment to serious news, and as the number of newspapers declines, cable news organizations do not make up for the difference. One third of households have no basic cable service and fewer than half have a premium service. Increasingly sports events that were once free on network television are now on cable. Similarly, the population that now goes to first-run cinemas, where the ticket price can be $10, is largely college educated with above-average incomes. As cellular phones predominate, pay telephone services have risen rapidly in price. A local toll phone call is 50 cents in many regions.

Access to new forms of communication is a public good. Moreover, some of the new media contain the seeds of renewed democratization. If hardware and subscription costs can be subsidized for poorer American families, e-mail use is less expensive than the traditional telephone. Cell phone costs can also be low and may prove more democratic than the traditional telephone. The VCR has provided a less expensive form of cinematic entertainment. But these issues must be understood and addressed. Access to information is a key to growth. The government should invest in universal access to computers in public schools.

Areas of Neglect

There is ample evidence of neglect in many important areas. To take but one example, spending on education and transportation infrastructure has fallen to half the proportion of GDP that it was in the 1970s. But these are classic public goods. The benefits of decent education, healthcare, and transportation spread well beyond the individual to the entire nation. Each of these areas is considered briefly in the following sections.

Education

Contrary to widespread belief, the quality of public education on average seems to have risen over the past two decades. College board test scores, for example, have been rising even as the proportion of students taking them has grown. But this is not necessarily satisfactory, for several reasons. For one thing, international comparisons suggest that while primary school children fare well compared to those in other nations, high school teenagers are below average. Second, in a changing economy, education standards keep rising. To do better is only to stand still.

Third, and most important, the nation's public education system is highly unequal because it is largely supported by local taxes. The urban, suburban, and rural poor suffer. Efforts to broaden and equalize tax support are imperative. An especially fruitful reform may be mixing poor and middle-class children in public schools.

Some observers insist that the nation is investing enough money in public schools. But if properly adjusted, the level of federal, state, and local spending has been lagging significantly. Most new spending has gone to special education for disabled children, a stunning and proud achievement. But much less remains for spending on traditional education. Also, the after-inflation dollars spent are lower than generally realized because the inflation of education costs, which is very labor intensive, is higher than inflation on average. When these facts are taken into account, investment in education from kindergarten to twelfth grade has risen at about 1 percent per year, less than half the rate of growth of the economy.

At the same time, college tuitions in the past twenty years have risen at three times the rate of average incomes. Yet subsidies for college education have not nearly kept pace, driving tuition costs still higher.

In sum, spending on education from kindergarten through twelfth grade is smaller as a proportion of GDP than in the past. The cost of college to families is higher than ever before. Moreover, because of its labor intensiveness, the cost of education will continue to rise fast.

More spending on education is therefore necessary. Some believe it should take the form of vouchers to enable families to choose schools and to promote competitiveness between these schools. Others believe direct public control and spending will remain most equitable. One of America's enduring strengths since the mid-1800s has been its universal free education system. It has been a great source of economic growth. Vouchers may well fragment the nation still more by leaving poorer or less socially adjusted families to languish in poor schools.

Healthcare

The two main problems for healthcare are inequality of access and inexorably rising costs. The proportion of Americans without health insurance grew in the 1980s and 1990s and only stabilized in 1999 at a high level. Some 43 million Americans have no such coverage. Meanwhile, costs rise rapidly. A nation that allows such a large segment of its population to get poor care is losing valuable productive workers, both through ill health and lack of motivation. As a benchmark, consider that the cost for one year of a moderate-quality family healthcare plan is equivalent to buying twenty-four high-quality VCRs and equal to the typical lease payment on a $30,000 car.

Infrastructure

Traffic congestion has risen dramatically in America. Researchers at Texas A&M report that it takes three times as long to commute to work as it did in 1970. Airport congestion is similarly worsening. The only consolation is that conditions may be as bad in other nations.

There is ample economic evidence that investment in infrastructure promotes economic growth. For example, the work of Ishaq Nadiri, based on another methodology, also suggests strongly that government investment in infrastructure produces returns to the economy as high as returns on private capital investment. Nadiri finds that the same relationship holds for investment in communications infrastructure, which reinforces the case that the government should invest in this area as well.

A Changed Economy's New Needs

Global competitiveness, the age of consumer choice, more sophisticated work, rapidly rising costs of education and healthcare, and the two-worker family have created new needs that, left unaddressed, have retarded economic growth. In the past, the nation met many of these changing needs. It created public schools and primary schools and subsidized colleges. It created unemployment insurance and Social Security. It built public healthcare systems and vaccinated entire populations. In the slow-growing era at the end of the twentieth century, the nation abandoned its long-standing confidence that it could deal with change.

Childcare

The great social revolution of the late 1900s was the two-worker family. Spouses went to work, partly out of desire but equally out of need. Male wages largely stagnated in these years. In 2000, two-thirds of women worked, but investment in high-quality childcare was modest at best. In the late 1990s, there was substantial investment by state and local communities in public childcare, but its quality was widely suspect. In fact, daycare development was so haphazard that at this writing there are no trustworthy measures of quality. Those that exist suggest that childcare is mediocre on average. Mediocre will not do.

Education

A sophisticated economy requires sophisticated workers. The initial assumption is that the first requirement is technical skills in dealing with computer technology. But it is increasingly clear that we really need a broad set of skills that enable workers to make decisions even at lower levels. We are moving more toward an office economy of white-collar work, where most workers must make key decisions and deal effectively with each other and with customers. The UPS driver is a good example; he or she is a sort of white-collar worker now. Higher levels of education allow people to develop such skills, including those that enable workers to keep learning well into their careers. The gap in pay between college graduates and high school graduates is higher than ever before, suggesting that even as more than half the population attends at least two years of college, the nation may still not be satisfying its needs for a sophisticated workforce. A large proportion of the population do not now get decent jobs compared to what the same education qualified them for in previous eras. These workers are unproductive for the nation. Yet college tuitions have risen far faster than incomes, and federal and state support has been expanded only modestly, or even reduced.

Job Security

A more flexible economy, facing intense global competition and consumer demands for more and better products, has meant less security for workers, and probably will continue to do so. Job security has unequivocally been reduced in several ways in recent decades. The proportion of temporary workers has risen, and they typically earn less and have few corporate benefits. The number of layoffs is much higher than it once was. Many of those laid off get new jobs, but they usually take a substantial pay cut when they do so. Although economists have argued over whether job tenure has been reduced, the evidence increasingly suggests that people hold jobs for less time than they once did. Companies are also eliminating healthcare benefits or asking workers to contribute to the cost. Defined contribution pension plans, such as 401(k)s, which are dependent on the contributions of workers, now replace defined benefit plans. But the evidence is that such plans benefit well-off workers far more than they do middle- and low-income workers. Lower-income workers are doing worse than they did with conventional pension funds, when corporations promised fixed benefits on retirement.

The financial security provided by having a good job has been undermined as the economy changes. Either new requirements on corporations or a new role for the federal government is necessary to compensate for this. Some observers will argue that workers must simply bear more responsibility for the lost security. But this undermines the purchasing power of workers as well as their confidence and motivation to work. It reverses the long trend in American history toward increased financial security.

Children

A higher proportion of children are poor in America than anywhere else in the advanced world. As economist Timothy Smeeding shows, this holds true even when adjusting for differences in purchasing power in individual nations. This cannot continue. The best way to reduce child poverty is to raise the wages of low-income workers. High-quality early education must be made available to the poor. Research convincingly shows that early care is critical to children's capacity to learn and to stay healthy.

Caring Labor

In a changed economy, our teachers, healthcare workers, eldercare workers, and childcare workers are more critical than ever before. But the nation pays them far less than workers in other fields. A large-scale plan is needed to subsidize the education of these caring workers, based on how long they do their jobs.

An Aging Population and the Environment

The aging population has been widely discussed, and concerns over financing old age pension and insurance plans are strong arguments for rapid economic growth. As the population ages, proportionally fewer workers will be paying Social Security or Medicare taxes. The imbalance might be so great in forty years that a reduction in Social Security benefits will be required. But the crisis has been exaggerated. Even a 0.5 percent increase in the rate of productivity growth will postpone any such benefit reduction indefinitely. Economic growth and small benefit reductions, not privatization, are the answers for Social Security reform. As the experience with 401(k)s shows, many and probably most workers will do poorly if they are required to save and invest for their own retirements. America would face rapidly growing poverty among the elderly.

Some argue that rapid economic growth might endanger the environment still more. But a financially sound economy can afford environmental regulation and investment in technological innovation to improve the environment. Slower economic growth will make the environment worse.

Free Trade

Anyone who claims that the growth of markets is a key to productivity growth in general must favor free trade. The expansion of international markets is important. But in recent decades, advocacy of free trade has been subtly overtaken by the advocacy of capital investment. In developing nations, the general tendency is not merely to open domestic markets to foreign goods but also to open capital markets to foreign investment. Developing countries have been encouraged to do so to the neglect of their internal demand and public investment. It is generally thought that capital will flow to business opportunity and thereby create businesses and jobs. Both government investment in the conditions of internal growth and the level of wages are generally neglected in this model. It is a recipe for only short-term and unstable growth, not optimal long-term growth. The advantages of foreign investment can be critical, but short-term investments can be quickly withdrawn. The hidden cost of such investment, however, is that developing nations' governments, compelled to balance their budgets, often neglect their internal markets by reducing investment in education, healthcare, and infrastructure. A second cost is pressure to compete through low wages, rather than developing regulations to support decent wages and working conditions and programs to encourage children to go to school.

For advanced nations, free trade and capital flows are also complex issues. Capital investment can flee too rapidly to regions with low wages, few corporate benefits, and no environmental regulations. This, in turn, can undermine the domestic market of the investing nation as it loses investment, businesses, and jobs, and reduces the wages it pays to workers at home. Free trade should be pursued, but at a more modest rate, and with greater sensitivity both to America's internal market and to the internal markets of developing nations, which also need rising wages and fair labor practices. The world's rich nations should open markets more aggressively to the world's poor.

The final concern of the emphasis on foreign capital flows is financial instability. One of the sources of the financial crisis in Asia in 1997 was "hot capital"—short-term loans— of major investors, which was withdrawn almost immediately from local countries as fears arose. A slower march toward capital liberalization is necessary, and the Federal Reserve and other regulatory bodies need to pay closer attention to overspeculation and abuse of financial markets. The Enron incident and its aftermath, involving many large formerly respected companies, is a clear signal of lax vigilance on the part of lawmakers.

Financing the Future: Progressive Taxes

In the 1980s, America fully experienced the dangers of outsized federal budget deficits. The most prominent consequence was that investors, fearing high inflation and the crowding out of private investment by federal borrowing needs, drove up interest rates by selling bonds. For the same reasons, the Federal Reserve maintained tight policies. But the fear of federal deficits has been exaggerated and their constructive uses underemphasized. Such deficits are entirely justifiable if there is an underinvestment in public goods. They are also justifiable if the economy is not generating sufficient production and employment.

But practically speaking, financial markets will remain sensitive to federal deficits, as will the Fed. Nor is there an unlimited amount the federal government can borrow.

Raising income tax rates for higher-income individuals is the right solution to this problem. As Edward Wolff points out, the federal tax system is no longer progressive. Once, those who made higher incomes were taxed at a higher rate. Income taxes, which are graded according to levels of income, have been reduced substantially in the past thirty-five years, while Social Security and other payroll taxes, which take a fixed proportion of income, have been raised. Workers are now taxed at the same rate, and once they make a given amount, they are not taxed on any further income at all. The combination of income tax reductions and rising payroll taxes has made the total federal tax bite flat.

At the same time, the incomes of wealthy individuals have soared. An astonishing 90 percent of all gains in personal income, including wages, salaries, and capital gains on investment, were earned by the top 1 percent of all earners in the 1990s. There is ample room for increased tax rates on high earners, and it will produce significant revenues for the nation.

What Can Be Accomplished

This new agenda calls for an emphasis on the internal market, equality, and public investment, and for adequate response to a changing economy. It will raise the U.S. economy's potential to grow by enlarging the market and maintaining its rapid growth, thereby creating the incentives for capital investment, technological advance, and, ultimately, productivity growth. One can be fully convinced of the importance and benefits of large markets but also realize that blind devotion to laissez faire principles will undermine it. The new agenda will improve the other conditions necessary for growth that are consistent with economic history. It will include more of the American population as productive workers. It will raise the optimism and motivation of a broader cross-section of the public, which should generate greater investment in education and confidence in the future.

What it may not do is raise the rate of growth of the living standard to its historical level. Intense global competition, new regional markets, and the fragmenting of markets that come with the age of choice may well mean that incomes cannot grow as they once did, no matter how optimal the nation's policies are. Yet future needs will not diminish. Trying to raise wage growth to old levels may be self-destructive if it reduces profitability too much.

But attention to the internal market, so long neglected, is now necessary. At the same time, the nation must realize that workers cannot manage their new needs on their own in an age of slower income growth. The conflicts between profits and wages, between capital investment and the promotion of demand, and between markets and government, must be reconciled productively. All this will require a new social contract, one that America may not be prepared to undertake.

11

Why We Won't Do It

THE MAIN RISK TO AMERICA'S ECONOMIC FUTURE MAY WELL BE its own national character. The agenda necessary to maximize America's potential conflicts with some of our most deeply held convictions. This prospect is disturbing. To restore rapid economic growth, we must understand our own history better to see how we truly grew into a great nation and call on some qualities that are not part of our national self-image.

The very phrase "national character" chills some scholars. A nation as complex as America, to whose development so many groups of people have contributed, cannot have a single national character. The exploration of a nation's or even a community's character, so popular among scholars ranging from anthropologists to political scientists in the mid-twentieth century, gave way in later years to careful scrutiny of the variability and diversity of cultures.

But certain attitudes have persisted throughout American history, as well as that of most other nations, that at least suggest a common set of experiences that are brought to bear on how decisions are made. This "national character" seems to affect the decisions and policies a people and a nation make. The confusion may lie in assuming that a national character must somehow be true to history. "The real problem of history," wrote the political scientist David M. Potter nearly half a century ago, "is to separate academic and rational theories of national character from chauvinistic and mystical theories, and to do this rigorously and with finality." Potter no doubt recognized the power of mythology, especially in a nation's formative years. But he may have been determined to show that national character was based on something unique and historically real. This is misleading.

That America has some kind of national character that sets it apart from most other nations is evident. The forest is a little clearer than the trees, in this case. Suspicion of government, for instance, is one of the nation's most decided characteristics. Distaste for taxes is a corollary. A strong sense that individuals must be responsible for their own well-being is another. Americans typically believe their success is entirely due to their own efforts. The community and government have little to do with it, which is partly why there is natural resistance to paying taxes. More than people in most other nations, Americans believe anything is possible, and optimism is generally considered a virtue in itself. There is, in addition, a disdain for history and tradition. Ralph Waldo Emerson, one of the great shapers of the nation's mythology, expressed that disdain so explicitly and beautifully as to be convincing. No tradition is sacred in America, or so our national character tells us. (This last is far from true; it seems to me we consider the nation itself quite sacred.) All of these national ideas, as we might call them, were established early in the nation's history.

National character is a partly mythological set of unique beliefs about why one's nation has succeeded. By a nation's success is meant that it remained independent, lived by its own social contract and set of laws, and grew in population and wealth. What incipient nation did not have such a set of mythological beliefs? Herodotus wrote that all people believe their ways are best. How can that be true when they are often so contradictory? But a burgeoning people that faces the great risk of starting anew apparently requires some irrational belief in the uniqueness of its principles.

Such a set of beliefs provides a nation with energy and courage. Rarely does it fully account for its success, however. This is the point about assertions of national character that today's scholars constantly refer to and deeply resent. Many other factors contribute to a nation's success, but the nation often attributes its success to a relatively few ideas. Those few do make contributions, but they are frequently contradicted or cast aside as the nation deals with new challenges and changing times. Pragmatism fortunately often intervened and overrode faith in some of America's deepest values. When allegiance to the supposed national character was too strong, it was often damaging.

The American mythology is as strong as any nation's. Individualism and self-reliance are quasi-religious tenets. Opportunity is rarely withheld to anyone, by nature or human, according to American principles. The great transgressor of individual rights is not your neighbor or your landlord or your boss but your government. The social contract between a government and its people is therefore a highly restricted one. Government is to be restrained; individual freedom is to be exalted.

For these reasons, Americans have the fewest social programs among advanced nations—the shallowest social net. What social programs they have are usually linked to work. Americans will give as a community to others only if they show themselves deserving by hard work. Unemployment insurance eligibility is determined by one's wages. Social Security benefits are a function of annual earnings and length of employment. We partially subsidize colleges, but only if one goes to college. If a person does not, he or she gets no analogous subsidy from the federal government. Welfare deeply bothers Americans; it is seen as getting something for nothing. Those who have the best healthcare get it through their jobs. Government healthcare is restricted to the elderly or the very poor. People are not entitled to excellent healthcare merely because they are American.

The true reasons for America's extraordinary success are more complex, of course, than the national character suggests. Government played an enormous part in America's development. Commu-

nity had as large a role as individualism. Egalitarianism, which sometimes clashed with individualism, was a potent American force.
America preached equal opportunity for all but often had to make
that opportunity equal through law and regulation. The nation
wanted to believe it had created a "new man," but instead it benefited from new circumstances. These particular American circumstances came together with the optimism of Europe's Enlightenment, which included the novel idea, at least to the extent that it was
widespread, that a person could control his or her life. Immigrants
added their own courage and ambition to this mixture. Nowhere in
the world were physical circumstances more congenial to Enlightenment ideas and individual ambition than in America, and physical
opportunity in turn reinforced our faith in these ideas.

In times of political and economic difficulty, the national character became a set of instincts we relied on to relieve confusion and restore lost confidence. Thus the nation became less generous to those
in need and exalted individualism over equality after the moral and
economic exhaustion of the Civil War and again after the Vietnam
War. In times of prosperity, when the nation was most confident, it
was more open to uses of government and more demanding of what
we might call social justice. These times included the Progressive
Era and the Great Society, but also the ages of Jefferson and Jackson.
America's progressive attitudes were stengthened by prosperity and
usually inhibited by national insecurity.

On the face of it, the development of government programs during the deprivation of the Depression of the 1930s would seem to be
an exception to the rule that prosperity generated progressivism in
America. But the New Deal was the extension of the strong momen-
tum of the Progressive Era. Furthermore, the reforms of the New
Deal were hardly "progressive" by European standards. Both unemployment insurance and Social Security were tied to an individual's
work. Financing for Social Security came out of new payroll taxes,
not general revenues. Franklin Delano Roosevelt dared not nationalize the banks despite their widespread failures.

The paradox America now faces is that, since the slow economic growth and high unemployment that characterized the nation's economy starting in the early 1970s, the nation has again resorted to its narrow sense of national character for answers. But America will need a broader set of solutions to regain prosperity. The nation must reinstate those aspects of its past that do not necessarily conform to its national character but were critical to its success, in particular, its egalitarian inclusiveness and confident pragmatism. It must reaffirm its belief in equal circumstances and answer the call of change, as it had done habitually in the past. This will not happen without the acceptance of community sacrifice and the active use of government. It will not be sufficient to sing out "every person for himself or herself."

The central national problem is that only during prosperous times has the nation used its government to reinvigorate its inclusive ideals and adjust pragmatically to the new needs of changing times. The Progressive Era evolved during the extraordinary prosperity of the age of Robber Barons. The New Deal was its ultimate extension, and was preceded by the 1920s, the decade of greatest growth and change in the nation's history. The New Frontier and Great Society were products of the prosperity of the immediate post-World War II years. In the 1950s and 1960s, family incomes doubled, and for the first time a majority of Americans considered themselves middle class. The great democratic reforms of the early 1800s were also born in periods of prosperity and were conceived as ways to protect access to prosperity for broad numbers of Americans. In such periods, or during war, Americans were willing to pay more taxes to support the social programs or new government institutions they thought they needed. Business itself expanded the benefits it offered workers and invested in training, stable long-term work, and ongoing research.

It is by no means obvious that prosperity, by which we mean rapid economic growth, will now continue. Although America has improved its condition since the mid-1970s, it may not return to the sustained rapid growth to which it was long accustomed. Without such prosperity, America's tendency to resort to its narrow national character will further inhibit growth. The nation is not even vaguely aware of this threat to its future.

○   ○   ○

When David Potter wrote his influential book, *People of Plenty*, published in 1954, scholars often attributed America's national character to its immigrants or its rapidly growing population. Potter helped to reinstate an old view, first popularized by Frederick Jackson Turner. Turner, who badly oversimplified history but did so with powerful clarity and vision, saw the source of American character in the economic opportunity of the frontier. For Potter, the source was material abundance in general. "It suffices to note that, by the general consent of all observers," he wrote, "this state of relative abundance, of material plenty, has been a basic condition of American life and that it has had pervasive, if undefined, influence upon the American people."

This premise is, I believe, fundamentally true. "The United States is a child of the Industrial Revolution," wrote Theodore J. Lowi. This can hardly be denied. The nation's history is entirely conterminous with the Industrial Revolution that began in Britain. Is there any more important fact in its history?

What reinforced America's individualistic sense was the wide availability of cheap, fertile land. By 1800, Charles Sellers writes, half of Americans were living at a subsistence level, but on their own land. This was far better than in the Old World, which they had not merely courageously, but also intelligently, escaped. The Industrial Revolution soon created demand for their produce, especially the tobacco and cotton of the South. Modern scholarship finds that Americans were much healthier on average than their peers in the Old World. Birth weights were higher, as was life expectancy. Americans were on average much taller than Britons, a reflection of their better diets and relative freedom from famine and plague. This was indeed something of a miracle on Earth, and it was easy for Americans to believe that they created their fortune by their individual hand, or perhaps by Adam Smith's invisible hand of the market, but surely not by the hand of government, which represented the oppression of the Old World. In America, freedom meant economic individualism.

As the historian Joyce Appleby wrote:

> The Jeffersonians unified ordinary voters through a vision of class-lessness. Its intellectual origins were as old as Hobbes' and Lockes' social contract theories, but its material base owed much to the recent changes in the Atlantic economy, which put a premium on commodities reaped on American farms. With this substantial underpinning, Jeffersonians could persuade practical men that the only relevant status was that of the "the free and independent man." Their utopia was a society of aspirants bound together by a common need to liberate themselves and human nature from the implicit slurs of elite doctrines.

But the Industrial Revolution was not a sufficient condition for the development of the national character. Ideas were borne from the British and European Enlightenment, which when cultivated in the United States took vivid flower. These ideas were so palpably successful that they were carried to an extreme. America was the experiment that proved their value. What were these basic ideas and values of a changing Old World? "[N]o one can move from the fifteenth to the sixteenth, still more to the seventeenth, century," wrote Harold J. Laski, who taught in London, "without the sense of wider and more creative horizons, the recognition that there is a greater regard for the inherent worth of human personality, as sensitiveness to the infliction of unnecessary pain, a zeal for truth for its own sake, a willingness to experiment in its service, which are all parts of a social heritage which would have been infinitely poorer without them."

This is not quite the American character, but it well describes the great change in Europe that sustained it. America gravitated to a narrower view, best exemplified in the seventeenth-century works of John Locke, that was based on an exaltation of the individual's status and natural rights. Government was more a necessary evil than a force for good, whose primary duty was to protect natural rights, in particular the right to private property.

Political and social experimentation was abundant in early America and critical to its development, but it was not truly a conscious part of the nation's character. Nor was a zeal for truth. Rationality was in the air, but not as a maker of nations or a mover of peoples. Americans believed in their own inevitability. They separated religion from the state, but their confidence was based on a mystical faith in their chosenness. It was easy to believe America had created a "new man" and not merely new circumstances. Religion, with the Second Great Awakening that began in the early 1800s, provided spiritual approbation for material success. To risk an oversimplification, to the early Protestants, being well-off on Earth meant one was among the chosen. To the new religions of America's 1800s, anyone could be among the chosen with faith and hard work, and the payoff on Earth was proof of it. Religion was both democratized and fully materialized. "Our secular mythology renders almost incomprehensible the religious mythology that organized experience for rural America," writes Sellers.

As Potter and many others since have pointed out, both government and a sense of one person's obligations to another played a much larger part in American success than was recognized or than was incorporated into its national character. "There is a widespread belief in the United States," wrote Potter,

> that the basic policy of our government underwent a sudden change
> . . . with the advent of the New Deal. According to this belief, the
> American Republic had been a thoroughgoing laissez faire state dur-
> ing its first century and a half—a state where government scrupu-
> lously refrained from intervention in the economic sphere, and pri-
> vate enterprise alone shaped the country's economic progress. . . .

[W]e need to be aware of the strands of continuity. . . . If we are to appreciate the links with the past, we must recognize that laissez faire was not the unique principle of policy in our eighteenth- and nineteenth-century development but that one of the key principles was certainly the constant endeavor of government to make economic abundance of the nation accessible to the public.

Here is a piece of American history we are rarely taught. Government was vitally used to make sure that economic opportunity was available to all. In the nation's early years, democracy and equality meant expanding opportunity to all, in large part because there was so much opportunity to go around. So the country relied not on laissez-faire principles alone, but also on government. "We must recognize that laissez faire was not the unique principle of policy in our eighteenth- and nineteenth-century development but that one of the key principles was certainly the constant endeavor of government to make the economic abundance of the nation accessible to the public," wrote Potter. "The tactics by which this was done changed as the form of abundance itself changed, but the basic purpose—to keep our population in contact with the sources of wealth—has remained steadily in the ascendant throughout our history."

What did government do? First, when the ownership of land meant economic subsistence and political independence, the federal government actively protected the right to land for most Americans. It progressively reduced the price of that land, made more government property available for sale, and protected the rights of squatters. The landowners fought bill after bill, but they passed time and again. In these years, and in such ways, democracy and egalitarianism meant the spread of economic opportunity. Government was required to enforce and ensure the opportunity to own land.

Democracy itself became institutionalized. America was the first of the developed nations to grant universal white male suffrage; in most states, it became law in the 1820s. Britain and Europe did not pass such laws until the middle of the century. It was democracy that demanded broad protections for all and thus served economic growth so well. Government, including both federal and state institutions, built roads and canals and subsidized the development of the railroads, obeying for the most part the will of the people. There would have been no strong markets without such investment. Government, under democratic ideals, also broadened competition. In the Old World, corporate charters were usually reserved for the elite. In America they were granted to many if not most comers. Eventually, the nation granted full legal rights to corporations.

In the 1830s, state and local governments were already developing the free and mandatory primary school system. Democracy was its guiding principle, economic growth its beneficiary. "Education then, beyond all other devices of human origins, is a great equalizer of the conditions of men—the balance wheel of the social machinery," wrote the great educator, Horace Mann, as long ago as 1848. The federal government regulated monopoly and prohibited the abuse of workers. In the early 1900s, state and local government built and ran the nation's high schools. Federal and state government supported countless universities. The sanitation of the nation's cities was accomplished by government and contributed enormously to growth by making large metropolises inhabitable.

Throughout most of the nineteenth century, America's financial system was unstable, supporting capital investment at some points and stoking overspeculation at others. Every recession of the nineteenth century was preceded by a severe financial panic. In 1912, the Federal Reserve was formed to stabilize financing, the currency, and inflation. During the New Deal, unemployment insurance and Social Security were created, and deposit insurance was established. The Securities and Exchange Commission was created. By ensuring reasonable fairness for investors and a flow of information, this agency did not restrain corporations by imposing more costly paperwork but rather accomplished the opposite. Good information was vital to free markets and capital investment and enabled America to grow.

In the post-World War II period, government built the highways, sent the veterans to college (making the ultimate spread of high technology possible), and vaccinated the nation's children against polio. Defense research led to the transistor and the Internet. In the 1960s, civil rights were at last seriously afforded the protection of the law, one hundred years after the Civil War freed the slaves.

We can argue about the specific uses of government. But its contributions, here only partially reviewed, is remarkable, especially given that they are so little acknowledged. In truth, the uses of government were broadly resisted throughout the nation's history from all parts of the political spectrum. The early Jeffersonian Republicans did not want to build the roads. Jackson undermined the nation's central bank. Grand plans for public improvement under John Calhoun and others were always defeated. There was a battle to keep even primary schools private. Government failed to end racial prejudice and disadvantage.

But time and again, America ultimately resorted to government to adjust to changing times. And times always changed. The nation might have been better served if it were not so suspicious of government. Most important, it might have built better roads earlier, as well as a more stable banking system. It might not have tolerated slavery for so long and have worked harder after the Civil War to ensure civil rights for the African-American population, arguably the greatest failure. But, ultimately, government was used and needed. And the reasoning was pragmatic, not ideological. Even though government was critical to growth, Americans to this day do not readily admit it; it never made its way into American ideology. It is not part of the national character. Even the convincing economic evidence advanced by mainstream economists today about the value of public investment receives almost no public attention.

Prosperity returned time and again to America, for the variety of reasons outlined in chapter 4. Growth became rapid after the Civil War and, except for recessions, it consistently maintained the pace. (In Europe, economic growth was generally slower.) Incomes grew as a result. Some argued that the reason America had no strong Socialist party was that its incomes were so high. No doubt the issue was more complex, but prosperity was a great tonic. Similarly, its organized labor movement was far less radical and weaker than Europe's. One reason might be the early adoption of universal (white male) suffrage. Another was surely fairly widespread prosperity. The two in truth went hand in hand; democracy meant prosperity for more in America. Even in 1900, average wages in America, according to the best estimates, were about 50 percent higher than in Europe.

The historian Richard Hofstadter believed that a national character is formed early in a nation's history and does not change. Henry Steele Commager, a historian in the mythologizing romantic tradition, wrote, "Circumstances change profoundly, but the character of the American people has not changed greatly or the nature of the principles of conduct, public and private, to which they subscribe."

This may well be true, and if so it is a tragedy. To the social reformers of the 1960s, the individualistic national character seemed outmoded or irrelevant. Americans supported new social programs for African Americans and the poor in a tradition that seemed on the surface to extend from the Progressive Era of Theodore Roosevelt and Woodrow Wilson. But prosperity was never greater in America. Opportunities seemed limitless. Few could have foreseen how the nation's traditional character would resurface strongly under the guidance of Ronald Reagan in the 1980s. By then, Americans had suffered nearly a decade of high unemployment and high inflation. Government, for a variety of complex reasons, became an easy scapegoat. Reagan was the rhetorician of the traditional national character. "It is morning again in America," he eloquently claimed, and the nation reverted to its old suspicions of government, its longing for a crude individualism, and a nostalgia that has debilitated it.

But it was slow economic growth, not Ronald Reagan, that returned Americans to their old instincts. Resistance to taxes was strengthening in the 1970s before the Reagan presidency, for example, as inflation and unemployment undermined standards of living. Inclusiveness, that great early American ideal, had once meant more for everybody; now, with slow growth, it seemed to mean less for most. Now we had to give something up to help others. Inclusiveness in America was the godchild only of prosperity. Taxes redistributed money from the middle class to the relatively poor, but now the middle class was no longer doing as well. Reagan mined the disaffection effectively. Social programs were easy to denigrate in a period of slow growth; they seemed to fail. Individualism and self-reliance were considered the keys to American success. This was partly true and, as important, partly false. The ideal touched the deepest of American instincts, and they had that most attractive of benefits in difficult financial times: These ideals meant lower taxes.

"Why does government think it can take my money?" I have been asked constantly when addressing groups across the country. There is little gratitude to a government that educates a business's workers, collects its garbage, builds its roads, provides for its safety and national defense, regulates its financial markets, creates a stable financial system, insures those who save in its banks, protects it from fraud, provides legal recourse for grievances, takes care of its elderly workers, and so forth.

America, it must be remembered, only instated a progressive income tax to fight wars, first World War I and then World War II. (There was a temporary income tax during the Civil War as well.) The income tax proved the great source of federal revenue of the twentieth century, without which we would have been a much different and much lesser nation, but it was never adopted as a solution to social problems. As family income fell, or at best grew at historically slow rates, Americans were less trustful of the social vision enacted by Theodore Roosevelt, Franklin Roosevelt, John F. Kennedy, and Lyndon Johnson. It was much easier to believe government was the cause of the problem and that markets unrestricted by government would lead back to rapid growth.

In some instances, less government was decidedly good. Deregulation of industries should be promoted where possible. Privatization is useful. Taxes should not be high. Freedom to pursue new ideas should be as widespread as possible, and this typically requires decentralization and the freedom to pursue profit. Moreover, and perhaps most important, we live in a much larger and more sophisticated world than we once did. Government was often needed in the past to mobilize capital and gather the best minds for a given project. Now private financial institutions can manage many of these tasks, as can local governments, where the level of expertise has leaped forward. Corporations can control much more complex bureaucracies and can call on a far more educated population of workers than a hundred or even fifty years ago. We should take advantage of these beneficial circumstances. Central government is no longer needed for some purposes and is not as good at some tasks as local government or private business.

But the "embrace of markets" or the diminution of government was by no means the wellspring of growth in the 1990s, as so many in the media casually and absurdly claimed. For one thing, government was hardly diminished at all, down only a couple of percentage points as a percentage of GDP. For another, economic growth was at its height in the 1950s and 1960s, when tax rates were very high and government was growing rapidly. The great sources of growth in the late 1990s were similar to what they always had been in the past, even if growth itself was less durable.

Government, then, is a pragmatic affair. It should not be avoided for ideological reasons, just as it should not be used for ideological reasons. Public goods, and in particular public investment, have been badly neglected in America, not for pragmatic reasons but for ideological ones, because their neglect appealed to the national character in a time of economic stringency. Similarly, the rise of inequality and the slow growth of wages, which have undermined the strength of domestic markets and led to unsustainable levels of borrowing, have been deemed beyond the grasp of government solutions, again, not for pragmatic or justifiable reasons but for ideological ones.

The national character also misleads us about the proper role of private enterprise. We are somehow easily convinced as a people that the goals of these enterprises were always the narrow pursuit of profit. As business got larger in the mid-nineteenth century, it certainly became abusive. But during the twentieth century, American business expanded its obligations. The best executives understood that their businesses were members of a community and actively supported local social programs and charities. They expanded benefits to their workers, increasingly provided health and pension benefits, and improved working conditions. They provided education and training and tried to make work more meaningful. There were many exceptions, of course. The American record is still poor on worker safety, for example. But on average and in general, the trend was toward a greater sense of obligation, which in the long run served the nation's profits well.

In recent decades, this trend has been reversed. The corporation has abandoned its embrace of the workers. Benefits were reduced, wage increases were resisted until the late 1990s, layoffs reached record levels, and factories were easily moved to other countries. Organized labor has been further weakened. Corporations turned to temporary workers, who usually received no benefits. In the recession of 2001, workers were fired at a record pace. Worker insecurity has risen sharply as a result.

There is a tradeoff for companies that pursued these tactics. Lower wages and more flexible work certainly contributed to higher profits in the 1990s. In a time of intense domestic and foreign competition, this had its benefits. But it also detracted from the nation's potential growth by reducing demand in the domestic market. Margaret Blair and other economists have written that in their own self-interest, corporations should attend to their workers' needs. For example, one result of greater flexibility in the workforce is that job training, ever more important, is increasingly neglected. Why invest in training workers if the priority is to be able to fire them when necessary? Why should workers give their all or try to improve themselves, if they know their employment is short-term?

A more flexible workforce has of necessity made job training more of a public good than in the past. Job training will benefit the economy as a whole, but individual companies will invest relatively less than they otherwise would because workers are now likely to leave or be asked to leave. If what we need is a flexible business sector, with fluid workforces, government-sponsored job training becomes the optimal recourse.

If the nation believes that secure pension benefits and healthcare are valuable in themselves and may also contribute to a strong economy, these too become increasingly public goods as private corporations reduce their commitments. Even though by reducing their commitments individual companies became more flexible and competitive, they also damaged the economy as a whole by reducing the ability of its people to buy goods and services. Our national character shed light on only one side of this equation.

Economics has never been free of political ideology. One of the objectives of Adam Smith's *Wealth of Nations* was to combat the rich mercantilists who wanted to restrict trade. Robert Malthus, who warned about the inevitable damage of population growth, was determined to protect rich landholders, and David Ricardo was determined to undermine them.

Ideally in the search for knowledge, we should seek objectivity. No goal is more important. But we should recognize how difficult it is to achieve. What a relief it would be if the nation's major academic economic departments included in their coursework a module or two on the ideological underpinnings of their theories. For the most part, they do the opposite. Intent on proving themselves scientists, they exaggerate the objectivity of their claims. Few academic departments require a course in the history of economic thought. The evident swing of the economics profession toward "the embrace of markets" has some justification but has been carried beyond what the evidence can support. The malleability of statistical techniques is too great to make them more than suggestive in most cases, and the ambiguity of the empirical facts and of the analyses based on them are often understated.

Economic ideology, then, is also an enemy of future growth. Mainstream economics, at least for the moment, has aligned itself closely with individualism and minimal government. We cannot ignore how some of the precepts of contemporary mainstream economics, from the free flow of capital to restrained government spending and emphasis on strong currencies, also are consonant with the foremost desires of the world's richest financial institutions. But, by the same token, there are many strands of economic theory that are promising. Behavioral economics, which argues that people are not as rational as theory has sometimes assumed they are, is breaking new ground, for example. Theories of economic development are being broadened. Concerns with imperfect information have potential for providing theoretical guidelines about the unequal distribution of resources. In general, economics should be seen as providing a set of extraordinary tools but not providing universal answers. Universal answers are for ideologues.

A Social Contract

The American national character has prevented the nation from adopting a new social contract to lead it forward. We do not even speak in terms of the social contract anymore because, implicitly, we do not give government sufficient status to enter into a contract with the people. These days, as large as government is, in the public mind it is an appendage and a burden, not a partner.

We should reinstate the concept of the social contract and it should be expanded to include two principles. The first is inclusiveness. All Americans must be able to fulfill themselves in a more sophisticated and demanding world. The second involves the adjustment to change. Americans should recognize that changing times present new obligations and require new responses. The nation's problems are not the consequence of government actions but of both change and neglect.

Inclusiveness and adaptation to change have always been critical to America's success. The old social contract was Lockean: Government must be minimal and largely protect only the rights to private property. Our sense of civil rights was as a protection from governmental tyranny—thus, democracy and free speech. Inclusiveness in the American national character is defined restrictively. Openness to change has always been a part of American development but not an explicit commitment that involved government.

A new inclusiveness will automatically make the domestic market healthier by involving everyone in it. It will involve addressing the inequality of income and providing adequate healthcare, education, and early childcare for all. It will make work possible for women and two-worker families. It will recognize that a flexible workforce, as befits the changed economy, places more obligations on society, not fewer, because business abandons such tasks as training or providing benefits. This inclusiveness would ensure that prejudice is eliminated at work and will recognize that some workers need more protections than others. The social ideal of inclusiveness is also an economic ideal. It will strengthen the markets for goods and services, make more Americans productive workers, and relieve the nation of the dependency of those who do not have an adequate chance.

Economic change is the driving force for this broader definition of inclusiveness. It is also creating new demands even for those with advantages. Jobs are more sophisticated, and they change more rapidly. Businesses must have the ability to hire and fire to remain competitive both domestically and internationally, which thrusts job training and benefits associated with work into the public sphere. Meanwhile, education and healthcare will inevitably become more expensive and take a larger share of the nation's income.

Government must set the new agenda of inclusiveness and adaptation to change. Those who adhere to the ancient national character will cry that individualism is being violated and that self-reliance is the only guarantor of a nation's success. But they ignore how radically the world has changed; that is, how much more sophisticated, complex, and competitive it now is. Giving everyone an equal chance is more complex now than it ever was. This is not a call for equal outcomes, but equal opportunities, as it always was, since government was needed to protect access to land.

The nation's survival is not jeopardized in the short run. We do not understand the nature of national decline. Recently a commentator claimed that federal deficits in the 1980s must not have been all that bad because the economy survived them. What would have constituted failure? A new depression? Lasting how many years? We have already seen how many were left out of economic abundance in the past twenty-five years, how incomes do not keep up with the costs of education and healthcare, how two-worker families are now necessities, how few high-quality daycare institutions we have, how debt and the trade deficit grew rapidly. The nation did not survive the 1980s well. It is still paying a price.

If America is to grow at its full potential, it must recognize that equal opportunity is no longer a matter of throwing an individual into a nation of vast fertile land or into an economy of constant rapid growth and a cascade of new, good-paying jobs. Since the early 1970s, slow economic growth has undermined America's ability to change. Its people have fallen back on a misleading sense of national character. The nation does not adequately address the need for better education, equal access to healthcare, and new family institutions. It does not address the issues of inequality. It does not do so precisely because it will not embrace government as a partner. There is no good reason to expect that attitude to change. However, if it does not, economic growth in America will not reach its potential. Without prosperity, the nation does not know who it is and is unlikely to restore the attitudes that contributed so much to its greatness.

The great moral thrusts of the post-World War II era dissipated some time ago, and America has been floundering since. The moral values it should embrace—inclusiveness and change—are not taken up with enthusiasm, despite their benefits to the economy. America's best values are in jeopardy, not immediately, but over time. They may erode so slowly that it will not be noticed.

Notes

Chapter 1

page

2   *This book argues that the growth of markets through trade, colonization, and domestic expansion was the predominant factor in Western economic development. . . .* In particular, we stress the growth of domestic markets. Economists have debated such issues in the past, and still do, although the predominant view can now be called "supply side." The minority view rarely if ever reaches the public discourse. Economic growth theory today is now dominated by the central idea that it is what we put into the economy that matters for growth—capital investment, technological advance—not what we pull through it. The importance of demand was better thought of in the past. A quote from the economist Nicholas Kaldor is illustrative: "[I]t is the competition between these large, frequently transnational or multinational enterprises which generates the rapid technological change in an environment of expanding total demand, which is both the cause and the reflection of the growth in markets." Nicholas Kaldor, *Causes of Growth and Stagnation in the World Economy*, eds. Carlo Filippino, Fernando Targetti and A.P. Thirlwall, *Raffaele Mattioli Lectures* (New York: Cambridge University Press, 1996). This source is a series of lectures given in 1984.

There was a period from the 1930s until around the early 1980s when effective demand, based on the ideas of John Maynard Keynes, was a dominant concept in macroeconomics. The theme of this book is only a cousin of this idea. The view proposed here is closer to Adam Smith's idea about markets, but it is nevertheless related to the idea of effective demand, if not the same thing. For other views that support, see Kohn in the next footnote. See also Rick Szostak, *The Role of Transportation in the Industrial Revolution* (Montreal: McGill-Queen's University Press, 1991), which argues that the fall in transportation costs enabled markets to expand rapidly and was a central cause of growth. In general, the great French historian Fernand Braudel supports this point of view. In his classic work, *Civilization and Capitalism*, volume 3, he writes about the British Industrial Revolution as follows: "[W]hat really gave the impetus to industry and probably to innovation as well, was the substantial enlargement of the domestic market" (New York: Harper & Row, 1999), 544.

There was a reaction years ago among some growth economists to this emphasis on demand, epitomized by Nathan Rosenberg: "Rather than viewing either the existence of a market demand or the existence of a technological opportunity as each representing a sufficient condition for innovation to occur, one should consider them each as necessary, but not sufficient, for innovation to result; both must exist simultaneously." Nathan Rosenberg, *Inside the Black Box* (New York: Cambridge University Press, 1982), 231–32. Joel Mokyr has become probably the leading historian in favor of technological emphasis. See, in particular, *The Lever of Riches: Technological Creativity and Economic Progress* (New York: Oxford University Press, 1990).

Where this book differs from the Rosenberg approach is in his emphatic case that markets do not matter more than other factors, and the implication, which essentially if implicitly holds, that demand actually matters less than supply factors. Even Braudel argued in the 1970s that technology had been too neglected (566), but now the reaction has become the dominant, conventional wisdom. "There is no good a priori reason in theory why 'market demand' factors should be dominant in motivating innovative activity," Rosenberg continues (231–32). This book holds that there are very good empirical and historical reasons to think just that, and that it is theory that is lacking, but I also maintain that there is no single dominating cause of growth, only a tendency of markets to be first among equals. What is clear is that the supply side view has gone too far. Even those disposed to a Keynesian view of macroeconomics often say the economy is Keynesian in the short run, and classical, meaning supply side, in the long run. I argue that economic growth is demand driven both in the short run and the long run, if nevertheless complex and organic at all times. The policy implications of this view are critical.

3   *The possibility of trading goods in large volume was a major source of growth beginning at least in the Middle Ages. . . .* Among the best and most recent summaries of this position is Meir Kohn, "The Expansion of Trade and the Development of European Industry to 1600," Working Paper 00–20, Dartmouth College, January 2001.

3   *But legal institutions, or semilegal ones, including judicial systems, were more the consequence of growing markets and trade than their cause.* The current conventional view, which argues the central importance of these institutions, is expressed best by Douglas C. North, *Structure and Change in Economic History* (New York: W. W. Norton, 1981). Perhaps the most thoughtful recent version of the conventional view is by William Baumol, *The Free Market Innovation Machine: Analyzing the Growth Miracle of Capitalism* (Princeton, NJ: Princeton University Press, 2002). A popular application of the view to developing economies is by Hernando de Soto, *The Mystery of Capital* (New York: Basic Books, 2000). But it seems obvious on the face of it that property rights are not a sufficient cause of economic growth. The Netherlands had secure property rights, for example, and was easily usurped by Britain. Also, growth often occurred when property rights were still being developed, as in the United States and certainly early Britain. The most illustrative modern example is rapid economic growth in China, which has occurred without property rights on the Western or Japanese model. It is also clear that as the economy developed, property and contractual rights were increasingly strengthened in Britain, a consequence more than a cause of growth.

4   *Towns and cities were integral to economic growth in Britain and Europe, . . .* See Kohn,"Expansion of Trade."

4   *For now it is important to recognize that exchange itself improves welfare,* . . . This is fundamental to classical economics.

5   *As Adam Smith wrote, "Give me that which I want, and you shall have this which you want.* . . . This is of course fundamental to modern economics. Adam Smith, *An Inquiry into the Nature and Causes of the Wealth of Nations* (New York: Oxford University Press, 1993), book I, chapter ii, 22.

5   *It is assumed that the savings will then be invested, and that capital investment in turn is the engine of growth* . . . Adam Smith argued that savings were essential. He did not consider the contradiction between savings and the strength of the market: if there is more savings there is less demand. See Smith, *Inquiry into Nature and Causes*, book II, chapter iii.

6   *But financial institutions are classic followers, not leaders, somewhat to the right on our continuum.* . . . For a recent example of the conventional view, emphasizing modern venture capital institutions, see Michael J. Mandel, *The Coming Internet Depression* (New York: Basic Books, 2001). See also *The Economic Report of the President 2000*, Council of Economic Advisers, Washington, D.C.

6–7   *Relatively free markets, as Karl Polanyi pointed out, were social constructions of government.* . . . This was a theme of Polanyi's great work, *The Great Transformation* (Boston: Beacon Press, 1944), 139 ff.

7   *Finally, many observers, notably Joseph Schumpeter, argue that entrepreneurialism is the great source of economic growth,* . . . Joseph Schumpeter, *Capitalism, Socialism, and Democracy* (New York: Harper, 1950).

7   *The same can be said for the importance of managerial competence and innovation, so forcefully brought to our attention by the historian Alfred Chandler.* . . . Chandler provides the classic history not only of management in the United States but also of mass production and, as important, mass distribution. Alfred D. Chandler Jr., *The Visible Hand* (Cambridge, MA: Harvard University Press, 1977).

9   *However it is implemented, economic growth will not occur unless a people has a drive toward material betterment,* . . . Adam Smith takes this instinct for granted, and does allude to it. But obviously it has been the central theme of much Anglo-Saxon philosophy going back to Hobbes and Locke at least.

10–11   *In such earlier and purer cases, natural resources and geographical differences were probably closer to first causes of growth than they are in modern economies.* . . . Jared Diamond provides the most readable analysis and summary of these early civilizations, I believe. For his basic theme about the primacy of environmental influences, see the "Prologue," 13–32. Jared Diamond, *Guns, Germs, and Steel* (New York: W. W. Norton, 1998).

Chapter 2

13   *As The Economist wrote, a "big idea" was necessary to explain the sudden and surprising prosperity of the late 1990s in the United States,* . . . "How Real is the New Economy?" *The Economist*, July 24, 1999, 21–23.

14   *Americans were confused and disappointed by the economy's poor performance between 1973 and 1995.* . . . All economic data are based on the National Income and Product Accounts compiled by the Bureau of Economic Analysis, U.S. Department of Commerce.

14   *"Perhaps at no time since World War II has the performance of the U.S. economy been more mystifying," . . .* "Slower Growth, An Inflation Bias or a New Dynamic" *Business Week*, June 1, 1981, p. 60.

15   *In 1985, Business Week devoted a special issue to "the most revolutionary economic change in a century—the emergence of a 'new economy' of services and high technology." . . . Business Week*, January 21, 1985, pp. 68–78.

15   *The next year, a U.S. News cover hailed a "Brave New Economy." . . .* "Brave New Economy, *U.S. News & World Report*, April 14, 1986, p. 43. The *U.S. News* new economy had to do with breaking the back of inflation, not a significant rise in information technology: "Unleashing the private-enterprise system to do its thing." *Fortune put "America's New Economy" on its cover in that year as well. . . .* "America's New Economy," Arthur M. Lewis, *Fortune*, June 23, 1986, pp. 18–29. *Fortune* reported that "things look brighter than they have in decades." Than the 1960s? The market crashed the next year, and faith in the dollar soon had to be restored at the Louvre. This was followed by another seven or eight years of slow economic growth and no improvement in productivity.

15   *For example, Ronald K. Shelp, a business executive, and Gary W. Hart, the former senator, co-authored an article, Understanding a New Economy, that was largely about the requirements of a services economy.* "Understanding a New Economy," *Wall Street Journal*, December 23, 1986, 1.

15–16 *Business Week's cover in 1988 ironically announced: "The New Economy: Say Hello to the Lean Years." . . .* November 16, 1987, p. 164.

16   *For example, Robert Reich, President William Clinton's labor secretary, repeatedly discussed a "new economy," in which good manufacturing jobs were being lost to overseas competitors. . . .* Op-ed piece by Reich, "The Americas: Trade with Mexico Is a Boon for U.S. Workers" *Wall Street Journal*, April 30, 1993, p. A13.

16   *An extensive search of newspapers and magazines in the 1980s and early 1990s shows the phrase "new economy" being used to describe the services economy, the information age, deindustrialization, wage stagnation and inequality, deregulation and privatization, lower tax rates, high levels of debt, and of course early computer technology. . . .* Computer search of Lexis-Nexis Academic Universe and Dow Jones Interactive Services for articles with references to "the new economy." Such references, for example, increased from 325 in all business press in 1995 to nearly 23,000 in 2000. Thanks to the Joan Shorenstein Center for Press and Politics, Harvard University, for generous support of this research.

16   *"This is truly the second industrial revolution, and it will change every aspect of people's lives," said John T. Chambers, the CEO of Cisco Systems. . . .* Quoted in *Business Week*, August 28, 2000, 210.

16   *Business Week was more consistent than most and, by the mid–1990s in any case, claimed that the new economy rested on two factors, globalization and the advance of information technology. . . .* "The Triumph of the New Economy," *Business Week*, December 30, 1996, p. 68.

17   *They added deregulation and corporate restructuring to these two in a definition it proposed in 1997. . . .* "Debating Myth or Miracle Behind a New Economy," Steven Pearlstein, *Washington Post*, November 11, 1997, p. D7.

17   *As corroboration, speculators drove the prices of high technology stocks to levels that the economist Robert Shiller showed were on average without historical*

precedent. . . . Robert J. Shiller, *Irrational Exuberance* (Princeton, N.J.: Princeton University Press, 2000), 7–14.

17 *Given the poor rates of growth of the economy since 1973, they certainly suggested an improvement, but compared to similar exuberant periods in the past, such as the 1920s, 1950s, and 1960s, they were actually below average. . . .* National Income and Product Accounts, Bureau of Economic Analysis, Washington, D.C. See also, in general, *Historical Statistics of the United States. Colonial Times to 1970* (Washington, D.C.: U.S. Bureau of the Census, 1975).

17 *If this was a new economy, there had been many new economies in U.S. history. . . .* This issue is discussed at greater length in Chapter 5. My favorite history of technology in the United States remains Chandler, *The Visible Hand.* See also Rosenberg, *Inside the Black Box.* See also, Carroll Pursell, *The Machine in America* (Baltimore: Johns Hopkins University Press, 1995). Finally, see the *Cambridge Economic History of the United States* (New York: Cambridge University Press, 2000).

18 *Railroads also began to take hold, supplementing the waterways and soon overtaking them as efficient modes of transportation. . . .* The classic history of the U.S. railroads is George Rogers Taylor and Irene D. Neu, *The American Railroad Network* (Cambridge: Harvard University Press, 1956). The postal service and education are discussed in later chapters.

18 *Large wholesalers and retailers distributed them via rail and steamboat to every corner of the nation, and new highly productive retail chains such as the Atlantic & Pacific Tea Co. (the A&P) sold packaged goods and machine-made clothing conveniently and at low prices. . . .* Alfred Chandler is especially convincing about the role of distributors, especially; see *The Visible Hand,* 209–39.

19 *(it was the "age of aspirin," eventually wrote the playwright Clifford Odets). . . . The Country Girl,* act 2, scene 2.

19 *A dozen years after World War II, a highway system leading to a network of paved roads connected 90 percent of U.S. homes. . . .* See Eric Beshers for a good analysis of highway development, "High Returns on Public Spending," in *Unconventional Wisdom,* edited by Jeff Madrick (New York: Century Foundation, 2000).

19 *"The nineteenth century moved fast and furious, so that one who moved in it felt sometimes giddy, watching it spin," wrote Henry Adams in 1905. . . .* Henry Adams, *Mont Saint Michel and Chartres* (New York: Penguin Books, 1986), p. 35.

20 *When the complex arguments of some sophisticated economists were boiled down, for example, they maintained that because there will always be technological advance, we can simply count on ongoing economic growth. . . . A leading example of an excellent economist who subscribes to such a view is Paul Romer.* I think his ultimate trust in technology is incorrect, but his central works are seminal. See Romer, "Increasing Returns and Long Run Growth," *Journal of Political Economy* 94, no. 5 (1986):1002–1037. See also "Implementing a National Technology Strategy with Self-Organizing Industry Investment Boards," in *Brookings Papers on Economic Activity, Volume 2,* edited by Martin Neil Baily and Clifford Winston (Washington, D.C.: Brookings Institute, 1993); and "Why, Indeed, in America? Theory, History, and the Origins of Modern Economic Growth," Working Paper no. 5443, National Bureau of Economic Research, January 1996.

20 *In other instances, talented economists, even while criticizing the assumption that computers were the driving force in a new economy, assumed that Amer-*

ica's most rapid economic growth earlier in the century was largely the consequence of the internal combustion engine, the electric dynamo, and a few other key inventions. . . . A leading economist who holds such a view is the talented and protean Robert Gordon, who if always provocative, I think is mistaken in his emphasis here. "American Economic Growth: One Big Wave?" working paper, Northwestern University, March 1993.

20   *Probably most influential, the accomplished economic historian Paul David hypothesized that the rapid growth of the early twentieth century was the consequence in large measure of the adoption of electricity. . . .* Paul David, "Computer and Dynamo: The Modern Productivity Paradox in a Not-Too-Distant Mirror," in *Technology and Productivity: The Challenge for Economic Policy* (Paris: OECD, 1991).

21   *It is widely agreed that the Industrial Revolution started in Britain in the second half of the 1700s. . . .* The Industrial Revolution is discussed at length in Chapter 4. One of the classic histories on which this account relies, and which contains much of the cited information in this chapter, is David S. Landes, *The Unbound Prometheus* (London: Cambridge University Press, 1969). It has a technological point of view. The other key work is Braudel, *Civilization and Capitalism,* which is more congenial to the importance of demand. But even Landes has a demand-pull aspect in his work, when he discusses how innovation was often a response to challenges in the production systems, not independent of them (as we shall see).

22   *He warned sarcastically about stressing "the element of invention as much as many writers do." . . .* Joseph Schumpeter, *The Theory of Economic Development: An Inquiry into Profits, Capital, Credit, Interest, and the Business Cycle* (Cambridge: Harvard University Press, 1934), 89. The fuller quote is as follows: "Economic leadership in particular must hence be distinguished from 'invention.' As long as they are not carried into practice, inventions are economically irrelevant. . . . Besides, the innovations which it is the function of entrepreneurs to carry out need not necessarily be any inventions at all. It is, therefore, not advisable, and it may be downright misleading, to stress the element of invention as much as many writers do."

24   *On balance, there was no increase in national savings and, therefore, there was no independent injection of more funding into the economy in the 1990s. . . .* Alan S. Blinder and Janet L. Yellen, *The Fabulous Decade* (New York: Century Foundation, 2001), 83–4.

25   *In the seminal Wealth of Nations, published in 1776, Smith made clear that the accumulation of a nation's savings for capital investment was critical to economic improvement. . . .* Book II, chapter iii.

26   *The overwhelming causal factor of growth for Adam Smith, in my reading of him, was in fact the large market discussed previously. . . .* The pin factory example is in Smith's first chapter in *Wealth of Nations.* Smith can of course be somewhat contradictory. He also emphasizes that it is important to save. But it is quite clear, in his writing, that markets are the sources of the division of labor and productivity growth.

27   *"As it is the power of exchanging that gives occasion to the division of labour, so the extent of the division of labour must always be limited by the extent of*

the market," Smith wrote explicitly and early. . . . *Wealth of Nations*, Book I, chapter iii.

28   *The Austrian economist Frederick van Hayek long ago correctly criticized economists' references to capital equipment as too general, with their assumptions that such capital was unchanging and always optimal.* . . . This is not an easy set of issues, but see van Hayek's *The Pure Theory of Capital* (London: Routledge & K. Paul, 1941), in particular, for a fairly clear representation of his concerns.

29   *(These factors are discussed in greater detail in Chapter 7.)* . . . Many of these issues are discussed in some detail in subsequent chapters, and sources are given there, where they are most relevant.

Chapter 3

32   *The sum of all goods and services produced and provided by business and government each year is the nation's gross domestic product (GDP).* . . . GDP is derived from the National Income and Product Accounts. These are by and large a way of analyzing the economy that is fairly young. The great American pioneer was Simon Kuznets, who published his *National Income 1929–1932* and *National Income Since 1869* in 1946, and, probably most important, *Modern Economic Growth: Rate, Structure and Spread* (New Haven and London: Yale University Press, 1966). The study of national income accounting occupied a great deal of economics education in the 1950s, when it was still relatively new. Now we take it for granted—probably too much so. Kuznets was in truth more skeptical of the procedures and meaning of the accounts than are his successors.

33   *Because of America's fast rate of growth, its annual GDP was already larger by the late 1800s than the annual output of goods and services of its nearest rival, Britain, which had stood as the most powerful economy in the world over the preceding one hundred years.* . . . These data are largely based on the enormous database compiled by Angus Maddison. See *Monitoring the World Economy, 1820–1992* (Paris: OECD, 1995). An important earlier work is *Dynamic Forces in Capitalist Development* (New York: Oxford University Press, 1991). Maddison rarely develops data himself but rather takes the best compilations from economists in each nation and makes them comparable.

34   *The level of GDP reached in 1929 turned out to be a high point for the next decade.* . . . See Maddison, *Monitoring the World Economy;* and *U.S. Historical Statistics.* Data for the United States are found in Maddison and also in *Historical Statistics.*

35   *The health of the nation deteriorated in the nineteenth century as it industrialized, but by the twentieth century Americans were living far longer and much healthier lives.* . . . We will discuss this further, but in general see Dora L. Costa and Richard H. Steckel, "Long-Term Trends in Health, Welfare, and Economic Growth in the United States," in *Health and Welfare During Industrialization,* edited by Richard H. Steckel and Roderick Floud (Chicago: University of Chicago Press, 1997).

36   *On average, a single worker could thresh about seven bushels of wheat per day in the early 1800s on American farms.* . . . Information on threshing is taken

from J. Sanford Rikoon, *Threshing in the Midwest, 1820–1940* (Bloomington: Indiana University Press, 1988).

38   *Economic historians calculated that productivity for the American economy as a whole, excluding government but including all business goods and services, grew by more than 2 percent per year on average after roughly the end of the Civil War. . . .* See Maddison, *Dynamic Forces in Capitalist Development.*

39   *Threshing was not the only task in the harvesting of wheat. . . . Many new tools were created, including eventually the tractor, to harvest and prepare the wheat.* Robert C. Williams, Fordson, Farmall, and Poppin Johnny, *A History of the Farm Tractor and Its Impact on America* (Urbana, IL: University of Illinois Press,1989), 8.

40   *That is to say, American farmers were on average producing about three times more per hour of labor in 1900 than they were in 1800. . . .* Lance Davis et al., *American Economic Growth, An Economist's History of the United States* (New York: Harper & Row, 1971), 371ff.

40   *But the best evidence to date suggests that American wages rose on average over the entire nineteenth century by about 1 percent per year. . . .* See Robert Margo, *Wages and Labor Markets in the United States, 1820–1860* (Chicago: University of Chicago Press, 2000). See also Robert Margo, "The Labor Force in the Nineteenth Century," in *The Long Nineteenth Century,* Volume II of *Cambridge Economic History of the United States* (New York: Cambridge University Press, 2000).

46   *Wages increased significantly for all levels of workers. . . .* The most comprehensive analysis of these data is by Lawrence Mishel, Jared Bernstein, and John Schmitt, *The State of Working America, 2000–2001,* Economic Policy Institute, (Ithaca, NY: Cornell University Press, 2001).

46   *Those under forty were at last buying homes in large proportion again. . . .* The U.S. Bureau of the Census and the Joint Center for Housing Studies, *The State of the Nation's Housing,* Harvard University.

46   *People were buying new cars again in a volume that was at last more commensurate with the rate of buying in the 1960s. . . .* Industry statistics have long shown that the number of new cars bought per worker in America is far lower than in the 1960s and 1970s. Economists assumed that Americans bought fewer cars because they were more durable, but this only partly explained the phenomenon. The slow growth of wages accounted for much of the reduction. As wages rose, car sales rose to become more commensurate with earlier periods of prosperity. In fact, there was probably considerable pent-up demand. See American Automobile Association, *Total Vehicle Sales and Vehicles in Use,* annual publication.

Chapter 4

47   *But for almost every assertion about industrial revolution, there seems to be a contrary one. . . .* Joel Mokyr offers the best summary of the varying views and controversies about the British Industrial Revolution, although his own point of view is evident. Joel Mokyr, "Editor's Introduction, The New Economic History and the Industrial Revolution," in *The British Industrial Revolution,* edited by Joel Mokyr (Boulder, Colo.: Westview Press, 1999) 1–127. See also in general, Roderick

Floud and Donald McCloskey, eds., *The Economic History of Britain Since 1700*, (Cambridge: Cambridge University Press, 1981, second edition, 1994.

47   *I can find no simple or adequate definition of "industrial revolution," but for our purposes, the Industrial Revolution marks the point at which productivity began to grow consistently. . . .* There is considerable controversy about the early data, how strong growth was, or even when it began. For a summary of alternative views, see C. Knick Harley, "Reassessing the Industrial Revolution: A Macro View," in Mokyr, *British Industrial Revolution*, 160–203. See also 10–17.

48   *It was the beginning of an inexorable rise of productivity. . . .* Again, Angus Maddison (1991) provides the most comprehensive analysis of long-term growth rates.

48   *"The history of the English working classes begins in the second half of the eighteenth century with the invention of the steam engine and of machines for spinning and weaving cotton," wrote Friedrich Engels in 1845. . . .* Engels, *The Condition of the Working Class in England in 1844* (London: Allen & Unwin, 1952) (originally published in 1848), quoted by Harley, "Reassessing the Industrial Revolution," 161.

48   *Toynbee wrote that society was "suddenly broken in pieces by the mighty blow of the steam engine and the power loom."* Quoted by Harley, "Reassessing the Industrial Revolution," 162.

48   *David Landes, for example, argued that the textile industry was the lead industry of Britain's Industrial Revolution, even as he emphasized the cultural changes that were necessary to make it possible. . . .* Landes, in *Unbound Prometheus,* for example, argued that cotton textiles was the lead industry of Britain's Industrial Revolution, even as he pointed out how complex economic development was (41–44).

48   *Carlo Cipolla argued that all aspects of society contributed to the economic awakening, but singled out iron and coal as the leading factors. . . .* Carlo Cipolla's history of economies during the Middle Ages is among the best available. Carlo M. Cipolla, *Before the Industrial Revolution* (New York: W. W. Norton, 1976), 241–42.

49   *Hierarchy and bureaucracy emerged. . . .* See Jared Diamond, *Guns, Germs, and Steel,* in general for a masterly summary of what we know of these early civilizations.

50   *Around the year 1,000 A.D., an age of advanced tools and machines was launched in Europe that improved the productivity of many of these societies. . . .* A seminal work on medieval technology is Jean Gimpel, *The Medieval Machine* (New Yok: Holt, Rinehart & Winston, 1976).

50   *The improvements in farming methods included crop rotation so as not to deplete the resources of the land (a practice used in ancient Rome). . . .* Gimpel, *Medieval Machine,* 39–43.

51   *But during the Middle Ages manorial agriculture evolved into family farming, with plots large enough, and incentives great enough, to encourage productivity gains. . . .* Meir Kohn has written a provocative tract on this subject. Kohn, "The Expansion of Trade and the Transformation of Agriculture in Pre-industrial Europe," Working Paper, 00–13, Dartmouth College, 2001.

51   *One reason we know horseshoes were valuable was that ferries charged twice as much to transport a horse with horseshoes across a river as one without them. . . .* Cipolla, *Before the Industrial Revolution,* 139.

52   *"The heavy plow, the open fields, the new integration of agriculture and herding, three field rotation, modern horse harnesses, nailed horseshoes . . . had combined into a total system of agrarian exploitation by the year 1100 to provide a zone of peasant prosperity stretching across Northern Europe from the Atlantic to the Dnieper."* . . . Lynn White, "The Expansion of Technology 500–1500," in *The Fontana Economic History of Europe*, volume 1 (London, 1972), 153, quoted in Cipolla, *Before the Industrial Revolution*, 138.

52   *"It is an astonishing concept to the modern mind that medieval man was surrounded by machines,"* wrote the historian Jean Gimpel. . . . Gimpel, *Medieval Machine*, 1–2.

52   *When William the Conqueror sent his surveyors across the land in 1086 to collect taxes, as recorded in the Domesday books, they found more than 5,600 water mills, or one per fifty families.* . . . Gimpel, *Medieval Machine*, 10–12.

52   *The windmills generated up to 20 or 30 horsepower, but their use was more limited by the vagaries of weather.* . . . Cipolla, *Before the Industrial Revolution*, 142–44. Cipolla's account of the mills is excellent and is the source of information in the following paragraphs.

53   *Again, it appears that the market, not technology, was the first mover. The earliest use of water mills in the 600s was for grinding grain.* . . . Kohn, "Expansion of Trade," 4; and throughout the paper.

53   *"The economic rise of Flanders in the twelfth and thirteenth centuries is one of the wonder stories of medieval economic history,"* wrote the historian M. M. Postan and Edward Miller. . . . Postan and Miller, *The Cambridge Economic History of Europe*, Vol. II (Cambridge: Cambridge University Press, 1987), ii, 668.

54   *The value of the goods on which duty was paid in Genoa, for example, rose by four times in only the twenty years between 1274 and 1293.* . . . The quotes and facts cited in this paragraph are from Cipolla, *Before the Industrial Revolution*, 195–98.

54   *Some historians have referred to the economic advances of the 1200s as the "first industrial revolution."* . . . Braudel credits E. M. Carus-Wilson with this concept in, "An Industrial Revolution of the 13th Century," *The Economic History Review*, vol. 11, no. 1 (1941): 39–60.

55   *Florence, for example, may have lost half its population.* . . . Cipolla, *Before the Industrial Revolution*, 130–32.

55   *People of Placenza live at present in a clean and opulent way and in the houses they now possess implements and tableware of a much better quality than seventy years ago.* . . . Cipolla, *Before the Industrial Revolution*, 203.

56   *At one point, a book cost as much as two cows. In the 1400s, a professor's annual salary could buy only four medical books.* . . . Cipolla, *Before the Industrial Revolution*, 148.

57   *David Landes has estimated that, with the rise in wages of the 1400s, although the distribution of wealth was often execrable, wages for peasants and workers were three times higher in about 1500 than they were five hundred years previously.* . . . Landes, *Unbound Prometheus*, 14.

57   *Fabulous wealth was temporarily created in Flanders and the Italian city-states, including Venice and Florence, as well as regions of France and Spain.* . . . See, in general, Richard A. Goldthwaite, *The Building of Renaissance Florence* (Baltimore: Johns Hopkins University Press, 1980).

57   *"The bursting of Europe's oceanic boundaries at the end of the fifteenth century is one of the central events in history," wrote historian Lynn White. . . .* Quoted by Cipolla, *Before the Industrial Revolution*, 148.

58   *By the Renaissance, Europe was probably wealthier (some, as usual, disagree) than any other region in the world. . . .* See Kenneth Pomeranz, *The Great Divergence* (Princeton, N.J.: Princeton University Press, 2000).

58   *Spain eclipsed Italy in the sixteenth century as Europe's leading economy, due partly to the extraordinary flow of gold from its conquests in the New World. . . .* On Spain, see Cipolla, *Before the Industrial Revolution*, 237–40, 23.

59   *Several thousand productive windmills were dedicated to manufacturing a wider range of products than in the leading economies of the past, including oil, wood, grains, cloth, paper, and hemp. . . .* See Cipolla, *Before the Industrial Revolution*, 249–59, for a rich description of the Dutch ascendancy. See also Maddison, *Dynamic Forces in Capitalist Development*, 30–34. Also, of course, Braudel provides his customary stunningly broad and comprehensive assessment of events, *Civilization and Capitalism*, 177–276.

59   *In other words, by 1700, almost twice as much output was produced in a single hour of work as in 1600. . . .* Extrapolating from Maddison, *Dynamic Forces in Capitalist Development*.

59   *"Wages were notoriously high," concluded Carlo Cipolla. In this wealthy environment, painting in particular thrived, and the University of Leyden rose to a preeminent place in Europe. . . .* Cipolla, *Before the Industrial Revolution*, 257.

60   *Some accused the Dutch of complacency and nostalgia, the indulgence of social elites living off their past glory. . . .* For varying views of Dutch history, see Margaret C. Jacob and Wijnand W. Mijnhardt, *The Dutch Republic in the Eighteenth Century* (Ithaca, N.Y.: Cornell University Press, 1992); Simon Schama, *Patriots and Liberators* (New York: Alfred A Knopf, 1977); Braudel, *Civilization and Capitalism*, 227–76.

61   *No other domestic market approached its efficiency in these years. . . .* Much is made of Britain's early exports, and they were especially important for cotton and steel. But the home or domestic market was more important. See Landes on its development, *Unbound Prometheus*, 45–54. There is a great deal of anecdotal information, says Landes, about higher wages, greater equality, and better living conditions in England than the continent: "[P]urchasing power per head and standard of living were significantly higher than on the Continent" (47). See also Braudel, *Civilization and Capitalism*, 353–85. Also, Stanley L. Engerman, "Mercantalism and Overseas Trade," in Floud and McCloskey, eds. 182–204.

62   *It took time for the power looms to replace handlooms, but by 1838, David Landes has noted, one man with an inexperienced assistant could produce twenty times the output of a hand worker. . . .* Landes, *Unbound Prometheus*, 86. On textile inventions generally, information is taken from 84–88.

62   *"Britain," wrote the economic historian Joel Mokyr, "had no monopoly on invention, but when it was behind, it shamelessly borrowed, imitated, and stole other nation's technological knowledge." . . .* Mokyr, *Lever of Riches*, 107. A wide range of historians emphasize this point, including Rosenberg and Landes.

62   *He called the dialectical relationship "challenge and response." . . .* Landes, *Unbound Prometheus*, 84 is, I believe, the first mention of this phrase.

63   *Britain smelted less iron than did France, but by the mid–1800s, the nation was producing 2 million tons per year, more iron than the rest of the world. . . .* Landes, *Unbound Prometheus*, 95.

64   *Organization of labor was a key contribution in the Industrial Revolution.* . . . Landes, *Unbound Prometheus*, 114.

64   *The economist Walt Whitman Rostow reflected the early post-World War II conventional wisdom when he hypothesized in the 1960s that economies always "take-off" on the basis of a handful of basic industries, such as steel. . . .* All the other economists have been cited. Rostow's main work is *The Stages of Economic Growth* (Cambridge: Cambridge University Press, 1960).

64   *In 1860, Britain imported 1.4 billion pounds of cotton at 7.5 pence per pound, the same it paid in 1800 when the industry was a small fraction of the size; expanding demand was readily filled. . . .* Landes, *Unbound Prometheus*, 83.

65   *At that point, and for the rest of the century, Britain's productivity grew at an estimated rate of 1.2 percent per year on average compared to the 0.3 percent per year achieved in the Dutch Golden Age of the 1600s. . . .* Maddison, *Dynamic Forces in Capitalist Development*, 1991.

66   *To take one example, cotton imports rose fourfold between about 1820 and 1845 alone, an extraordinary rate of increase of 5 percent per year.* Landes, *Unbound Prometheus*, 238.

66   *Overall, economists estimate that GDP per capita rose from about $1,200 in 1780 to $3,300 in 1890 (in 1985 prices), nearly a threefold increase, although more of the gain came after 1830 than originally believed. . . . In the case of wages, the general consensus among economic historians is that for manual laborers, real wages actually rose in the first half of the 1700s in the decades leading up to the Industrial Revolution, stagnated or fell in the second half, and then began to rise again in the early 1800s. . . . .* Roderick Floud and Bernard Harris provide an excellent brief summary of the latest debate over these issues, "Health, Height and Welfare 1700–1980," in Steckel and Floud, *Health and Welfare During Industrialization*, 91–94.

66   *But research by economic historians over the last generation suggests that, despite the wrenching changes, real wages rose, mortality decreased, and literacy spread during these years. . . .* See Floud and Harris, "Health, Height and Welfare 1700–1980," 91–126. Also see Mokyr, *British Industrial Revolution*, for a more contentious view.

67   *European nations eventually followed Britain's lead: first France, then Germany and Belgium, and later Switzerland and Sweden. . . . .* Steckel and Floud, *Health and Welfare During Industrialization*, in general. Their work generally shows that standards of living rose, if occasionally irregularly, as industrialization proceeded, corroborating the view of the material benefits of rising productivity over time.

Chapter 5

69   *It was the large continentwide market, I believe, that ultimately made the nation unique. . . .* See Richard R. Nelson and Gavin Wright, "The Rise and Fall of American Technological Leadership: The Postwar Era in Historical Perspective,"

Journal of Economic Literature, vol. 30, no. 4(December 1992): 1931–64. This is a seminal piece on the subject.

70   *By the 1830s, America had an efficient postal system. By the mid–1800s, it was laying telegraph wire across the nation. The number of its newspapers was astounding. . . .* See Richard D. Brown, "Early American Origins of the Information Age," in *A Nation Transformed by Information,* edited by Alfred D. Chandler Jr. and James W. Cortada (New York: Oxford University Press, 2000).

70   *At first, as the economic historian Nathan Rosenberg has illustrated, America's basic technology was mostly borrowed from Britain and the Continent. . . .* The main work on this was done, conclusively, by Nathan Rosenberg, *Technology and American Economic Growth* (White Plains, NY: M.E. Sharpe, 1972).

70   *By the 1830s, the railroads were being built. In the 1830s and 1840s, railroad lines were short, connecting cities such as Boston and Lowell, New York and Philadelphia, and Baltimore and Washington, but they would soon surpass the canals. . . .* Rogers Taylor and Neu, *American Railroad Network,* is the classic history. Chandler supplements this history in *Visible Hand.* Another good summary of railroad development, among other issues, can be found in Lance E. Davis et al., *American Economic Growth, An Economist's History of the United States* (New York: Harper & Row, 1972).

71   *. . . "For the first time in history, freight and passengers could be carried overland at a speed faster than that of a horse," wrote the business historian Alfred Chandler. . . .* Chandler, *Visible Hand,* 83. Time and again improvements in transportation, as well as extensions of transportation, were the key to expanding markets.

71   *But this evidence also suggests that productivity was optimized only when demand grew rapidly, even in colonial times. . . .* On colonial times, see Winifred B. Rothenberg, "The Productivity Consequences of Market Integration," in *American Economic Growth and Standards of Living Before the Civil War,* edited by Robert E. Gallman and Joseph Wallis (Chicago: University of Chicago Press, 1992).

71   *Lowell, Massachusetts, with its access to waterpower, was the nation's textile capital, and the largest Lowell mills employed several hundred workers each by the 1830s. . . .* The first factories were concentrated in the textile industry; iron makers were a distant second. Chandler, *Visible Hand,* 60.

72   *Visiting Britons in the 1850s were stunned by what became known as the "American system of manufacture," which raised productivity dramatically over the next half century and was the basis of mass production, . . .* The famous American system is widely cited, Chandler, *Visible Hand,* 74–75. See also Davis et. al., *American Economic Growth,* 253–59.

72   *By the 1890s, the American market was already more than twice as large as Britain's in terms of money spent on goods and services. The market was some four times larger than Germany's. . . .* Author's calculations based on Maddison, *Dynamic Forces in Capitalist Development.*

73   *A market that was twice as large would be more than twice as advantageous due to the division of labor and economies of scale because costs per unit were lower in large markets than in smaller ones. . . .* This important point is surprisingly rarely made in economists' discussion of growth and the size of markets.

73   *The cost of distilling a barrel of kerosene, for example, fell from 6 cents per pound in the late 1860s to 1.5 cents in 1882, a 75 percent reduction. . . .* Harold F.

Williamson and Arnold R. Daum, *The American Petroleum Industry: The Age of Illumination* (Evanston, IL: Northwestern University Press, 1984), 282.

73   *A machine invented by the Briton James Bonsack in 1881, and cleverly imported to America by James Buchanan Duke, could produce by the late 1880s 120,000 cigarettes a day compared to at best 3,000 a day rolled by hand. . . .* Chandler, *Visible Hand*, 249–50. In general, the classic history is Richard B. Tennant, *The American Cigarette Industry* (New Haven: Yale University Press, 1950).

74   *The cost of steel rails fell from $67.50 per ton in 1880 to $17.63 per ton by about 1900, a stunning reduction in perhaps the key material of the time. . . .* Alfred D. Chandler, Jr., *Scale and Scope: The Dynamics of Industrial Capitalism*, (Cambridge: Belkap Press, 1990): 129. See also, in general, Peter Temin, *Iron and Steel in Nineteenth Century America* (Cambridge: MIT Press, 1964).

74   *In such a market, a wide range of services, from transportation to retailing to communications, also became highly productive. . . .* This is one of Chandler's key points and is repeated throughout *Visible Hand* and *Scale and Scope*. His history of wholesalers and retailers and their importance to the economy is especially interesting. See also Harold Barger, *Distribution's Place in the American Economy Since 1869* (Princeton, N.J.: Princeton University Press, 1955).

75   *Americans created the breakfast cereals industry to utilize the full productive potential of milling. . . .* Chandler, *Visible Hand*, 294.

75   *He taught America how to smoke by aggressively marketing and advertising. . . .* Chandler, *Visible Hand*, 290–92. On Singer, see Chandler, *Visible Hand*, 303–5.

75   *The young nation raised the commercial culture it had inherited from Britain to a new level, stimulated by a diligent work ethic and a broad, commercially approving religious conversion in the 1800s, known to later historians as the Second Great Awakening (the first occurred a century earlier, and was not commercially oriented). . . .* On the Second Great Awakening, see Nathan O. Hatch, *Democratization of American Christianity* (New Haven, CT: Yale University Press, 1989). See also Gary Wills, *Under God* (New York: Simon & Schuster, 1990); and Gary Wills, *Reagan's America* (New York: Penguin, 1988).

75   *The federal government, notably under President Andrew Jackson, aggressively protected access to land, even protecting the rights of squatters. . . .* On America's unusual land policies, see Daniel Feller, The Jacksonian Promise: 1815–1840, (Baltimore: Johns Hopkins University Press, 1995). See also Charles Sellers, *The Market Revolution: Jacksonian America, 1815–1846*, (New York: Oxford University Press, 1991), 310–13.

76   *These companies professionalized research and marketing, as well as basic management, in the late 1800s and early 1900s. . . .* This is one of Chandler's major themes in almost all his works. See in particular "Integration Completed," *Visible Hand*, 345–76, and "Conclusion: The Managerial Revolution in America," *Visible Hand*, 484–500. *Scale and Scope* compares managerial strategies in the United States to those in Germany and the United Kingdom. The comparisons are instructive.

77   *By modern statistical standards, which adjust for quality improvement, growth was perhaps a full percentage point per year faster on average, or 3 percent per year on average. . . .* Growth data from Maddison, *Dynamic Forces in Capitalist Development*, and author's calculations.

77   *Between 1870 and 1910, overall consumer prices fell on average by an estimated 40 percent. . . .* U.S. *Historical Statistics, Bureau of Labor Statics, 2000.*

77   *"Labor time expended in making a Model T dropped from 12 hours and 8 minutes to 2 hours and 35 minutes per car." . . .* Chandler, *Visible Hand,* 280.

77–78 *By 1916, the price of the Model T had fallen to $360 from $950 in 1909, and demand for automobiles, aided by the plentiful supply of inexpensive gasoline, rose dramatically. . . .* A classic history of mass production is David A. Hounshell, *From the American System to Mass Production* (Baltimore: Johns Hopkins University Press, 224).

78   *Factories and homes were widely electrified between 1910 and 1930. . . .* On factories, see Warren D. Devine Jr., "From Shafts to Wires: Historical Perspectives on Electrification," *Journal of Economic History*, vol. 43, no. 2 (June 1983): 347–72. On homes, see Stanley Lebergott, *The American Economy: Income, Wealth and Want* (Princeton, N.J.: Princeton University Press, 1976).

78   *In 1920, only one in four families owned a car. In just nine years, three out of five families owned one, as the car evolved from a plaything of the rich to a middle-class requirement in less than a decade. . . .* Stanley Lebergott, *Pursuing Happiness: American Consumers in the Twentieth Century* (Princeton, N.J.: Princeton University Press, 1993), 130. Lebergott, a leading expert in American consumption patterns, paints a glowing picture of U.S. material achievement in the latter book, but he provides invaluable data on overall patterns, if not on distribution of these goods or on the availability of public goods.

78   *In 1920, there were three radio stations; in 1923, there were 500. . . .* Shiller, *Irrational Exuberance.*

78   *By the 1930s, half of all Americans got all their news over the radio, . . .* Phillip Seib, *Rush Hour* (Fort Worth, Tex.: The Summit Group, 1994), 157.

78   *there were 80 million admissions to the "talkies" each week,* Gerald Mast and Bruce F. Kawin, *A Short History of the Movies,* (Boston: Alwyn & Bacon, 2000).

78   *and half of all families owned refrigerators. . . .* Lebergott, *Pursuing Happiness.*

79–80 *It seems almost obvious, to this writer at least, that the automobile came when it did more because of economic and social changes than because of technological change as such. . . . A good case can e made for the contention that among the indispensable conditions for the coming of the automobile age were relatively high levels of income, at lest for the middle-income classes, and an individualistic society.* J. Schmookler, "Changes in Industry and in the State of Knowledge as Determinants of Industrial Invention," in *The Rate and Direction of Inventive Activity,* edited by Richard Nelson (Princeton, N.J.: Princeton University Press, 1962). Quoted by Mowery and Rosenberg, *Paths of Innovation: Technological Change in 20ᵗʰ Century America,* (New York: Cambridge University Press), 1998, 10.

80   *The rapid spread of the radio set, the average price of which fell from about $130 in 1929 to $10 in 1935, created a new advertising network that was competitive with newspapers and provided another informational outlet to supplement the nation's multitude of newspapers. . . .* Mowery and Rosenberg, *Paths of Innovation,* 105–6. The basic source for this information is S.H. Schurr et al, *Electricity in the American Economy* (New York: Greenwood Press, 1990).

81   *"The large size of the American market had introduced American firms at an early stage to the problems involved in the large-volume production of basic products . . . wrote economists* David Mowery and Nathan Rosenberg. . . . Mowery and Rosenberg, *Paths of Innovation,* 78–79.

81   *In 1910, only 9 percent of seventeen-year-olds received high school diplomas; by the end of the 1930s, more than half did, almost all from public schools. . . .* Claudia Goldin, "America's Graduation From High School: The Evolution and Spread of Secondary Schooling in the Twentieth Century," *Journal of Economic History, vol. 58, no. 4* (December 1998): 1118–1146.

82   *In the 1990s, all these costs together came to roughly $3 a week for the average family (still less for the median, or typical, family. . . .* Author's 1998 estimates based on network ad revenues.

83   *By the 1950s, 90 percent of all homes were reachable on a paved road, and America's transportation system was never more efficient, . . .* Beshers, "High Returns on Public Spending."

84   *But when economists tried to verify these contentions empirically and statistically, they found that they needed other variables such as economies of scale, managerial innovation, and educational attainment to make sense of how economies grew, . . .* The original growth theory work was based on a seminal article by Robert Solow, "Technical Change and the Aggregate Production Function," *Review of Economics and Statistics* 39 (1957): 312–320. See also Moses Abramowitz's pioneering piece, "Resource and Output Trends in the United States since 1870," *American Economic Review* 46 (1956): 5–23. The pioneering work on seeking other sources of growth is the classic research of Edward Denison, *The Sources of Economic Growth in the United States and the Alternatives Before Us* (New York: Committee for Economic Development, 1962).

84   *Such "learning-by-doing" and "learning-by-using" were central to America's development. . . .* Learning by doing was first raised in a seminal piece by Kenneth Arrow, "The Economic Implications of Learning by Doing," *The Review of Economic Studies,* vol. 29, no. 3 (June 1962): 155–73. Nathan Rosenberg amplified the concept. See especially *Inside the Black Box,* 120–33.

84   *New theory incorporated this idea, claiming that technology was "endogenous" to a well-functioning economy, not an exogenous creation of lone inventors. . . .* Paul Romer is the leading contemporary theoretician on so-called new growth theory. See Romer, "Endogenous Technological Change," *Journal of Political Economy,* vol. 98, no. 5 (October 1990): 71–102.

84   *Total factor productivity is an attempt to measure how well labor and capital work together, . . .* Based on Bureau of Labor Statistics quarterly estimates.

85   *In fact, as they became useful, natural resources such as oil were increasingly discovered and developed around the world. . . .* See a seminal paper on this issue, Gavin Wright, "The Origins of American Industrial Success, 1979–1940," *American Economic Review,* vol. 80, no. 4 (September 1990): 651–668.

Chapter 6

89   *But profitability (profits divided by capital) had been falling for years, and inflation was already a concern, especially as America spent tens of billions of dol-*

lars to fight the war in Vietnam, . . . See Robert Brenner, *The Boom and the Bubble*, (New York: Verso, 2002):17–42. Also, in general, Madrick, *The End of Affluence* (New York: Random House, 1995). *The Economic Report of the President*, published annually by the Council on Economic Advisers, was the basis of information used here. It usefully summarizes key government data each year from several agencies.

91   *The number of new products introduced each year expanded dramatically,* . . . "New Product News" (Chicago), a newsletter no longer published, kept track of such products, and undertook analyses for the author, 1995.

91   *Basic new car models alone increased from 30 to 150 during this period,* . . . The classic accessible book on this is by James P. Womack, Daniel T. Jones, and Daniel Roos, *The Machine That Changed the World* (New York: HarperCollins, 1991).

92   *The real interest rate of the thirty-year Treasury bond rose from a point at which it was actually negative in 1980 (inflation exceeded interest rates) to well over 7 percent in the mid–1980s,* . . . Author's calculations based on *Economic Report of the President*.

93–94 *America's imports rose from 4 percent of consumption and business spending in the 1960S to 10 percent in the mid–1980s, and its trade balance fell into chronic deficit (imports consistently exceeded exports).* . . . Trade data from *Economic Report of the President*, 2002.

94   *In the 1980s, the number of manufacturing jobs in America declined for the first time in its history.* . . . Jeffrey D. Sachs and Howard J. Shatz, "Trade and Jobs in U.S. Manufacturing," Brookings Papers on Economic Activity, vol. 0, no. 1, 1994: 1–69. working paper presented to Brookings Institution panel, 1994.

94   *All of these items consume an increasing share of a typical family's budget,* . . . Family budget estimates are made by the Bureau of Labor Statistics.

95   *The difference between the earnings of a worker with a college degree and one with only a high school diploma kept widening in the 1980s and 1990s.* . . . Mishel et al., *State of Working America*, 2000–1: 152–56.

95   *On average, college graduates have twice as much debt today, adjusted for inflation, as they had in 1970.* . . . State Public Interest Research Groups, in Diana Jean Schemo, "More Graduates Mired in Debt, Survey Finds," *New York Times*, March 7, 2002. Average college debt was $17,000 compared to half that level in 1992.

95   *(Welfare reform in 1996 did provide more funds for childcare, but the quality of the new services was as yet hard to measure.)* . . . Barbara Wolfe and Deborah Lowe Vandell, "Child Care for Low-Income Working Families," *Focus*, vol. 22, no. 1 (2002).

97   *The most influential research in this area, as noted, was conducted by the economic historian Paul David.* David, "Computer and Dynamo: The Modern Productivity Paradox in a Not-Too-Distant Mirror."

97   *Around 1900, the rate of productivity growth in manufacturing slowed markedly, but services productivity kept growing strongly.* . . . These are Paul David's own estimates, by phone interview, 1994. See also Moses Abramovitz, "The Search for the Sources of Growth: Areas of Ignorance, Old and New," *Journal of Economic History*, vol. 53, no. 2 (June 1993): 217–43. See also Maddison, *Dynamic Forces in Industrial Capitalism*.

98   *The economist Daniel Sichel proposed one plausible explanation for slow growth through the mid–1990s. . . .* See his important book, the best representation of this view. Sichel, *The Computer Revolution* (Washington, DC: The Brookings Institution, 1997).

99   *Only in the late 1990s did Sichel and a colleague, Stephen Oliner, find that the rate of investment rose rapidly enough to raise the stock of capital in new technologies significantly enough to affect productivity, . . .* Oliner and Sichel, "The Resurgence of Growth in the Late 1990s: Is Information Technology the Story?" Finance and Economics Discussion Series, Federal Reserve Board, May 2000.

100   *Several interesting books written in the 1990s offered counter-arguments, in which the authors claimed that much of the work done by computers was superfluous or even created unnecessary or unproductive work. . . .* See Sichel, *Computer Revolution*, 32–35, for a good summary. Robert J. Gordon may offer the best ideas about the nonproductive aspects of computers, "Does the New Economy Measure Up to the Great Inventions of the Past?" *The Journal of Economic Perspectives*, vol. 14, no. 4 (Fall, 2002): 49–74.

101   *The age of consumer choice more or less began with Japanese car manufacturers, led by Toyota. . . .* Womack et al., *Machine That Changed the World*.

103   *Wal-Mart, through aggressive computer use, is one of the most productive services giants in the world, . . .* See "Retail Trade," *U.S. Productivity Growth 1995–2000* (Washington, D.C.: McKinsey Global Institute, 2001).

103   *In the mid–1950s, only six cars accounted for 80 percent of sales in the United States, and a single model might sell nearly 1 million units. . . .* Womack et al., *Machine That Changed the World*, 43. The total sales of six cars came to 5.5 million in 1955.

103   *But by the mid–1990s, some 15,000 new food products of all kinds were introduced each year. . . .* New Product News, 1995.

104   *Similarly, in the early 1970s, there were a few hundred mutual funds. By the 1990s, there were twenty times as many, offering investors a wide range of specialized products to meet various needs. . . .* Lipper Analytical Services, New York. This is among the most remarkable changes of the past twenty-five years.

105   *In 1976, the economist Tibor Scitovksy published an influential book called The Joyless Economy, in which he expressed dismay at the monotony of American products, . . .* Tibor Scitovsky, *The Joyless Economy*, rev. ed. (New York: Oxford University Press, 1992). Scitovsky's strong view (to which I am quite sympathetic) that, no matter the variety and quality of material goods, they are inherently boring, and a full life requires other pursuits. These, one can note, are often more expensive than the mass market material goods Scitovsky dislikes the surfeit of.

107   *Now the three networks together reached on average only 50 percent of the audience, and the cable outlets divided up the rest of the market, . . .* Estimates of A. C. Nielsen & Co.

108   *According to one consulting study by McKinsey & Company, and countless anecdotes, marketing costs rose significantly in this period. . . .* Productivity in the Processed Food Industry (Washington, D.C.: McKinsey Global Institute, 1993).

109   *In New Rules for the New Economy, Kevin Kelly insisted that plentiful amounts of down time—what was waste only in the "old" economy—were necessary*

for the creative ideas of the new economy. . . . . Kevin Kelly, *New Rules for the New Economy* (New York: Viking, 1998), 147–54.

109   *In addition, they increasingly hired temporary workers, which according to some estimates increased their productivity in aggregate by several tenths of 1 percent in the late 1990s.* . . . . Louis Uchitelle, "Temporary Workers are on the Increase in Nation's Factories," *New York Times,* July 6, 1993.

110   *Research by the economists Anthony Carnevale and Stephen Rose show that the great rise in jobs came in just such "office" activities in this period, not in the high-technology areas of the economy.* . . . Carnevale and Rose, *Education for What? The Office Economy* (Princeton, NJ: Educational Testing Service, 1998).

111 Also, the greater increase in the demand for services in the past twenty five years came less from consumers than from businesses themselves. The best summary of this is in Gordon C. Bjork, *The Way It Worked and Why It Doesn't: Structural Change and Declining U.S. Growth* (New York: Praeger, 2000.

112–13   *Thus, any such adjustments are misleading for the standard of living in general; quality and choice probably benefited better-off Americans more than other Americans.* . . . . A comprehensive review of what economists know about prices can be found in. Charles Schultze, et. al., At What Price: Conceptualizing and Measuring Cost-of_Living and Price Indexes, National Academy Press for the National Academy of Sciences, Washington DC, 2002. See also Jeff Madrick, "Cost of Living, A New Myth," New York Review of Books, March 6, 1997.

114   *Some observers, such as historian Robert Brenner, make a strong case that these were the elements that at last led to rapid growth in the 1990s* . . . Brenner, *The Boom and the Bubble.* Most of the last half of the book is devoted to this subject, but see in particular 238–55.

Chapter 7

115   *In the late 1990s, productivity grew at nearly 2.5 percent per year, and GDP itself grew by more than 4.0 percent per year.* . . . . All productivity calculations are based on Bureau of Labor Statistics estimates.

116   *The recovery of manufacturing profitability actually began with the fall of the U.S. dollar beginning in 1985 after its long, debilitating rise since the late 1970s.* . . . The best recent history of this period is Brenner, *The Boom and the Bubble.* For this period, see in particular chapter 2, "American Economic Revival, 48–93. On the Plaza and Louvre Accords, see 84–89.

117   *Robert Brenner points out that real hourly wages rose by only 0.15 percent per year between 1986 and 1993 in the United States, compared to nearly 3 percent in Japan and Europe.* . . . . Brenner, *The Boom and the Bubble,* 61.

117   *The failure of capital investment to rise over this period of profit growth, however, casts serious doubt on the thesis that these financial improvements and market-oriented government policies accounted for the rapid growth that started in 1996.* . . . . Based on Bureau of Economic Analysis data.

118   *Thus manufacturing sales overall grew slowly, and the industries that remained inevitably had more robust productivity growth.* . . . . As Brenner writes, "the initial step-up in the manufacturing profit rate that took place in the latter years of the 1980s was as yet unaccompanied by any significant improvement in U.S. man-

ufacturing dynamism." *The Boom and the Bubble*, 67. Brenner goes on to ascribe the lack of capital investment to use of finance for takeovers and leveraged buyouts. In my view, this was more a symptom of reduced opportunity or lack of innovative capacity than its cause, although no doubt the absorption with takeovers was a distraction. It also reinforced the drive toward lower wages, even as the appetite for debt increased. Debt servicing was acceptable in these years; higher wages were not.

118   *In 1999, for example, the rise in manufacturing profits accounted for half of all increased profits. . . .* These are nonfinancial profits, Brenner's solid point, *The Boom and the Bubble*, 68. But Brenner and many others underestimate the importance of services in the economic slowdown and the impact a changing economy has on them—indeed, more on services than on manufacturing.

119   *Reduced taxes and interest rates, stagnating wages, and deregulation did not produce rising capital spending in these nonmanufacturing industries until the mid–1990s, . . .* This failure to raise productivity in services is key to understanding what happened, as addressed in the previous chapter. Services do not inevitably have low productivity—*viz.* fast food, transportation, Wal-Mart.

119   *One piece of evidence in support was the rapid increase in investment in information technology in the latter 1990s, which as economists Dan Sichel and Stephen Oliner found, added significantly to the stock of high-technology equipment. . . .* Oliner and Sichel, "Resurgence of Growth in the Late 1990s."

120   *The new-economy advocates instead continually discussed information technology as something entirely new, a new way of doing business. . . .* See Kevin Kelly, *New Rules for the New Economy;* Stephen B. Shepard, "The New Economy: What It Really Means," *Business Week*, November 17, 1997: 38. For a post bubble-view, see Diane Coyle, *Paradoxes of Prosperity* (New York: Texere, 2001).

122   *In 1999, computer power, according to federal estimates, cost approximately 10 percent of what it did in 1990, and by far the largest part of that gain came in the last half of the decade; computer power fell in price by more than 30 percent per year from 1996 to 2000 compared to 15 percent per year before that. . . .* Bureau of Economic Analysis computer prices deflator. These are "quality adjustments." For an opposing argument, see Robert Gordon, "Does the New Economy Measure Up?," in which he argues that the returns on investment in computers are falling rapidly enough that the price declines are not offsetting the decline in uses. Gordon has also argued that priced declines were more rapid in the earlier years of computer development than reported by the federal government.

122   *The cost of transportation fell rapidly in the 1800s with the building of the canals and then the railroads, but neither as rapidly nor by as much as computer power. . . .* If we adjust for quality in historical products, the question of how fast prices of older key products fell is not as clear. If they were adjusted for quality, the prices would have fallen faster than reported. But even so, declines in prices of computers and related chips, with the exception of some declines in communications prices in the past, such as the telegraph (compared to alternatives), was almost certainly faster. One estimate is that the rate of decline of quality-adjusted prices in the early car industry was about half that of in the computer industry. D. M. G. Raff and M. Trajtenberg, "Quality-adjusted Prices for the American Automobile Industry: 1906–1940, in *The Economics of New Goods*, edited by T. F. Bresnahan and R. J.

Gordon (Chicago: University of Chicago press, 1997). Quoted by Mowery and Rosenberg, *Paths of Innovation,* 56. As more historical research is done and quality adjustments are made, the price reductions of computers may not seem so historically extreme, but they will still be significant. See next footnote.14 On the telegraph, see JoAnne Yates and Robert I. Benjamin, "The Past and Present as a Window on the Future," in *Information Technology and the Corporation of the 1990s,* edited by Thomas J. Allen and Michael S. Scott Morton (New York: Oxford University Press, 1994), cited by Sichel, *Computer Revolution,* 119.

124   *Both the sale of PCs and capital investment in information technology grew by more than 30 percent per year in the late 1990s. . . .* Adjusted for inflation. *Digital Economy 2002* (Washington, D.C.: U.S. Department of Commerce, 2002): 24–25.

125   *The large majority of software sold, for example, was prepackaged.* Mowery and Rosenberg, *Paths of Innovation,* 153.

126   *Cisco Systems, which made routers for the Internet, had 80 percent of its market. . . .* "A Kid No More," *Economist,* September 1, 2001, 59.

126   *Intel sold 90 percent of the computer chips in America. . . .* "Intel Sacrifices Share on ASP Altar," *Microprocessor Report* 12, no. 15, November 16, 1998, 1.

126   *Hewlett Packard made 50 percent of the nation's printers. . . .* "Sheltering from the Storm," *Economist,* September 8, 2001, 83.

126   *AOL had more than 44 percent of Internet subscribers. . . .* "Pricks and Kicks," *Economist,* August 14, 1999, 52–53.

126   *Microsoft's Windows NT had 50 percent of all workstations. . . .* "Microsoft's Contradiction," *Economist,* January 31, 1998, 65–68.

126   *The MS Word word-processing program had 90 percent of the market. . . .* Microsoft Company Profile/S&P Business Summary, *Business Week Online,* May 8, 2002.

126   In *October 2000, Business Week wrote: . . .* "The Four Horseman of the New Economy," *Business Week* October 2, 2000, 48.

126   *Wal-Mart, in particular, learned to pare costs to a minimum, and meet consumer needs, by adopting enormous coordinated purchasing and marketing operations across its markets. . . .* McKinsey, *Productivity in the Processed Food Industry.*

127   *Mortgage interest rates fell from 10.0 percent to 7.0 percent in this period. . . .* All interest rates are from U.S. Treasury Department or Federal Reserve Board.

127   *Alan Greenspan probably should have eased rates earlier.* Blinder and Yellin disagree. See their useful history of this period, *Fabulous Decade,* 25–34. For the easing period in 1994–1996 as well as crises of 1997 and 1998, mentioned later in this paragraph and chapter, see 35–55.

129   *A high volume of sales was critical to these improvements, as were the sales of higher value goods to better-off customers, which generated more dollars per sale. High stock prices also made financial companies more productive in this period for the same reasons: They raised both the volume of transactions and dollar value of each one. . . .* McKinsey, *Productivity in the Processed Food Industry,* on both retailing and financial industries.

130   *The evidence suggests that there was modest growth of productivity among the users of computers, but much of it was dependent on rapid cyclical*

growth. . . . Robert Gordon originally proposed that almost all total factor productivity gains that could not be attributed to a cyclical rise in the economy were made in the suppliers of information technology. Both Oliner and Sichel and Kevin Stiroh and Dale Jorgenson, utilizing sophisticated total factor productivity estimates, showed gains that were broader, although they conceded that a lot of productivity growth was generated by the suppliers of information technology. The breadth of the productivity gains, if we discount for the effects of greater cyclical demand, are not yet entirely clear, although there is probably at least some structural gain. See Sichel and Oliner, "Resurgence of Growth in the Late 1990s," also published in *The Journal of Economic Perspectives* (Fall 2000), and Robert J. Gordon, "Does the New Economy Measure Up To the Great Inventions of the Past?" *Journal of Economic Perspectives*, vol. 14, no. 4 (Fall 2000): 49–74. Both Oliner and Sichel and Gordon have updated their work since, but as of this writing the papers have not been published. See also Dale W. Jorgenson, Mun S. Ho, and Kevin J. Stiroh, "Projecting Productivity Growth, Lesson from the U.S. Growth Resurgence," paper presented at Federal Reserve Bank of Atlanta, January, 2002; and Dale W. Jorgenson and Kevin J. Stiroh, "Raising the Speed Limit: U.S. Economic Growth in the Information Age," *Brookings Papers on Economic Activity* 30, no. 1, 2000: 125–211. For a useful overall summary, see Martin Neil Baily, "Distinguished Lecture on Economics in Government: The New Economy: Post Mortem or Second Wind," *Journal of Economic Perspectives*, vol. 16, no. 2 (Spring 2002): 3–22.

131 *Workers were probably also increasingly dissatisfied, but their anger was channeled at government, not work. . . .* See in general Kevin Phillips, *Wealth and Democracy* (New York: Broadway Books, 2002).

131 *The problem with attributing the boom to new financial "institutions" is timing, . . .* Brenner, *Boom and Bubble,* 224–25.

Chapter 8

134 *It is difficult to determine whether this is a high or low figure. . . .* For a sophisticated analysis that argues the United States is not saturated, see Federal Reserve Board economists Jason G. Cummins and Giovanni L. Violante, "Investment-Specific Technical Change in the U.S. (1947–2000), Management and Macroeconomic Consequences," *Review of Economic Dynamics*, vol. 15, no. 2 (April 2002): 243–84.

135–36 *We have had many communications revolutions since, including the railroads' and steamships' carrying the mail and newspapers in the 1830s and 1840s, the telegraph in the mid–1800s, the telephone in the early 1900s, the radio in the 1920s and 1930s, and television in the 1950s.* Chandler and Cortada, *A Nation Transformed by Information,* is the best compilation of essays on all these.

137 *The term "information economy" was commonly used in the 1970s. . . .* See Gordon, "Does the New Economy Measure Up," 69–71. He argues that much of the information on the Internet is merely duplicative and replaces other forms of access, such as sales catalogues. He also argues that the Internet causes time wasting at businesses, a fact that is hardly deniable. The question is whether workers simply had other ways to waste time, which they have now replaced.

137   *In my view, the greater value of the Internet and intranets is to create price, quality and distribution competition among potential suppliers.* This is one of the rare areas involving the Internet in which some economic research has documented the improvements. . . . A pioneering early analysis of how the Internet affects the efficiency of markets was by Michael D. Smith, Joseph Bailey, and Erik Brynjolfsson, "Understanding Digital Markets: Review and Assessment," in *Understanding the Digital Economy,* edited by Brynjolfsson and Brian Kahin (Cambridge, MA: MIT Press, 1999).

137   *The central benefit that new economy advocates attribute to the Internet, however, is that it is a network unlike all others.* Carl Shapiro and Hal R. Varian raise this point in the only serious book I have read about changes in markets brought about by the Internet. But they do not pursue the implications fully; that is to say, it is simply an extension of the mass production argument of the last century. It will require still greater marketing costs, giving the advantage to bigger not smaller companies. Shapiro and Varian, *Information Rules: A Strategic Guide to the Network Economy* (Boston: Harvard Business School Press, 1999).

139   *Nonfinancial corporate debt rose from about 3.5 percent of sales in the mid–1990s to a record of nearly 10 percent of sales in 2000. Household debt stood at a record level of nearly 100 percent of disposable income.* . . . Brenner, *Boom and Bubble,* 191–92, based on the Federal Reserve Board Flow of Funds accounts. The amount of annual household borrowing did not reach the record level of the late 1980s.

139   *Because Americans save so little on average, a smaller flow of capital to U.S. markets can have damaging results.* . . . The Commerce Department reported that America's personal savings rate was a negligible 1 percent on average in 2000 and 2001, and was at times negative.

Chapter 9

144   *Family incomes were only modestly higher in 2001 than they were in 1989, discounted for inflation.* . . . Mishel et al., *State of Working America, 2000–1,* 33–102. The authors provide a thorough summary of contemporary and historical data.

144–45   *Yet according to Census Bureau data, half of male workers who are fifty or so today earn less, discounted for inflation, than they did when they were thirty. This probably never happened before in American history over such a long period of time.* . . . Author's calculations of synthetic cohorts based on U.S. Census Bureau data. See also Stephen Rose, "Measuring Earnings Mobility and Career Paths in the U.S." *Indicators,* Fall 2002.

What follows is a table that shows how a typical male worker's fared over this period, based on age. This is an estimate, based on the median income of each succeeding age group over time. It strongly suggests that many and in some age categories most males, even as they grew more experienced, actually made less money over time. This was especially true for older workers, as seen in the second table.

How Male Workers Fared Over Time If They Earned the Median Income for Their Age Group (1998 $)

Year in which age 25 to 34	Percentage gain in income ten years later	Year in which age 35 to 44	Percentage gain in income ten years later
1948	51 percent	1948	23 percent
1958	55 percent	1958	32 percent
1968	26 percent	1968	12 percent
1978	21 percent	1978	02 percent
1988	23 percent	1988	-1 percent

Source: Author's calculations, Bureau of the Census

Older Male Workers Earn Less Over Time (Median Income)

Year in which age 45 to 54	Percentage gain or loss ten years later
1948	17 percent
1958	24 percent
1968	-0.2 percent
1978	-12 percent
1988	-20 percent

145   *Even as families could afford VCRs and new food items, they could not buy nearly the same amount of education, healthcare, drugs, housing, or public transportation as they could a quarter century earlier because the prices of these key goods and services rose much faster than typical incomes....* Author's calculations based on Bureau of Economic Analysis data. Median family income rose by 5.3 percent per year before inflation between 1973 and 1998. But the cost of health insurance rose by nearly 8 percent per year, the cost of higher education by 7 percent per year, and the cost of drugs by 6 percent per year. To put it more graphically, over the full twenty-five-year period, income rose 3.6 times. While the cost of electronic products fell, the costs of health insurance rose by 7 times, the cost of higher education by nearly 5.4 times, and the cost of drugs by 4.3 times.

Here we see how prices of housing, education and healthcare, among others, rose faster than median family incomes.

Key Prices Rise Much Faster Than Incomes

	Annual rate of increase 1973–98	Multiple increase from 1973 to 1999
Median Family Income	5.3 percent	3.6

Key Prices Rise Much Faster Than Incomes (continued)

Prices of goods that rose slower than average inflation, wages and male income	Annual rate of increase 1973–98	Multiple increase from 1973 to 1999
Automobiles	3.7 percent	2.6 x
Food	4.5 percent	3.2 x
Clothing	1.5 percent	1.5 x
Video/audio/electric	Negative	-40 percent
Computers and related	Negative	-90 percent
Prices of goods and services that rose faster than average		
Housing	5.3 percent	3.8 x
Drugs	5.8 percent	4.3 x
Health Insurance	7.8 percent	7.0 x
Higher Education	6.7 percent	5.4 x

145   *Moreover, for family incomes to increase during these years, both spouses typically had to work, yet the nation did not supply adequate childcare to support these changing needs.* Far more women now work than did in the past, as can be seen in the following table.

	Females over 16 working
1900	20 percent
1973	45 percent
1999	60 percent

145   *Consumers generally "kept up with the Joneses" only by borrowing against their homes and credit cards. . . .* For the latest data on personal wealth, see Edward Wolff, *Retirement Insecurity: The Income Shortfalls Awaiting the Soon-to-Retire* (need place: Economic Policy Institute, 2002).

145–46   *In fact, an annual growth rate of 2.5 percent under modern data gathering methods was at best equal to the annual long-term rate of productivity growth since the Civil War. More likely, it was below the average. . . .* Author's calculations based on Commerce Department data.

146   *When one adds factors such as the widening inequality of incomes; the longer hours worked by families; and the rapidly rising costs of education, healthcare, and drugs, claims of prosperity made by both Republicans and Democrats over*

this period are callous and perhaps even deliberately deceitful. . . . A contemporary look at income inequality is still disheartening, even after the 1990s boom. The ratio of family income at the 95th percent compared to the 50th percentile, the median, was 3.15 in 2000, 2.89 in 1989, and 2.59 in 1979. Calculations by Jared Bernstein, Economic Policy Institute, for the author.

148   *Moreover, the growth of the late 1990s depended on factors that may not be repeatable. . . .* Blinder and Yellin provide a clear account of some of the temporary factors that helped growth in this period, including the high dollar, which kept prices down; the rising stock market, which supported consumption; and unusually low wages, which added substantially to corporate profits. Their documentation is very valuable, as is their admitted surprise, given that they were policy insiders, at what they call these wage and price "shocks." *Fabulous Decade*, 38–55.

151   *In the* Wealth of Nations, *Adam Smith made an especially revealing observation: "As the operations of each workman are gradually reduced to a greater degree of simplicity, a variety of new machines came to be invented for facilitating and abridging these operations." . . .* 160.

151–52   *Smith implied that an entrepreneur was at the center of such decisions, but he did not explicitly define such a role. . . .* Mark Blaug makes this point in *Economic Theory in Retrospect*, 5th ed. (New York: Cambridge University Press, 1996), 91.

152   *The early-nineteenth century French economist Jean-Baptiste Say asserted that supply must constitute demand because a business making a capital investment to expand production will pay workers for their labor, will pay other companies for their machines, and will pay bankers interest on their loans. . . .* It was Keynes who rewrote Say as meaning that "supply creates its own demand"; Say advocates take exception to this. See W.W. Hutt, *A Rehabilitation of Say's Law*, (Athens, OH: Ohio University Press, 1974). But as I now argue, if one insists that he meant *contain*, the point is awfully close to a tautology or at the least nothing more than an identity. It says nothing about the causal direction, in other words. But causal direction is the question. For much of Say, I think Blaug is especially useful. *Economic Theory in Retrospect*, 143–59.

154   *The economic historian Joel Mokyr quotes an eighteenth century partner of the great steam engine inventor, James Watt, as follows: "It is not worth my while to manufacture (your engine) for three counties only; but I find it very worth my while to make it for the whole world," . . .* Mokyr uses this quote at least twice. Probably the first use is in *Lever of Riches*, 245. The direct Mokyr quote is on the same page. Mokyr, as a reminder, is a technological determinist, not a subscriber to this book's main thesis. He goes on to note Britain's excellent transportation system of canals and roads, as well as political cohesion, and notes that the nation became "an integrated market system."

155   *Some economists, including Mokyr, assume that scale does not matter after a certain rather low volume of sales. But large scale has turned out to be far more potent than was originally thought, and certainly more so than Adam Smith could have imagined. . . .* This is a key point. Mokyr writes in *Lever of Riches*, 147, that in the twentieth century, gains from trade and capital accumulation (now conventional growth theory) suffered from diminishing returns. "Technological progress alone can support sustained growth, because it alone has not run into diminishing returns." By contrast, there is a large and growing literature about increasing returns.

Romer, "Increasing Returns and Long Run Growth," was one of the pioneers of the resurgence of this view. But even support of shock therapy in transition economies, such as Russia, depended on a view that market size was perhaps the key in gaining rapid production efficiencies. See, for example, Andrei Schleiffer, Kevin Murphy, and Rob Vishny, "Industrialization and the Big Push," *The Journal of Political Economy*, vol. 97, no. 5 (October 1989): 1003–26. I think simple empirical observation tells the story best: television economics, for example, and the falling price of microprocessors, are dependent on enormous markets to drive economies of scale. The Internet, as I argued in chapter 8, may make huge markets even more valuable, especially as they become the foundation of enormous marketing costs. The narrow view of economies of scale depends on a manufacturing production model, pure and simple, that in itself is outdated, but also ignores the importance of marketing, finance, and other requirements.

156   *Jumping forward in history, David Mowery and Nathan Rosenberg have made the following observations about the contribution of a large market to America's technological development: . . .* Mowery and Rosenberg, *Paths of Innovation*, 169.

158   *This was Keynes's main point, and a basis for his view that demand must occasionally be supported, even if government budget deficits are created. . . .* John Maynard Keynes, *The General Theory of Employment, Interest and Money*, 1st Harbinger ed. (Boston: Harcourt Brace, 1964), 26. On this single page, Keynes offers a precise statement on this subject.

160   *Both domestic and international markets should be encouraged to grow rapidly to support the general Smithian principle of the division of labor and its related principle, economies of scale. Ricardian principles also suggest that growth will improve through exchange. . . .* See Blaug, *Economic Theory in Retrospect*, on Ricardo. But in another Blaug work, he offers a brief but penetrating summary of the differences between Smith and Ricardo, the first dependent on induction, the second on deduction with all its alleged certainties. The general equilibrium theory that dominates mainstream economics today has Ricardo as its father more than Smith, I think. Certainly claims for economics as a science with a kind of certitude of findings is Ricardian. See Blaug, *The Methodology of Economics*, 2d ed. (New York: Cambridge University Press, 1992), 51–54.

Chapter 10

163   *Savings never increased substantially in the United States even with the 1993 Clinton tax increase. . . .* See Blinder and Yellin, *Fabulous Decade*, 83.

163   *Interest rates fell in the second half of the 1990s largely because bond investors, and then the Federal Reserve, came to believe that inflation was defeated and were therefore willing to buy bonds at higher prices, or that reduced deficits meant a slower rate of economic growth and less demand for funds. . . .* On the psychological behavior of bond markets, see Blinder and Yellin, *Fabulous Decade*, 23.

164   *Profits are a key component of savings. . . .* Some economists argue that a low savings rate will not inhibit growth because it will lead to high total savings, as profits are increased. See Wynne Godley, *Seven Unsustainable Processes: Medium-Term Prospects and Policies for the United States and the World*, Special Report, The Levy Economics Institute of Bard College, 1999. See also Lance Taylor, *Recon-*

structing Macroeconomics: Structuralist Proposals and Critiques of the Mainstream (forthcoming from Harvard University Press, 2003).

164   *Modest federal deficits are not dangerous if they are used to support needed public investment, which will raise the growth rate over time. . . .* A key supporter of this view was the late economist, Robert Eisner, of Northwestern University. See, for example, Eisner, *The Great Deficit Scares*, (New York, Twentieth Century Foundation, 1997).

164   *Families in the 95th percentile of income earned 3.15 times what the typical family earned in 2000, compared to 2.59 times in 1979. . . .* Inequality was stabilized in the late 1990s but not reduced. Computations for author by Jared Bernstein, as noted previously, Economic Policy Institute.

165   *Markets cannot solve all problems of scarcity because some goods—public goods—produce benefits well beyond the businesses or individuals that invest in them. . . .* For a general view of the theory of public goods, a good resource is Alan Shipman, *The Market Revolution and Its Limits* (New York: Routledge, 1999), 47–63. This section gives both sides of the issue.

167   *The Fed, for example, probably pushed up rates too quickly in 1993. . . .* Blinder and Yellin, in *Fabulous Decade* argue that the tightening was not excessive, based on their models. They also give valuable insight into the thinking of the Fed and Greenspan at the time. In my view, they probably overestimate to what degree inflation would have risen had policy been loosened in this period (25–33). One important insight that has been overlooked is that the authors say the Fed was prepared to raise rates again in 1997, but the Asian financial crisis forced it to loosen policy. Would we have had the boom without the Asian crisis? It is a reasonable question, but inflation did not rear up. On the other hand, loosening in these years probably fed excessive speculation in stock prices, in my view. Blinder and Yellin, 53–55.See long-standing debates, as well as the latest contemporary debates on this key macroeconomic issue, in Shipman, *Market Revolution and Its Limits*. Shipman reviews well the arguments in opposition to the point of view in this book.

167   *It was, ironically, generally regarded as a social good that wages be kept down because this contributed to growing profits and reduced pressure on corporations to raise prices. . . .* Many mainstream economists are open to the possibility that fear of unemployment reduced workers' demands for wages. Blinder and Yellin offer some evidence, *Fabulous Decade*, 38–43, as well as alternative explanations.

168   *Direct contribution pensions have reduced the cost of retirement benefits to corporations but have failed to provide adequate pensions for middle- and low-income workers. . . .* See Wolff, *Retirement Insecurity*.

168   *In addition, too few poorer workers have even minimal healthcare benefits. . . .* See Barbara L. Wolfe and Timothy Smeeding, "Poverty, Health, and Healthcare Utilization: Health Needs and the Poor," paper prepared for the Allied Social Scientists Association Meetings (ASSA), January, 1999.

168   *At the same time, jobs are less secure. Temporary workers should be given corporate benefits after working a minimum number of hours with a firm. The drive toward flexibility has been costly to workers and to the strength of the internal market.*

Most important, as job dislocation becomes a way of life in a changed economy, the government should establish relocation policies that provide for assistance, income, and substantial training of workers.

The following tables show that the length of time at work hs declined and that the number of temporary jobs has increased. The sources are given, as shown.

The Decline in Job Tenure: Length of Time on the Same Job

Year	Male 35–44	Females 35–44	Male 45–54	Female 45–54
1993	7.3 years	4.1 years	12.8 years	6.3 years
1998	5.5 years	4.5 years	9.4 years	7.2 years

Source: Paul Osterman, *Securing Prosperity*, Century Foundation Book, (Princeton, Princeton University Press, 1999, 42.

The Number of Workers in Temporary Work

Year	Number	Share of all workers
1982	417,000	0.5 percent
1997	2.646 million	2.2 percent

Source: Mishel, et. al.

Some economist dispute Osterman's assumptions. But even dissidents agree that on average, a worker let go from one job takes a pay cut when he or she gets a new one.

169   *Chief executive officers of the largest companies earned 419 times the average wage of production workers in 1999, compared to 93 times in 1988 and 25 times in the 1960s. . . .* Phillips, *Wealth and Democracy*, 151–56.

169   *One third of households have no basic cable service and fewer than half have a premium service.* U.S. Statistical Abstract, 2001, U.S. Census Bureau.

169 *The population that now goes to first-run cinemas, hwere the ticket price can be $10, is largely college-educated with above average incomes.* MPAA Worldwide Market Research, Motion Picture Association of America, 1999.

170   *To take but one example, spending on education and transportation infrastructure has fallen to half the proportion of GDP that it was in the 1970s.*

The table below clearly shows the decline in the proportion of GDP spent by the federal government on public investment.

The Decline in Public Investment in R&D, Transportation, and Education

Year	Non-defense federal investment as % of GDP
1970	2.5 percent
1975	2.6
1980	2.6
1985	1.9
1990	1.7
1995	1.9
2000	1.9

Source: Office of Management and Budget

170   *Contrary to widespread belief, the quality of public education on average seems to have risen over the past two decades. College board test scores, for example, have been rising even as the proportion of students taking them has grown.* . . . These are widely accepted conclusions. They are also supported by the National Assessment of Educational Progress, National Center for Education Statistics, and Department of Education. See in general *The Economic Report of the President 1998*, 111–13.

170   *Third, and most important, the nation's public education system is highly unequal because it is largely supported by local taxes.* . . . A wide range of studies support this, including the benchmarking studies of TIMSS, Lynch School of Education, Boston College. See also *Economic Report of the President 1998*, 113–14. The disparity in achievement between the best schools and the worst schools based on standardized tests is enormous.

171   *But if properly adjusted, the level of federal, state, and local spending has been lagging significantly.* . . . On these adjustments and where the money has been spent, see Richard Rothstein and Karen Hawley Miles, *Where's the Money Gone?* (Washington, DC: Economic Policy Institute, c1995, c1996).

171   *At the same time, college tuitions in the past twenty years have risen at three times the rate of average incomes. Yet subsidies for college education have not nearly kept pace, driving tuition costs still higher.* . . . Tristan Mabry, "College Tuition Outpaces Inflation Again," *New York Times*, March 12, 1999. Based on Department of Education data. For an excellent summary of tuition increases and reduced subsidies see Robert E. Martin, "Cost Control and the Social Contract in Higher Education," *Challenge* (July/August 2002): 88–108.

172   *Traffic congestion has risen dramatically in America.* . . . See "2001 Urban Mobility Study," Texas Transportation Institute, Texas A&M University. Also, see Department of Transportation studies.

172   *There is ample economic evidence that investment in infrastructure promotes economic growth.* . . . See Beshers, "High Returns on Public Spending," for a good summary of the research. Nadiri's early publication, after which there have been many updates, is M. Ishaq Nadiri and Theofanis Mamuneas, *Contributions of Highway Capital to Industry and National Productivity Growth* (Washington, D.C.: Office of Policy Development, Federal Highway Administration, Department of Transportation, 1996). See Barbara Wolfe and Deborah Lowe Vandell, "Child Care for Low-Income Working Families," *Focus* 22, no. 1, University of Wisconsin, Madison, 2002 : 106–11.

173–74   *A more flexible economy, facing intense global competition and consumer demands for more and better products, has meant less security for workers, and probably will continue to do so.* . . . References to the points raised in this paragraph have already been cited previously in this chapter. In general, Osterman offers a good summary of these issues and the growing insecurity of American workers, where once that insecurity was inexorably reduced.

174   *As economist Timothy Smeeding shows, this holds true even when adjusting for differences in purchasing power in individual nations.* . . . See Timothy Smeeding, "No Child Left Behind," *Indicators* (Summer 2002): forthcoming. Smeeding finds that child poverty is significantly higher in the United States than other developed nations, when measured in comparable ways. Adjusting for purchasing power parity, he finds that children in the bottom 10 percent in America have a lower absolute standard of living than children in the bottom 10 percent in

other advanced nations measured, except Britain. The gap between rich and poor children is much higher in the United States than anywhere else.

175 *In a changed economy, our teachers, healthcare workers, eldercare workers, and childcare workers are more critical than ever before. . . .* See Nancy Folbre, *The Invisible Heart* (New York: The New Press, 2001).

175 *As the population ages, proportionally fewer workers will be paying Social Security or Medicare taxes. The imbalance might be so great in forty years that a reduction in Social Security benefits will be required. But the crisis has been exaggerated. . . .* See Bob Ball for an experienced hand's measured assessment of the issues, *Insuring the Essentials* (New York: Century Foundation Book, 2000). On the exaggeration of the crisis, see Dean Baker and Mark Weisbrot, *Social Security: The Phony Crisis* (Chicago: University of Chicago Press, 1999).

178 *There is ample room for increased tax rates on high earners, and it will produce significant revenues for the nation. . . .* An excellent summary of tax issues in the United States is Joel B. Slemrod, ed., *Does Atlas Shrug? The Economic Consequences of Taxing the Rich* (New York: Russell Sage Foundation, 2000). See in particular the first chapter by Slemrod himself.

Chapter 11

179 *A nation as complex as America, to whose development so many groups of people have contributed, cannot have a single national character. . . .* A representative book that takes the position that American character, or even economic determinism, is not a fixed quality is Sean Wilentz, *Chants Democratic* (New York: Oxford University Press, 1984).

179 *The exploration of a nation's or even a community's character, so popular among scholars ranging from anthropologists to political scientists in the mid-twentieth century, gave way in late years to careful scrutiny of the variability and diversity of cultures. . . .* There are many prominent examples. A volume edited by Seymour Martin is representative: *Culture and Social Character,* Seymour Martin Lipset and Leo Lowentahl, eds. (Glencoe, Ill.: Free Press of Glencoe, 1961). See essays in particular by Margaret Mead (chapter 2) and Lipset (chapter 7). The book is dedicated to the work of David Riesman, whose major work is also about America's national character. Indeed, Riesman's first sentence is, "This book is about 'character' in the contemporary scientific sense of 'social character'" *The Lonely Crowd* (New Haven, CT: Yale University Press, 1950). Riesman cites Santayana from his work, *Character and Opinion in the United States:* "I speak of the American in the singular, as if there were not millions of them, north and south, east and west, of both sexes, of all ages, and of various races, professions, and religions. Of course the one American I speak of is mythical; but to speak in parables is inevitable in such a subject, and it is perhaps well to do so frankly."

179–180 *"The real problem of history," wrote the political scientist David M. Potter nearly half a century ago, "is to separate academic and rational theories of national character from chauvinistic and mystical theories, and to do this rigorously and with finality." . . .* Potter wrote the classic modern book on an economically determined national character. I believe in large part it still holds up. David M. Potter, *People of Plenty* (Chicago: University of Chicago Press, 1954), 31.

180   *All of these national ideas, as we might call them, were established early in the nation's history. . . .* The extraordinary historian, Richard Hofstadter, for example, endorsed a popular idea: "Our mold as a nation was established by the early nineteenth century," in *The American Style*, edited by Elting E. Morrison (New York: Harper, 1958), 357.

180   *Herodotus wrote that all people believe their ways are best. . . .* See Neal Ascherson, *Black Sea* (New York: Hill and Wang, 1995), 78.

181   *Government is to be restrained; individual freedom is to be exalted. . . .* This is our early heritage from John Locke. I am especially grateful to a former professor, George C. Lodge, for making me aware of these issues early in my reading of American history. See his *The New American Ideology* (New York: Alfred A. Knopf, 1974). He cites in particular C. B. Macpherson. *The Political Theory of Possessive Individualism: Hobbes to Locke* (Oxford: Clarendon Press, 1962).

181   *Americans will give as a community to others only if they show themselves deserving by hard work. . . .* See Theda Skocpol's now classic work on government welfare programs after the Civil War, *Protecting Soldiers and Mothers* (Cambridge, MA: Belknap Press, 1992).

182   *Franklin Delano Roosevelt dared not nationalize the banks despite their widespread failures. . . .* On the limits of the New Deal, see the classic study, Alan Brinkley, *The End of Reform* (New York: Alfred A. Knopf, 1995). See also Richard Hofstadter, *The Age of Reform* (New York: Knopf, 1955).

183   *The great democratic reforms of the early 1800s were also born in periods of prosperity and were conceived as ways to protect access to prosperity for broad numbers of Americans.* See Arthur M. Schlesinger Jr., *The Age of Jackson* (Boston: Little, Brown, 1947).

184   *Turner, who badly oversimplified the history but did so with powerful clarity and vision, saw the source of American character in the economic opportunity of the frontier. . . .* Frederick Jackson Turner, "The Significance of the Frontier in American History" (1893), in *The Frontier in American History* (Tucson: University of Arizona Press, 1986).

184   *"It suffices to note that, by the general consent of all observers," he wrote, "this state of relative abundance, of material plenty, has been a basic condition of American life and that it has had pervasive, if undefined, influence upon the American people." . . .* Potter, *People of Plenty*, 67.

184   *"The United States is a child of the Industrial Revolution," wrote Theodore J. Lowi. . . .* Lowi, *The End of Liberalism* (New York: W. W. Norton, 1969), 3.

184   *By 1800, Charles Sellers writes, half of Americans were living at a subsistence level, but on their own land. . . .* Charles Sellers, *The Market Revolution* (New York: Oxford University Press, 1991), 3–28. Wrote Sellers, "In the beginning was land . . . ," 3.

184   *Modern scholarship finds that Americans were much healthier on average than their peers in the Old World. . . .* For a thorough review of this history, see Costa and Steckel in Steckel and Floud, *Health and Welfare During Industrialization*, 47–89.

185   *As the historian Joyce Appleby wrote, . . . elite doctrines. . . .* Joyce Appleby, *Capitalism and the New Social Order* (New York: New York University Press, 1994), 78.

185   *"[N]o one can move from the fifteenth to the sixteenth, still more to the seventeenth, century,"* wrote Harold J. Laski, *who taught in London, "without the sense of wider and more creative horizons, the recognition that there is a greater regard for the inherent worth of human personality, as sensitiveness to the infliction of unnecessary pain, a zeal for truth for its own sake, a willingness to experiment in its service, which are all parts of a social heritage which would have been infinitely poorer without them."* . . . Laski, *The Rise of Liberalism* (New York: Harper, 1936), 10.

186   *Government was more a necessary evil than a force for good, whose primary duty was to protect natural rights, in particular the right to private property.* . . . See Lodge in general, *New American Ideology*, and Macpherson, *Political Theory of Possessive Individualism.*

186   *Religion, with the Second Great Awakening that began in the early 1800s, provided spiritual approbation for material success. . . .* See Hatch, *Democratization of American Christianity* .

186   *"Our secular mythology renders almost incomprehensible the religious mythology that organized experience for rural America,"* writes Sellers. . . . Sellers, *Market Revolution*, 29ff. Sellers provides a forceful assertion of the religious principle in America that accommodated capitalism, even if it often started out against it.

186   *"There is a widespread belief in the United States,"* wrote Potter, . . . *". . . to the public."* . . . Potter, *People of Plenty*, 123.

187   *"We must recognize that laissez faire was not the unique principle of policy in our eighteenth-and nineteenth-century development but that one of the key principles was certainly the constant endeavor of government to the public,"* wrote Potter. . . . Potter, *People of Plenty*, 123.

188   *In America they were granted to many if not most comers. . . .* On corporate charters and how they led to general incorporation laws, see Gordon S. Wood, *The Radicalism of the America Revolution,* (New York: Alfred A. Knopf, 1992): 318–22.

188   *"Education then, beyond all other devices of human origins, is a great equalizer of the conditions of men,—the balance wheel of the social machinery,"* wrote the great educator, Horace Mann, as long ago as 1848. . . . Quoted in *Living Ideals in America*, edited by Henry Steele Commager (New York: Harper, 1951), 568.

188   *Every recession of the nineteenth century was preceded by a severe financial panic. . . .* See in general Charles Kindleberger, *Manias, Panics, and Crashes* (New York: John Wiley & Sons, 1978).

189   *Grand plans for public improvement under John Calhoun and others were always defeated. . . .* On Calhoun, Sellers is particularly instructive and interesting, *Market Revolution*, 150–52.

190   *Some argued that the reason America had no strong Socialist party was that its incomes were so high. . . .* Werner Sombart, *Why Is There no Socialism in the United States?*, (Tubingen J.C.B. Mohr [P. Siebeck], 1906).

190   *Even in 1900, average wages in America, according to the best estimates, were about 50 percent higher than in Europe. . . .* Jeffrey Williamson, *The Evolution of Global Labor Markets Since 1830*, Discussion Paper No. 1571 (Cambridge, MA: Harvard Institute of Economic Research, 1991).

190   *Henry Steele Commager, a historian in the mythologizing romantic tradition, wrote, "Circumstances change profoundly, but the character of the American*

people has not changed greatly or the nature of the principles of conduct, public and private, to which they subscribe." In Commager, ed., *Living Ideals in America*, xviii.

190   *America, it must be remembered, only instated a progressive income tax to fight wars, first World War I and then World War II. (There was a temporary income tax during the Civil War as well.)* . . . See W. Elliot Brownlee, "Historical Perspectives on U.S. Tax Policy Toward the Rich," in Slemrod, ed., *Does Atlas Shrug?*, 29–73. This is an excellent historical review.

193   *But on average and in general, the trend was toward a greater sense of obligation, which in the long run served the nation's profits well.* . . . This is a key issue as I read Chandler, *Visible Hand.* Good management has often coincided with the betterment of workers. Even Henry Ford famously argued that he wanted to pay his workers $5 a day so they could afford to buy his cars.

193   *Margaret Blair and other economists have written that in their own self-interest, corporations should attend to their workers' needs.* . . . See Margaret M. Blair, *Ownership and Control* (Washington, DC: The Brookings Institution, 1995).

194   *Intent on proving themselves scientists, they exaggerate the objectivity of their claims.* . . . As noted, Mark Blaug believes this is the heritage of Ricardo, not Smith, or we might say the ultimate victory of Ricardo. The pendulum may yet swing the other way. Blaug, *Methodology of Economics*, 51–54.

195   *But, by the same token, there are many strands of economic theory that are promising.* . . . There are indeed many strands to explore, including institutional economics, social choice, behavioral economics, game theory, and information economics, little of which makes it into the public discourse. An unheralded book in which much of this is discussed and made relevant is Kaushik Basu, *Prelude to Political Economy* (New York: Oxford University Press, 2000).

Index

A&P. *See* Atlantic & Pacific Tea Company
Accounting, 148
Adams, Henry, 19
Advertising, 39, 72, 80, 82, 83, 104, 107, 138, 156
African Americans, 189, 190
Agriculture, 18, 19, 36–37, 43, 59, 69, 89, 152
  early, 49, 54, 56
  productivity in, 39, 39(n), 50–52, 62, 65, 71, 81, 85
Air conditioning, 99
Airlines, 99–100, 104, 113, 136
AOL, 125, 126
Appleby, Joyce, 185
Arabia, 5
Aspirin, 19
Assembly lines, 25, 77, 79, 99, 152
Atlantic & Pacific Tea Company (A&P), 18, 44, 74, 94, 125
Automobiles, 18, 21, 32(n), 35, 44, 46, 77–78, 79–80, 90, 91, 101–102, 112, 120, 155, 157, 206, 218
  basic models, 102, 103

Banks, 6, 15, 25, 31, 32, 42, 55, 59, 65, 91, 100, 104, 131, 158, 182
  central banks, 90, 117, 189. *See also* Federal Reserve System
  computerization of, 108–109
Belgium, 67
Bicycles, 77, 80
Biotechnology, 28
Black Death, 55

Blair, Margaret, 193
Blaug, Mark, 223, 224, 231
Blinder, Alan, 223, 225
Bonds, 92, 93, 127–128, 163, 166, 177
Bonsack, James, 73
Borrowing, 6, 15, 23, 25, 28, 89, 90, 92, 95, 128, 131, 135, 151, 163, 192, 221
  against homes, 24, 145
  short-term loans, 176
Braudel, Fernand, 199, 200, 204
Brenner, Robert, 114, 117, 132, 217, 218
Britain, 4, 17, 21, 33, 46, 47, 50, 52, 53, 61–67, 70, 74, 151, 152, 155, 187, 200, 207, 209
  cotton imports of, 64, 65, 66
  Golden Quadrangle in, 61
  internal market, 60, 61, 156, 158, 223
  populations, 59, 61, 66
Budget deficits, 23, 24, 87, 88, 92, 127, 128, 158, 163, 164, 167, 177, 197
Bureaucracies, 49
Bureau of Labor Statistics, 113, 117, 227
Bush, George, 24
Business cycles, 34, 106, 146
Business Week, 14–15, 15–16, 16–17, 126, 202

Calhoun, John, 189
Canals, 17–18, 42, 59, 60, 61, 70–71, 75, 123, 156, 188
Capital, 3, 43, 76, 128, 139, 150, 160
  capital equipment, 27
  capital stock, 98–99, 101, 117
  hot capital, 176

venture capital, 131
See also Economic growth, and financial
    capital; Investments, capital invest-
    ments
Carnevale, Anthony, 111
Cartwright, Edmund, 62
Cereals industry, 75
Chambers, John T., 16
Chandler, Alfred, 7, 71, 77, 201
Change, 19, 20, 35, 43, 51, 66, 79, 113,
    190, 198
    adapting to, 140–141, 165, 183, 189,
        195–196, 197
    cultural and political, 130–132
    in markets, 88
    needs in changed economy, 172–175
Chemical industry, 80, 81, 84, 157
Chief executive officers, 169
Children, 75, 176, 189
    childcare, 94, 95, 140, 141, 145, 161,
        166, 173, 196
    child poverty, 30, 174, 227
China, 7, 62, 140, 200
Cipolla, Carlo, 48, 54, 64
Cisco Systems, 125, 126
Cities/towns, 4, 18, 21, 44, 53, 56, 66, 67,
    69, 81, 188
Civilization and Capitalism (Braudel), 199,
    204
Civil rights, 189, 196
Climate, 55, 69
Clinton, Bill, 24, 163
Cloth, 52, 58, 62, 64
Coal, 48, 60, 63, 64, 73, 78, 152
Colonization, 2
Commager, Henry Steele, 190
Commercial culture, 75
Common Market, 140
Communications, 3, 4, 8, 26, 28, 42, 70,
    73, 74, 80, 81, 84, 121, 164, 165, 166,
    169–170, 172
    revolutions in, 135–136
Competition, 4, 9, 37, 38, 41, 61, 75, 76, 84,
    88, 89, 104, 105, 111, 137, 176, 188
    foreign competition, 93–94, 96, 110,
        114, 140, 148, 167–168
Competitive advantage, 93, 94, 157
Computers/chips, 2, 13, 15, 16, 19, 28, 35,
    46, 73, 78, 83, 91, 96, 97, 98, 101,
    102–103, 104, 106, 108–109,

119–120, 126, 130, 134, 148, 155,
    157, 169
and total productivity, 99–100
See also Costs, of computers/computer
    power; Internet
Consultants, 108, 110
Consumer choice, age of, 96–97, 101–108,
    111, 113, 134, 139–140, 148
Consumer products, 18, 75, 79, 90, 91, 99,
    100, 122. *See also* Products
Consumption, 66, 90, 105, 129, 148,
    223
    and consumer satisfaction, 113
Continuous-process machines, 73–74
Contracting out, 110
Contracts, 6, 108
Corporate intranets, 136, 137
Corporate restructuring, 17, 94, 116
Costs, 4, 26, 28, 36, 39, 45, 63, 72, 73, 74,
    82, 90, 102, 115
    of books before printing presses, 56,
        123, 135
    of computers/computer power,
        121–122, 122–124, 125, 128,
        133–134, 140, 147(n), 218, 224
    and creative down time, 109
    of education, 30, 94, 148, 171, 222
    fixed/variable, 77, 138, 154
    of healthcare, 30, 148, 171–172
    of labor, 150
    marketing, 39, 99, 108, 221, 224
    reduced by technology, 120
    start up, 101, 106
    See also Prices
Cotton, 17, 48, 62, 65, 66, 69, 184, 207
    cotton gin, 18, 64, 70, 71
Crafts, 26–27
    new, 97, 106, 109
Creativity, 96–97, 106, 109, 111
Credit, 25, 65. *See also* Borrowing
Culture of opportunity, 42, 43

David, Paul, 20–21, 97–98, 111
Debt, 16, 92, 95, 117, 122, 128, 139, 148,
    162, 218. *See also* Borrowing
Deficits. *See* Budget deficits; Trade, trade
    deficits
Deindustrialization, 16
Demand, 3, 7, 26, 28, 42, 44, 46, 51, 56,
    64, 71, 73, 75, 77, 79, 85, 90, 92, 93,

114, 121, 128, 132, 133, 135, 151,
161. 164, 178, 184, 196, 199–200
for dollars, 140
and innovation, 62–63
for labor-intensive services, 94–95
for less standardized products, 88, 91
for more standardized products, 124
and productivity, 129–130
and supply, 152–153, 158, 159–160, 223
as supported, 158
Democracy, 56, 61, 69, 75, 169, 187–188,
190, 196
Department stores, 74
Deregulation, 2, 16, 17, 23, 29, 104, 116,
117, 119, 130, 192
Developing nations, 3, 11, 53, 176
Disease, 67, 81. *See also* Health issues
Division of labor, 25–26, 27, 36, 49, 50, 73,
88, 97, 151, 160. *See also* Labor
force, specialization in
Dollars, 28, 89, 93, 94, 116, 122, 128, 133,
139, 140, 148, 160, 161, 162, 202, 223
Domestic expansion, 2
Dot-coms, 134
Duke, James Buchanan, 73, 75

East Asia, 140, 176, 225
eBay, 137
Economic growth, 16, 48, 54, 67, 89, 190,
197
agenda for American, 163–178
causes/sources of, 3–12, 83–84, 120,
129, 132, 133, 143, 150, 162, 171,
172, 192, 199. *See also* Markets, market size and economic growth; Technology, as source of economic/pro-
ductivity growth
in early societies, 50
and financial capital, 23–25, 84
future challenges/prospects for,
133–141, 149(table)
government's role in, 23, 75–76, 95–96
history of, 152
myth of best path to, 148–149
necessary conditions for, 3, 7
organic model for, 9, 12, 13, 65
and productivity, 36–40, 46. *See also*
Productivity
sustained, 17, 20, 29–30, 42–43, 115,
149, 183–184

See also United States, periods of economic growth in
Economic theory, 11, 72, 84, 85, 116, 153,
195, 199, 224
Economies of scale, 8, 26, 28, 29, 56, 61,
62, 72–73, 77, 80, 81, 82, 83, 84, 96,
102, 115, 121, 123, 124, 128, 129,
132, 133, 138, 154–155, 157, 159(n),
160, 224
and success of companies, 125–126
Economies of scope, 80
Economist, The, 13
Economists, 20, 27, 31, 36, 74, 84, 87, 109,
115, 120, 133, 146, 152, 160, 164,
165, 189, 193, 194–195, 206, 225
Economy (term), 31
Education, 3, 4, 8–9, 15, 18, 19, 29, 42, 43,
70, 84, 95, 119, 131, 140, 145, 150,
161, 163, 165, 166, 176, 181, 197,
227
public education, 75, 76, 170–171, 188,
189
public investment in, 226
of workers, 173, 175, 191, 193
See also under Costs
Egalitarianism, 69, 182, 183, 187
Electricity, 8, 20, 21, 72, 73, 87, 97, 123
electric dynamos, 1, 20
electrical products, 18, 41, 78, 79
Electronics, 73, 80, 91, 93, 103, 110, 155,
222
E-mail, 41, 112, 124, 136–137, 169
Emerson, Ralph Waldo, 19, 180
Engels, Friedrich, 48
Enlightenment, 182, 185
Enron, 148, 177
Entertainment, 15, 108, 170
Entrepreneurialism, 3, 7, 8, 22, 23, 29, 40,
42, 59, 79, 83, 121, 130, 131, 149,
151–152
role of entrepreneur, 159
Environment, 34, 36, 175
Equality/inequality, 10, 16, 30, 35, 44, 66,
114, 131, 141, 145, 170, 171, 187,
192, 195
equal opportunity, 182, 197. *See also*
Culture of opportunity
See also Egalitarianism; Incomes, as
equal/unequal
Erie Canal, 70

Europe, 4, 17, 21, 24, 48, 50, 53, 57, 58, 64, 70, 79, 81, 85, 86, 106, 117, 130, 131, 140, 151, 182, 185, 187, 189, 190, 209

Exports, 17, 24, 27, 53, 58, 61, 62, 63, 64, 65, 69, 71, 93, 94, 106, 116, 133, 152, 161

Families, 14, 168, 183, 197. *See also* Incomes, family income

Federal Reserve System, 24, 28, 81, 92, 116–117, 121, 127–128, 133, 135, 138, 139, 160, 163, 166, 167, 176–177, 225
  formation of, 188

Fertilizers, 50, 81

Feudalism, 56, 59

Financing methods, 101, 103, 106, 111

Flanders, 53–54, 57, 59

Florence, 55

Food, 28, 50, 52, 53, 55, 103, 104
  fast-food chains, 15, 39, 83, 94, 218

Ford, Henry, 7, 25, 77, 79, 231

Fortune, 15, 202

France, 53, 54, 57, 63, 67–68, 156

Gap, The, 103, 112, 136

GDP. *See* Gross domestic product

Germany, 48, 67–68, 72, 117

GI bill, 83

Gimpel, Jean, 52

Globalization, 16, 96

Gold, 7, 58

Gordon, Robert, 219–220, 220–221

Government interventions, 41, 75–76, 88, 95–96, 130, 160, 168, 183, 186, 187, 188–189, 191, 194, 195, 197
  areas of neglect, 170–172, 174, 175
  spending, 23, 24, 29, 36, 42, 93, 114, 150, 158, 163, 164, 165–166, 167, 170, 171, 172, 192, 226. *See also* Subsidies
  and suspicion of government, 180, 181, 189, 190
  See also Reforms

Government revenues, 45

Grains, 17, 53, 71, 74, 152. *See also* Threshing

Great Depression, 33, 182

Greenspan, Alan, 16, 20, 24, 92, 124, 127–128, 148, 225

Gross domestic product (GDP), 32–35, 36, 45, 46, 65, 112, 113, 115, 122, 205
  per capita, 33, 34, 38, 48, 60, 66
  and services, 120–121
  and total wealth, 34

Guns, 72

Hargreaves, James, 62

Hart, Gary W., 15

Health issues, 3, 11, 18–19, 35, 66, 67, 68, 166, 184
  healthcare, 15, 29, 80, 94, 112, 119, 140, 141, 161, 163, 165, 168, 170, 174, 176, 181, 194, 196, 197. *See also* Costs, of healthcare
  health insurance, 45, 76, 112, 222

Hewlett Packard, 125, 126

Hierarchies, 49

History, 19, 141, 162, 178, 179–180, 184, 187, 194

Hofstadter, Richard, 190, 228–229

Home-buying, 24, 46, 145

Horses, 51–52, 71

Hundred Years' War, 57

Hunters/gatherers, 49

Ideology, 192–193, 194, 195

Immigration, 2, 4, 56, 59, 184

Imports. *See under* Prices

Incentives, 7, 8, 29, 42, 49, 50, 51, 56, 70, 71, 129, 167

Inclusiveness, 191, 195–196, 197, 198

Incomes, 2, 5, 14, 29, 30, 34, 35, 46, 80, 87, 144, 147, 149, 189–190, 205, 221–222
  and demand, 153
  as equal/unequal, 66, 114, 131, 141, 145, 157, 160, 164–165, 166, 167–168, 173, 196
  of executives/wealthy people, 169, 177–178
  family income, 164, 191, 222, 223
  and GDP, 32, 38, 45, 112
  See also Wages

India, 140

Individualism, 9, 56, 75, 80, 181, 182, 184, 185, 190, 191, 195, 197

Industrial revolutions, 16, 20

American, 69–86
causes of, 47–68
European, 67–68
Industrial Revolution (late 1700s), 1, 17, 21, 25, 46, 47–48, 50, 61–65, 156, 184, 185, 207
Industries, 64, 77, 94. *See also* Manufacturing
Inflation, 14, 20, 24, 28, 32, 33(n), 89–90, 92–93, 114, 116, 121, 127–129, 133, 135, 138, 139, 146(n), 149, 150, 160, 163, 166, 167, 171, 177, 190, 191, 225
Information, 3, 16, 49, 56, 68, 70, 120, 137, 159, 161, 188
and trade, 4, 53
See also under Markets
Information Rules: A Strategic Guide to the Network Economy (Shapiro and Varian), 221
Information technology, 2, 13, 17, 20, 21, 83, 88, 98, 102, 110, 120, 124, 127, 220–221
maturing, 27, 119, 128
See also Computers; Internet
Infrastructure, 163, 165, 166, 170, 172, 176
Innovations, 2, 7, 41, 49, 56, 57, 68, 71, 76, 84, 96, 103, 109, 122, 134, 200. *See also* Inventions; Technology; *under* Demand
Institutions, 3, 30, 131, 200
financial, 6, 192, 195
Insurance, 103, 104, 171–172, 175. *See also* Health issues, health insurance; *under* Unemployment
Intel, 125, 126, 133
Interest rates, 14, 24, 89, 90, 114, 116, 119, 121, 127–128, 139, 150, 160, 177
real/nominal, 92–93
Internal combustion engine, 20, 79, 87
Internet, 17, 19, 31, 39, 63, 82, 83, 100, 107, 112, 120, 121, 124, 125, 126, 128, 135–138, 148, 150, 155, 189, 220–221, 224
retailers, 134, 136
Intranets, 136, 137
Inventions, 1, 2, 7–8, 10, 17, 20, 22, 98, 204
from early civilizations, 50, 62
European, 21, 48, 62, 70

See also Technology
Inventories, 101, 103, 136
Investments, 8, 24, 29, 84, 99, 122, 129, 140, 148
capital investments, 61, 68, 87, 88, 90, 100, 116, 117, 118, 119, 121, 128, 135, 139, 150, 151, 160, 161, 164, 167, 176, 178, 199, 217
and demand, 153
in high technology, 100–101
See also under Markets; Savings
Iron, 48, 63, 64, 65
Italian city states, 54–55, 57

Jackson, Andrew, 75, 182, 189
Japan, 5, 85, 86, 101–102, 106, 117, 131, 136, 155
Jeffersonians, 182, 185, 189
Jobs, 14, 16, 30, 31, 35, 44, 46, 55, 111, 144
agricultural, 43
decline of manufacturing, 94, 118
job security, 166, 173–174, 193
job tenure, 226
job training, 15, 84, 156, 168, 183, 193–194, 196
in services, 118. *See also* Services, labor-intensive
See also Labor force; Unemployment
Johnson, Lyndon, 191
Jorgenson, Dale, 219
Joyless Economy, The (Scitovsky), 105

Kaldor, Nicholas, 199
Kelly, Kevin, 109
Kennedy, John F., 191
Kerosene, 73, 89
Keynes, John Maynard, 129, 153, 157, 199, 223
Kohn, Meir, 51
Kuznets, Simon, 205

Labor force, 29, 41, 42, 43, 55, 56, 64, 66, 68, 76, 99, 173, 221–222
benefits for, 76, 168, 183, 193, 196
flexible, 130, 139
household labor, 45
and new industries, 44
regard for working people, 169
and relocation policies, 168

replaced by machines, 36, 40
specialization in, 26–27, 49, 50, 68, 71, 72, 79
surplus labor, 38
temporary workers, 110, 130, 163, 168, 174, 193, 226
two-worker families, 30, 34, 45, 95, 131, 135, 145, 148, 166, 173, 196, 222
See also Jobs; Services, labor-intensive; Unemployment
Labor unions, 41, 108, 130, 190, 193
Land distribution/ownership, 10, 11, 75, 184, 187
Landes, David, 48, 57, 62, 64, 204, 207, 209
Laski, Harold J., 185
Lebergott, Stanley, 213
Lectures on the Industrial Revolution in England (Toynbee), 48
Legal issues, 3, 6, 10, 23, 42, 43, 100
Lifespan, 67, 184
Literacy, 3, 4, 10, 42, 43, 56, 66, 70
Locke, John, 186, 196, 201
Long Term Capital Management, 128
Lowell, Massachusetts, 71
Lowi, Theodore J., 184

McKinsey & Company, 108
Maddison, Angus, 65, 205
Managerial methods, 7, 22, 25, 49, 64, 71, 72, 79, 84, 91, 96, 101, 102, 104, 106, 129
scientific management principles, 80, 99
Mann, Horace, 188
Manufacturing, 15, 16, 25, 36, 37, 39, 55, 59, 61, 69, 74, 85, 93, 94, 97, 102, 116, 130, 133, 161, 162, 224
American system of manufacture, 72
and electricity, 78
first age of, 52
jobs in, 44
moved overseas, 110, 117, 118, 193
productivity after mid 1980s, 109–110, 111, 217
and product standardization, 28
sales, 117, 118
Marketing, 28, 39, 72, 75, 76, 80, 82, 83, 91, 101, 104, 106, 107, 138. *See also* Costs, marketing
Markets, 41, 53, 135, 143, 193
of developing nations, 176

embrace of markets, 192, 194
financial, 177
flexible, 168
fragmented, 88, 91, 95, 96, 103, 108, 111, 114, 121, 125, 126, 134, 137–138, 140, 141, 178
free markets, 4, 6–7, 88, 159, 191
growing, 151. *See also* Markets, market size and economic growth
and information, 2, 4, 8
and investments, 154–155
market share, 93–94, 101, 103, 126
market size and economic growth, 3, 4–5, 8, 18, 26–27, 28–29, 37, 41, 42, 43, 63, 65, 68, 69, 129, 149, 150, 175
market size and technology, 157
mass markets, 79–80, 83, 88, 121, 137, 138, 140
new, 7
regional, 148, 178
small, 56, 61, 154
strong, 167–169
weak domestic, 151
worldwide, 60
See also Britain, internal market; Netherlands, internal market; United States, domestic market in
Marx, Karl, 152
Mass production/distribution, 26, 28, 68, 70, 72, 78, 79, 81, 82, 88, 103, 105, 107, 120, 138, 201
Material well-being, 9–10, 184, 210. *See also* Standard of living
Mathematics, 9
Media, 13–14, 19, 20, 28, 30, 105, 169, 192. *See also* Television
Medicare, 45, 175
Metals, 7, 53, 72, 74
Microsoft, 107, 125, 126
Middle Ages, 1, 3, 4, 10, 11, 36, 50–51, 53, 57, 60, 63, 81
Middle class, 78, 80, 97, 105, 140, 171, 183, 191
Military power, 57
Miller, Edward, 53
Mills, 62, 69, 71, 73–74, 78. *See also* Water mills; Windmills
Minimum wage. *See under* Wages
Mokyr, Joel, 62, 64, 154, 155, 156, 223–224
Monopolies, 4, 40, 41, 188

Mortality, 66
Mortgage rates, 90, 127
Mowery, David, 81, 156–157
Mythology, 180, 181, 186

Nadiri, Ishaq, 172
National Academy of Sciences, 147(n)
National character. *See under* United
    States
Nation states, 56
Natural resources, 5, 10, 12, 41, 42, 43, 61,
    64, 69, 85, 121
Nature, 55, 67
Netherlands, 58–61, 63, 65, 66, 152, 156,
    158, 200
    internal market, 59, 60–61
New Deal, 182, 183, 186, 188
New economy, 13–30, 46, 82, 83, 105, 109,
    124, 137, 141, 202
    vs. former robust periods, 17–19, 20
    as invention of media and Wall Street,
        13–14, 19–20
    and productivity growth, 115
    and technology, 28, 101, 120
    use of term, 16
    See also United States, economy in
        1990s
New paradigm, 102
New Rules for the New Economy (Kelly),
    109
Newspapers, 44, 70
New York City, 70
Nike, 103
Nuclear energy, 8, 28
Nutrition, 67

Oil, 5, 18, 28, 72, 73, 81, 85, 120. *See also*
    under Prices
Oliner, Stephen, 99, 119, 219–220
OPEC. *See* Organization of Petroleum Ex-
    porting Countries
Oracle, 125, 126
Organization of Petroleum Exporting
    Countries (OPEC), 89

Pasteur, Louis, 21
Pensions, 168, 174, 175, 193, 194
People of Plenty (Potter), 184
Persia, 21, 52
Plaza Accord, 116

Pleasure, 9
Plows, 51
Polanyi, Karl, 6–7
Policy issues, 23, 24, 28, 88, 92, 116, 121,
    127, 132, 138, 148, 149, 151, 160,
    166, 168, 177, 179, 187
    fiscal policy, 167. *See also* Budget deficits
Political stability, 3, 42
Pomeranz, Kenneth, 64
Population(s), 2, 10, 33, 34, 38, 49, 56, 57,
    61, 140, 156, 184
    aging, 148, 175
    average height of, 67, 184
    in seventeenth century, 59
Postal system, 18, 70, 76
Postan, M. M., 53
Potter, David M., 180, 184, 186–187
Poverty, 11, 30, 61, 174, 175, 176, 227
Power loom, 62
Power sources, 63, 72, 73, 77, 78, 85, 97
Prices, 33(n), 37, 40, 41, 73, 77, 105, 115,
    145, 160, 218, 222
    agricultural, 89
    of computers. *See* Costs, of
        computers/computer power
    of imports, 93–94, 128, 161
    of Model T cars, 77–78
    of oil, 14, 89, 90, 123
    of radios, 80
    of services, 140, 145
    of telephone services, 169, 170
    See also Costs; Inflation; Stock market,
        stock prices
Printing press, 56, 57, 99, 138
Private property, 3, 196. *See also* Rights,
    property rights
Privatization, 16, 175, 192
Productivity, 26, 27, 29, 30, 33, 34, 41, 54,
    57, 63, 76, 112
    in Britain, 65–66, 67
    conditions for growth of, 43
    gradual acceleration vs. surge in,
        119–120
    growth of American, 38–39, 72, 73,
        74–75, 76–77, 79, 81, 82, 83, 86, 87,
        106, 109–110, 115, 119–120, 122,
        127, 132, 134, 143, 164
    growth of Netherlands, 59, 60
    growth rate of, 44, 45, 46, 49, 118, 145,
        146, 147, 175

and Industrial Revolution, 47, 48–49, 210
measuring, 110(n), 113, 146(n)
in Middle Ages, 50–51
slowdown in late twentieth century, 87–114
sources of slow growth of, 91–97
total factor productivity, 84–85, 219–220
and wages, 67
See also under Agriculture; Demand; Economic growth; Services
Products
new, 40–41, 81, 88, 91, 95, 96, 101, 103, 105, 106, 108, 112, 113, 121, 133, 134, 145
product awareness, 138
quality of, 35, 88, 91, 96, 101, 105, 112, 131, 141, 146(n), 216
See also Consumer products; Standardization of products
Profits, 8, 29, 32, 36–37, 41, 42, 45, 56, 84, 90, 93, 102, 103, 118, 130, 136, 144, 150, 154, 160, 163, 164, 168, 193, 223
profitability, 87, 89, 90, 93, 105, 114, 116, 117, 118, 119, 129, 139, 178
Progressive Era, 169, 182, 183, 190
Prosperity, 1, 13, 115, 183, 189, 190, 191, 197. *See also* Economic growth; New economy

Racial issues, 76
Radio, 78, 80, 107, 136, 169
Railroads, 18, 20, 39, 42, 44, 60, 61, 63, 65, 70–71, 72, 74, 75, 94, 123, 135, 188
miles of track, 71
Reagan, Ronald, 92, 116, 117, 190
Recessions, 14, 15, 16, 20, 25, 32, 33, 33(n), 45, 89, 90, 92, 167, 188, 193
Reforms, 66, 67–68, 95, 171, 175, 182, 183
Reich, Robert, 16
Religion, 75, 181, 186
Renaissance, 1, 57, 58, 99
Rents, 32
Research, 2, 72, 76, 80, 83, 131, 150, 151, 155, 165, 183, 226
Retailing, 3, 15, 17, 18, 28, 31, 39, 70, 74, 78, 85, 91, 94, 103, 104, 111, 113, 123, 126, 129
Internet retailers, 134

Ricardo, David, 93, 152, 159, 160, 224, 231
Riesman, David, 228
Rights, 4, 7, 43, 75, 141, 181, 187, 188
property rights, 6, 10, 23, 42, 186, 200
See also Civil rights
Roads, 18, 19, 42, 70, 76, 81, 83, 96, 156, 165, 188, 189
Robber Barons, 183
Role of Transportation in the Industrial Revolution, The (Szostak), 199
Rome (ancient), 21, 50, 53
Romer, Paul, 20, 203, 224
Roosevelt, Franklin Delano, 182, 191
Roosevelt, Theodore, 169, 191
Rose, Stephen, 111
Rosenberg, Nathan, 70, 81, 156–157, 199–200
Rostow, Walt Whitman, 64
Rubin, Robert, 148
Russia, 11, 128, 140, 224

Sanitation, 18, 21, 165, 188
Santayana, George, 228
Savings, 2, 11, 24, 29, 32, 87, 88, 131, 139, 140, 150, 163, 221, 225
and investments, 5–6, 8, 23, 25, 135, 153, 157–158, 158, 159(n), 163
Say's Law, 152–153, 157, 158–159, 159(n), 223
Scandals, 148
Schmookler, John, 79–80
Schumpeter, Joseph, 7, 22, 152, 204
Science, 80–81, 84, 99
Scitovsky, Tibor, 105, 216
Second Great Awakening, 75, 186
Securities and Exchange Commission, 188
Self-interest, 9, 193
Sellers, Charles, 184, 186
Semiconductors, 2, 98, 100, 104, 122, 157
Services, 3, 14, 15, 16, 29, 39, 44, 91, 118, 120–121, 161
and age of consumer choice, 102–103, 104, 109
complaints about, 113
demand from businesses for, 111
key services, 31—32, 141
labor-intensive, 94–95, 106, 108, 110, 111, 114, 118–119, 140
productivity in, 74, 85, 97–98, 101, 106, 111, 218

Sewage systems, 18, 81
Sewing machines, 18, 21, 35, 75
Shapiro, Carl, 221
Shelp, Ronald K., 15
Shiller, Robert, 17
Shipping/shipbuilding, 17, 57–58, 59, 69, 71, 135, 156
Sichel, Daniel, 98–99, 100, 119, 219–220
Singer Company, 75, 125
Slavery, 189
    slave labor, 18, 64
Smeeding, Timothy, 174
Smith, Adam, 5, 25–26, 27, 36, 41, 72, 93, 151, 157–158, 160, 194, 201, 204, 224
Social class, 157, 185
Social contract, 181, 185, 195–198
Social organization, 50, 59
Social programs, 181, 182, 183, 190, 191, 193
Social Security, 45, 150, 175, 177, 181, 182, 188
Sociology of knowledge, 14
Sony, 80
South Korea, 86, 106
Spain, 54, 57, 58, 59
Specialization. *See under* Labor force
Spinning wheels, 1, 21, 48, 50, 62
Sputnik, 83
Standardization of products, 28, 97, 99, 102, 103, 105, 107, 112, 131, 157, 160
    in 1990s, 115, 121, 124–127, 128, 132, 133
    See also Demand, for less standardized products
Standard of living, 30, 35–36, 37, 38, 46, 48, 59, 60, 67, 83, 112, 147(n), 178, 191, 209, 210
    of children, 227
    in early societies, 50, 54
Start-ups, 132
Steam power, 1, 17, 18, 21, 48, 61, 63, 64, 65, 72, 78, 97, 152, 154
Steel, 17, 18, 21, 28, 61, 63, 64, 65, 120, 123
    Bessemer process for, 74
Stiroh, Kevin, 219
Stock markets, 31, 121
    crash in 1987, 15, 116

mutual funds, 91, 104
stock prices, 16, 17, 19, 20, 28, 90, 92, 93, 116, 117, 122, 127, 128, 129, 132, 139, 144, 145, 148, 161, 223, 225
    See also Wall Street
Subsidies, 2, 42, 75, 78, 83, 95, 150, 164, 168, 171, 175, 181, 188
Suffrage, 187, 190
Superstores, 104
Supply. *See under* Demand
Sweden, 67–68
Switzerland, 67
Szostak, Rick, 199

Taiwan, 86, 106
Takeovers, 117, 217
Tariffs, 71, 156, 160
Taxes, 11, 16, 23, 24, 76, 87, 89, 127, 147, 164, 168, 170–171, 180, 183, 190–191, 192
    payroll taxes, 182
    progressive, 177–178, 191
    tax cuts, 92, 93, 116, 117, 119, 130, 167
    tax increases, 163
Taylor, Frederick, 80
Technology, 15, 19, 42, 100, 151
    and capital investment, 150
    maturing, 27, 119, 123, 128
    replacing one with another, 97–98
    returns on, 84, 101
    as source of economic/productivity growth, 1–2, 7–8, 11, 13, 17, 20, 21, 22, 23, 27, 43, 49, 50, 55–56, 84, 97, 98, 111, 134–135, 150, 154, 164, 199
    technological determinism, 20, 21
    See also Information technology; Inventions
Telegraphs/telephones, 18, 70, 71, 72, 80, 112, 121, 136, 138, 169
Television, 39, 41, 44, 73, 82, 83, 94, 99, 106–108, 121, 137, 138, 155, 156, 224
    cable, 104, 107–108, 112, 169
Textiles, 17, 18, 21, 48, 53, 61, 71, 93, 110, 207
Theory of Employment, Interest and Money (Keynes), 153
Threshing, 36, 37, 41, 42, 43, 71
Timber, 63
Tobacco, 17, 21, 69, 71, 73, 75, 123, 184

Tools, 49, 50, 51, 55, 63
  machine tools, 74
Total wealth, 34
Towns. *See* Cities/towns
Toynbee, Arnold, 48
Toyota, 101–102
Toys-R-Us, 103
Tractors, 71
Trade, 2, 3, 6, 49, 51, 54, 59, 69, 86, 154,
    157, 160, 194
  free trade, 159, 161, 175–177
  trade deficits, 25, 94, 139, 148, 151
  trade fairs, 53
  trade routes, 4
Transistors, 84
Transportation, 3, 4, 8, 15, 18, 19, 26, 28,
    31–32, 39, 56, 60, 65, 70, 74, 78, 81,
    83, 85, 96, 111, 123, 145, 163, 165,
    166, 170, 218, 226. *See also* Airlines;
    Automobiles; Canals; Railroads;
    Roads
Triage, 110
Truth, 185, 186
Turner, Frederick Jackson, 184

Unbound Prometheus, The (Landes), 204,
    207
Understanding a New Economy (Hart and
    Shelp), 15
Unemployment, 32, 34, 44, 87, 89, 90, 144,
    159, 160, 161, 183, 188, 190, 191, 225
  insurance, 150, 166, 181, 182
United Parcel Service (UPS), 109, 173
United States, 26, 46
  Civil War, 182, 191
  Defense Department, 83, 150
  domestic market in, 18, 69, 70, 72, 82,
    83, 85, 86, 106, 107, 114, 123, 155,
    156–157, 158, 160, 162
  economic future of, 179–198
  economy in 1990s, 2, 63, 98, 144–149,
    192. *See also* New economy
  industrial revolutions in, 69–86
  national character of, 179–186, 190,
    192, 193, 194, 195, 197
  periods of economic growth in, 17–19,
    21, 114, 145
  wages in, 117

See also Productivity, growth of Ameri-
    can
UPS. *See* United Parcel Service
U.S. News, 15, 202

Vaccines, 18, 19, 82, 189
Values, 198
van Hayek, Frederick, 27
Varian, Hal R., 221
Vietnam War, 89, 182
Volcker, Paul, 90, 92

Wages, 30, 32–33, 33(n), 38, 40, 41, 44–45,
    46, 55, 59, 66, 67, 76, 90, 91, 95, 96,
    105, 116, 119, 121, 141, 150, 159,
    161, 163, 167–168, 173, 178, 192,
    193, 206, 225
  average, 144–145, 190, 221–222
  efficiency wage, 67
  lower-wage nations, 110
  low wages, 117, 118, 130, 131, 135, 138,
    160, 166, 169, 174, 176, 218, 223
  minimum wage, 41, 168
  and supply and demand, 158
  See also Incomes
Wall Street. 13, 19, 28, 30, 105, 131. *See
    also* Stock markets
Wal-Mart, 103, 104, 126, 129, 156, 218
Wars, 57, 58
Washington Post, The, 17, 202
Water mills, 1, 21, 50, 52–53, 97, 152
Wealth of Nations (Smith), 25, 151, 194
Weaving, 54, 62
Welch, Jack, 130, 156
Welfare reforms, 95
Wheat, 39(n), 69. *See also* Threshing
White, Lynn, 57
William the Conqueror, 52
Wilson, Woodrow, 169
Windmills, 52, 55, 59
Wolff, Edward, 177
Wool, 53, 58, 62
Word processing, 100, 126
WorldCom, 148
World War II, 34
Writing, 49, 50, 100

Yellen, Janet, 223, 225